The Best of The Great Trail, Volume 2

The Best of
The Great Trail

Volume 2

British Columbia to Northern Ontario
on the Trans Canada Trail

MICHAEL HAYNES

Edited by Charles Stuart.
Cover and interior photographs by Michael Haynes unless otherwise indicated.
Maps prepared by Todd Graphic, www.toddgraphic.ns.ca.
Cover and page design by Julie Scriver.
Printed in China by MCRL Overseas Printing.
10 9 8 7 6 5 4 3 2 1

Goose Lane Editions acknowledges the generous financial support of the Government of Canada, the Canada Council for the Arts, and the Province of New Brunswick.

Goose Lane Editions
500 Beaverbrook Court, Suite 330
Fredericton, New Brunswick
CANADA E3B 5X4
www.gooselane.com

Library and Archives Canada Cataloguing in Publication

Haynes, Michael, 1955-, author
    The best of the great trail / Michael Haynes.

Contents: Volume 2. British Columbia to Northern Ontario on the Trans Canada Trail.
ISBN 978-1-77310-032-6 (v. 2 : softcover)

1. Trans Canada Trail--Guidebooks.
2. Trails--Canada--Guidebooks.
3. Canada--Guidebooks. 4. Guidebooks.
I. Title.

FC38.H39 2018   917.104'7
C2018-901161-0

The author has made every effort to ensure that the information contained in this book is correct. However, neither the author nor the publisher accept any responsibility, implied or otherwise, resulting from the use of this book or the trails described in it.

Contents

Foreword

In an increasingly complicated world, sometimes it's hard to find a connection. Today, with a click, we can find anything, and yet we still end up feeling a little lost.

Now, I don't know where your journey's leading you. Maybe you're just getting started, but isn't it great to know there's a place where we can meet up, breathe clean air, hear our hearts beat, see endless horizons, and celebrate the things that connect us deeply?

That's the kind of getting lost I could find a little more of!

Saying that The Great Trail connects Canada across 24,000 kilometres through 15,000 communities in an unprecedented coast-to-coast-to-coast system of inter-connected routes doesn't quite sum it up. It would be like saying the invention of the internet connected people. There's more to it than that – actually, a lot more. Connections like this change everything.

The Great Trail is a monumental accomplishment that allows all of us to access Canada's diverse and stunning beauty. But the Trail is more than a geographic entity. It also connects us to journeys of the heart and mind, and it can help us connect with each other. By allowing The Great Trail to dance with our imaginations, it becomes a network that symbolizes our country's collective commitment to community. Even when we don't see eye to eye, even when we have our differences, the Trail can keep us moving in a common direction. At its full potential, The Great Trail is a physical demonstration that we are more connected than we might believe. It's a massive instrument that will help us create a healthier, more unified future.

I'm proud to be a national Champion of the Trans Canada Trail, the creators of The Great Trail, and I'm excited about the journeys that this beautiful Canadian iconic project will inspire. As you use this guide and take your first steps on Canada's Great Trail, I hope that you will be as surprised and delighted as I have been each time I have discovered another section, another vista, another connection. The Great Trail will give back everything that you put into it – and then some.

We all have a connection to the Trail. Find yours.

Paul Brandt, Great Trail Champion,
Canadian Country Music Hall of Fame Member

Michael Haynes, Pukaskwa
National Park, Ontario

Why This Book?

Eastern and Western Canada are usually defined differently depending upon where in the country you live. To residents of St. John's, the West begins on the far side of Toronto. To Vancouverites, Winnipeg barely qualifies as part of the West. Volume 1 of *The Best of The Great Trail* started in Newfoundland and profiled thirty sections of the best hiking and cycling routes through to Central Ontario: the "East." Volume 2 is a guide to an area that begins at the Pacific Ocean and ends in Northern Ontario: the "West." Combined, both volumes feature sixty routes that represent the dramatic range and variety of Canada's Great Trail. The experiences include urban ambles and multi-day backpacking treks, family-friendly bicycle rides and hikes best suited for the experienced and adventurous.

British Columbia's routes, so many through rugged and deeply incised terrain, underscore just how mountainous the province truly is. Its many parallel ranges create a corrugated landscape, gloriously scenic and delightfully interesting to hike/bike.

Alberta shares the Rockies with BC but also contains the greatest variety of landscapes of any province. Alberta's best naturally includes routes near Banff and Canmore but also features pathways through prairie grasslands and the boreal forest in the province's north.

Saskatchewan boasts the Cypress Hills, rolling landscape that confounds the province's prairie stereotype. Douglas Park and its kilometres of sandy beaches on the shores of large Lake Diefenbaker will surprise those unfamiliar with the province's diverse landscapes.

Manitoba, like Alberta, straddles varied landforms. The Rossburn Subdivision traverses archetypal western grasslands and provides the anticipated prairie "big sky" experience. Yet the South Whiteshell Trail struggles through the western edge of the rocky and uneven Canadian Shield.

The routes in Northern Ontario are perhaps the most similar to each other of any in volume 2. Almost all work their way through the bleak and forbidding granite that borders Lake Superior, an area starkly beautiful and physically challenging. Only Kate Pace Way, near North Bay, provides a gentler alternative experience, a hint of the kinder landscape further south.

Nor are the great urban centres of the West ignored. Routes in Victoria, Edmonton, Saskatoon, and Winnipeg provide opportunities to explore some of Canada's most vibrant cities.

Perhaps what is best about The Great Trail is that it visits every province, every major city, every important landform of this massive country. When applied to Canada, the term "vast" is used so often as to become almost meaningless. Yet when one walks or bikes upon The Great Trail, especially in so many different parts of the country, perhaps then the word regains some meaning. Canada is a vast country, and perhaps can be best loved, and appreciated, by walking and biking. The Great Trail provides an unsurpassed opportunity for anyone to do exactly that.

No trail project has captured the Canadian public's imagination quite like The Great Trail. From its inception as the Trans Canada Trail (TCT) in the early 1990s, the vision of a connected pathway crossing Canada has both fascinated the average person and dominated the entire trail development community. In addition, almost from the first public introduction of the concept, individuals have been asking where it can be accessed. For more than two decades, public interest in The Great Trail has been significant and enduring, even when those curious are not necessarily outdoor enthusiasts.

From its relatively modest initial proposal to be a 5,000 km (3,100 mi) more-or-less direct pathway stretching from the Atlantic to the Pacific Oceans, The Great Trail has expanded to become an intricate and complex web of trail, road, and water connections from east to west and north to south, totalling approximately 24,000 km (14,900 mi). Its route has changed constantly, almost from its very first days, as new communities clamoured to be added and originally intended alignments were abandoned. Furthermore, with the recent addition of extended road and water linkages to span gaps, The Great Trail has never been identical from one year to the next. With a system so vast and disparate, it probably never will be.

In order to at least partially satisfy public curiosity about The Great Trail, I wanted to provide a guidebook profiling it. However an attempt to describe the entire and ever-changing route always seemed impractical. But if it is

11. Glenbow Ranch Provincial Park

unreasonable to profile the entire route, then perhaps a case can be made to out-line a sample. Instead of including everything, such as the 8,500 km (5,282 mi) of The Great Trail that is currently on roads and highways, I have selected some of the trail's finest and most interesting sections. The result is this book and its companion volume, which give everyone the opportunity to experience The Great Trail in every province but at a scale appropriate to most people's ability and allowable time frame.

Choosing the "Best"

Once I had decided that I would review and feature some, but not all, portions of The Great Trail, I had to determine what sections to select. Several concerns arose immediately. I had not, for example, traversed the entire trail myself, and every year the announced length of the trail was longer and more varied. Twenty-four thousand (plus) kilometres (more than 14,900 miles) is a daunting distance to contemplate. How could I know which sections were worthwhile, let alone superior, without seeing them all? How could I choose what to include, and what to exclude?

Later, when I was already advanced in my planning, the TCT Foundation began including long stretches of water routes, something they had previously excluded. Although I do canoe and kayak, my principal forms of recreation are walking and biking. Would I canoe the north shore of Lake Superior between Sault Ste. Marie and Thunder Bay? How about the 1,200 km (750 mi) Path of Paddle through Northwestern Ontario to Whiteshell Provincial Park in Manitoba?

In addition, nearly 8,500 km (5,282 mi) of the designated route of The Great Trail is currently located on roads, and sometimes for quite lengthy stretches. While many of these routes provide access to exceptional scenery, particularly in Northern Canada, few people would define or accept a paved road as their ideal choice as a "trail."

So I rather quickly decided that this work would profile neither water routes nor road connections, but restrict itself to off-road land pathways as much as possible, limiting itself to the original five core uses: walking, cycling, horseback riding, cross-country skiing, and snowmobiling. By doing this, approximately 15,500 km (9,632 mi) of The Great Trail's route could be removed from consideration. That still left nearly 9,000 km (5,593 mi) of trail from which to choose, but nevertheless this seemed to me a much more manageable figure.

Once I had the principal type of experience selected, hiking/biking on an off-road path, I immediately decided that I wanted to include at least one selection from every province, and to attempt to somewhat balance the number of choices I made both between and within each region. I did not want to select all mountain and coastal sections simply because those might be my personal preferences, but to highlight the best and most interesting in every part of the country. And as I was to discover, prairie grasslands might at first glance lack the overpowering presence of the Rocky Mountains or the Atlantic Ocean, yet they soon would reveal themselves to be in no way deficient of either beauty or grandeur.

Still, I was uncertain how to define the "best." Might it be the most scenic? The most remote? The longest wilderness hike? The most rugged terrain? Choosing these factors as selection criteria might seem reasonable to experienced outdoor persons, but what about the average or new Canadian, who might not have any experience in the outdoors at all yet still want to explore The Great Trail? The "best," for them, might be the closest, or most accessible. After all, within a few hours' drive of every major Canadian city there are sections of The Great Trail. Indeed, in many communities it passes through the centre of their urban area.

Fortunately, a workable solution was available, one that could access knowledge of the trail in places where I had none. When I was the Executive Director of the Nova Scotia Trails Federation, the provincial partner that coordinated development of the Trans Canada Trail (later The Great Trail), I frequently received telephone calls and emails from individuals wanting to know what parts I could recommend. Over several years, I identified those places where I was confident that visitors would (hopefully) enjoy their Atlantic Canada experience. My colleagues in the other provinces received similar requests for recommendations, and eventually we all developed our own informal list of favourites. So instead of me guessing where the "best" sections of The Great Trail were in other provinces, I contacted the provincial trail coordinators and asked them for their picks.

This did not completely relieve me from choosing, of course. Although some of my colleagues provided exactly the number of recommendations that I requested – Alberta, for example, furnished only the eight trail selections for which I asked – others did not: Le Conseil québécois du Sentier Transcanadien, for example, suggested twenty-five. Two provincial trail associations hesitated to provide any recommendations at all, and only did so at almost the last moment. In one Western Canadian province, I only received their final suggestion after I had hiked/biked all the others and was sitting by the side of the road trying to determine where I had to travel to next.

Interestingly, each association defined "best" slightly differently, with no two provinces classifying "best" in quite the same way. A few favoured remote and rugged trails, ones where hiking was the only use: this suited my tastes perfectly. Others preferred cycling pathways, and sometimes through their province's largest metropolitan centres. I undoubtedly looked somewhat out of place on these, dressed as I was for something more rugged. Still others attempted to select a representative and varied mixture of experiences spread geographically: urban, suburban, and rural. These I often found the most educational and quite interesting, as I moved from one to the other and attempted to understand what each revealed about its province.

Eventually I received recommendations from every provincial trail association. There were more provided than I had asked for, and many more than I could fit into one guidebook. As a result, I changed my original plan, from writing one book covering the entire Trans Canada Trail and comprising fifty route selections, to producing a two-volume work that would include sixty sections of The Great Trail, thirty in the East, and thirty in the West – although defining "East" and "West" also turned into a debate, and ultimately I had to split the country along a line that few will agree with but was necessary in terms of balancing the number of routes in each volume.

As a further complication, I had originally planned to limit the distance each route profiled to 10-25 km (6.25-15.6 mi). This, I thought, would provide walkers options ranging from an easy two or three hour ramble to an ambitiously long day of hiking. Perhaps unsurprisingly, nearly every provincial association made suggestions exceeding my 25 km (15.6 mi) limit, often recommending much longer routes that they insisted were essential to do in their entirety. Less commonly, there were also a few routes that were shorter than I intended, but so scenic that I believed that they needed to be included. As a result, there is a wider variation in distance than I intended between the trail sections profiled in these books, ranging from an easy 4.9 km (3 mi) to a rather more challenging 102 km (63.4 mi).

So does all this mean that these are the very best sections of The Great Trail? That can and probably will be hotly debated. We each have our favourites, and there are many excellent routes that could not be included. When selecting the best of anything, choices must be made.

But what I can promise is that I have consulted the people building the trail in each province, and I have used their judgment as the foundation of my eventual selections. In circumstances where a provincial association made firm recommendations, I used those. When there were options from which to choose, I made the final decision. In the majority of cases, these trails were new to me, so I was able to make my decision without preconceptions.

When I finished hiking and biking all the sections recommended by the various provincial trail associations, it turned out that these two volumes would profile slightly more than 1,600 km (994 mi) of pathway – though I had to trek most of them in both directions. This is less than 7% of the 24,000+ km (14,900+ mi) total distance of The Great Trail's official (2018) length – but more than 18% of the 8,500 km (5,282 mi) of its off-road land route. If you are able to travel them all, as I did, I think you will be able to claim that you have conducted a fair sampling.

I hope that you will enjoy discovering them as much as I did.

———

Where The Great Trail begins and ends is a matter of continuous debate. Both St. John's, NL, and Victoria, BC, have installed Kilometre Zero markers, for example. In order to respect both perspectives, the routes in the Eastern Canada volume are profiled from East to West, beginning in Newfoundland and ending in southern Ontario, while the routes in the Western Canada volume are profiled from west to east, beginning in British Columbia and ending in Northern Ontario.

Trail Signage
The Great Trail is a collection of hundreds of national, provincial, and municipal park trails, with many others developed and maintained by community volunteer groups. In addition, thousands of kilometres/miles of The Great Trail are currently located either on road or water. Each trail management authority makes its own decision on how many Great Trail signs it posts in addition to local signs, and some have elected to display none at all.

As of the writing of this text, in September 2018, there have been three main designs of Great Trail signs (see page 25).

The first, a red, brown, and green rigid maple leaf logo, was the original design and is still found on many trails, especially those that were completed before the mid-2000s.The second, a blue, yellow, and green wavy maple leaf, was a new design introduced after 2010 and is found on more recently developed routes. The most recent sign, reflecting the name change in 2015, is most likely to be found on provincially or municipally managed trails, but it will gradually be installed on every section of The Great Trail. Generally, only one of these designs will be found on any particular section of The Great Trail, although occasionally there is some overlap, particularly on trails managed by small volunteer community groups. However, be prepared for any of then – or even none at all, as some trail groups prefer to highlight the local trail identity above the provincial, national, or even international affiliations.

Trail Pavilions

Located in every province and territory of Canada are special pavilions that recognize donors to the Trans Canada Trail. From its inception, individuals could "buy" a metre of the then TCT and have their name displayed on one of these structures.

These pavilions range in size from single panel displays to a large, three-sided edifice. The original design was capped with a distinctive, steepled, red-metal roof. Beginning in 2018, an initiative was begun to update all the Discovery Panels and Trans Canada Trail Pavilions to reflect the name change to The Great Trail.

Routes in this book where trail pavillions can be found include Galloping Goose Trail, Edmonton River Valley, Athabasca Landing, Meewasin Trail, and Kate Pace Way.

Trail pavilions: original design (top) and the new design

Discovery Panels

Thanks to a generous donation from the Stephen R. Bronfman Foundation, an ambitious program of installing distinctively designed interpretive panels throughout the entire length of The Great Trail was instituted in the late 1990s. More than 2,000 of these bilingual panels were funded and distributed to the various local trail managers for placement where they wished.

Named "Discovery Panels," these colourful boards mostly profile flora and fauna commonly found along that pathway, including text and photographs or artwork. More occasionally, they detail distinctive geological and historical/cultural features. Some 170 different panels were designed with the assistance of 3 different Canadian museums.

In addition to the standard designs, trail groups were permitted to design and install their own unique panels following the Discovery Panel design format. They are few in number, and each one is unique; encountering one of these makes for a pleasant surprise.

I found Discovery Panels linked individual trail segments to the national route. Many trails have their own interpretive boards in addition to the Discovery Panels. Beginning in 2018, an initiative was begun to update all the Discovery Panels and Trans Canada Trail pavilions to reflect the name change to The Great Trail.

Trail Etiquette

With few exceptions, the entire length of The Great Trail is a shared-use pathway, something which requires all users to be aware of and follow basic rules of courtesy that will enhance their safety and everyone else's. Detailed codes of conduct are usually posted at trailheads, and many excellent ones can be found online with a simple search.

Generally, follow the rule that "wheels yield to heels." Cyclists should slow when passing oncoming walkers, and slow while ringing a bell when overtaking from behind. Both walkers and cyclists yield to horseback riders and should defer to the rider's judgment, as horse behaviour can be unpredictable. (Once, while cycling, I had to stop, dismount, and remove my helmet before a horse would sidle past me.)

On some routes ATVs are permitted. Although motorized users should always defer to walkers and cyclists, I found it easier, as a hiker, just to stop, stand aside, and let them pass.

In addition, most of The Great Trail is a thin ribbon of public right-of-way bordered by private land. The easiest way to respect landowners is to stay on the trail and only leave it at designated access points.

Learn the "Leave No Trace" Principles (www.leavenotrace.ca) and always practise them to ensure that the trails remain as pristine as possible, no matter how many times we visit them.

How to Use This Book

Begin your exploration with the "Trails at a Glance" table. This provides summary information on each of the thirty routes found in *The Best of The Great Trail, Volume 2*. The table displays each route's length, indicates the uses permitted when there is snow and when there is not, whether dogs are permitted on-leash or off-leash, or are prohibited altogether, and if there are fees required to use the trail. Finally, it lists the page in this book where a full route description is found.

Trail names: In most cases, I use the official name of the trail or trails on which all, or most of, the profiled route is found. Rarely does the route encompass the complete length of the named trails. For other routes, I use prominent features such as the names of the parks where they start and finish (e.g. Pukaskwa National Park or Pigeon River Provincial Park) or a geographic reference (e.g., Mount Gwynne) to name the route.

Length: The one-way trip distance in kilometres and miles, rounded up to the nearest tenth of a kilometre and mile. Double this distance should you intend to undertake the profiled route as a return trip.

Permitted Uses: These are the uses either formally permitted or considered likely to occur on the route being profiled. Typically, that means hiking, bicycling (touring and mountain), horseback riding, inline skating, and ATVs or other off-highway vehicles during spring, summer, and the majority of the fall when the trail is not covered by snow. During the late fall, winter, and early spring, those times of the year when the trail is potentially covered by snow, the uses are snowshoeing, cross-country (Nordic) skiing, and snowmobiling or riding other motorized winter vehicles. Many trails have official opening and closing dates for summer and winter uses, so check the trail website. Any item marked with an asterisk means that the use is not permitted throughout the entire distance but might be encountered along some sections of the profiled route.

Dogs: The majority of trails profiled have strict rules about dogs, particularly those within national and provincial park properties. Please respect non-dog owners and observe these regulations – and always "poop & scoop"! Whenever the rules vary for different sections of a route, I have highlighted the most restrictive rules and marked them with an asterisk (*).

Fees: Several of the pathways are either entirely located within or pass through portions of provincial and national parks. These often charge a daily visitor fee. Fees vary from park to park and year to year, so I have indicated where fees will be required by using a dollar sign ($). Where they apply to only a portion of the route, or only for some uses, I use a dollar sign with an asterisk ($*).

17. Cypress Hills	17.1 (10.6)	W, B*, H	S, X	L*	$*	194

In the example of Cypress Hills above, the route is 17.1 km (10.6 mi) in length. It permits walking and horseback riding throughout its entire length and biking on road sections. During the winter, snowshoeing and cross-country skiing are permitted. Dogs must be on leash in Fort Walsh National Historic Site but are permitted off-leash in the Interprovincial Park. Fees are charged for entry into Fort Walsh National Historic Site. They are not required for use of the park trails.

THE TRAILS

Once you have selected a trail, turn to the page indicated. In most cases I use the official name of the pathway(s) on which all or most of the profiled route is found. Rarely does the described section encompass the complete length of the named trail(s). For the other routes, I use a prominent geographic reference (e.g., Myra Canyon, Cypress Hills, and Winnipeg Forks).

Every route starts with a description of the area and some background about the trail. A detailed map for each route shows its path through the neighbouring terrain and key features identified in the text. These maps indicate nearby communities and main roads, as well as vital topographical information such as elevation and rivers. This is followed by:

Distance: gives the one-way — unless otherwise noted — trip distance in kilometres and miles, rounded up to the nearest tenth of a kilometre (and tenth of a mile). Double this distance should you intend to undertake the profiled route as a return trip. For a number of routes, because the starting trailhead is in the middle of the profiled section, or there are long side trails that must be travelled in both directions, the entire return distance is provided (e.g. Glenbow Ranch Provincial Park and Pigeon River Provincial Park). For two routes, Pinawa and Sleeping Giant Provincial Park, the profiled route is a loop.

Ascent and descent: provides the total ascent and descent, measured in metres (feet) of the profiled route in the direction with which I present it. Reverse these figures if travelling the route in the opposite direction.

Trail conditions: indicates all the types of treadway — trail surface — that will be encountered along the route profiled. Many pathways incorporate more than one surface type, although some of them often do so only for short distances, such as a paved section when it passes through a community. The possibilities are asphalt (paved roadway, concrete sidewalk), crushed stone (finely ground gravel or limestone crusher fines), compacted earth (dirt road, former forest roadway), and natural surface (woodland footpath, rock, sand, grass).

Cellphone coverage: indicates yes, no, or partial cellphone coverage on a route at the time when I traversed it. Please note that the coverage in some provinces varies considerably depending upon the service provider. I used Bell Canada; consult your provider's coverage map if you use a different service.

Hazards: brief cautionary notes in one or two words describing the potential dangers on the trail. Some, such as road crossings, are certain to be met. Others, such as ticks and poison ivy, are known to occur along the route but can be avoided with caution. Still others, such as wildlife or mountain weather, are possible hazards that are location specific and the occurrence of which will likely be unexpected. I consider mosquitoes and blackflies as part of the Canadian landscape, unavoidable and inescapable. Expect to encounter them in all but the most urban routes; late spring and early summer are usually when they are at their worst. Possible hazards include the following:

- **cliffs:** When I list "cliffs" as a hazard, it is because that particular trail features a section with at least one high, vertical drop with no guardrails – and where you are usually a long way from help.
- **coastal weather:** On a sunny, summer day, a walk alongside the ocean is one of the most relaxing experiences available. However, visit that same coastline when a northern gale is lashing it and you might think that you were undertaking an arctic expedition. There is often little to shield you from the full force of nature's power; discomfort is certain and hypothermia a distinct possibility for those unprepared. Like alpine weather, coastal conditions can change rapidly and unexpectedly. Cyclists and hikers should take precautions. (This is less common in Western Canada, although Lake Superior has similar weather.)
- **high usage:** On a few of the routes, particularly those passing through Canada's major metropolitan areas, the sheer number of people using the pathways is a significant hazard. Particular care must be taken by cyclists in these locations, because many of the trail users are families, novices, and others whose behaviour will be unpredictable. Where so many people share the trail, reduced speed is the only correct response.
- **hunting:** In some cases The Great Trail passes through areas where big game hunting is permitted for caribou, deer, or moose, usually during the fall.

- **isolated areas:** One route in this volume, the Pukaskwa National Park Coastal Trail, travels into one of the most remote regions of Ontario, far from any community or assistance. While trail users should always make adequate preparations and notify others of where they are hiking/biking and when they should be expected to return on every trail, this route requires particular thoughtfulness before it is undertaken. Most people rarely venture so far into the backcountry.
- **mountain weather:** In mountainous areas the weather is highly variable, and sudden, unpredicted storms often occur. Snow can persist on the ground until June, while severe snowstorms in September are not unusual. Adequate precautions should be taken to pack rain gear, warm-weather clothing, and other safety items when trekking in mountain regions.
- **poison ivy/giant hogweed:** These skin-irritating plants are increasingly found along the edges of many trails and fields. Managed trails will usually post warning signs, but as both poison ivy and other noxious plants, such as giant hogweed, are spreading and extending their range, poison ivy might be growing anywhere alongside the pathway. The best way to avoid poison ivy? Stay on the path.
- **road crossings:** Most longer trails, particularly those that have been created on former railways, require multiple road crossings. Quite often these will be over highways where the speed limits are 80 or 90 kph (50 or 55 mph), and in some cases road and trail cross each other at a diagonal, making visibility difficult for either the trail user or approaching automobile traffic. Of all the hazards trail users face, this is actually the most certain and truly dangerous.
- **rugged terrain:** The majority of the paths profiled in this book are wide, level, and surfaced in crushed stone. Others, however, wander over the landscape regardless of hills, rocks, rivers, or any other obstacle. When I thought that the terrain was of more than average challenge, I mentioned it.
- **ticks:** These tiny spider-like insects climb onto grass and scrub and climb onto animals and people when they rub against the plants. Although a tick bite is usually painless, ticks can transfer several diseases, including the serious Lyme disease, while they feed. For more information about Lyme disease, visit www.phac-aspc.gc.ca/id-mi/tickinfo-eng.php. Black-legged ticks are extending their range through much of southern Canada, heading north by more than 100 km (60 mi) per year; consult a provincial website for the most up-to-date information.

- **wildlife:** Concern about wildlife encounters tends to be what most people fear when hiking or biking on trails. Stories of bear attacks, though extremely rare, are usually gruesome and captivating. But in addition to bears, the wrong interaction with any wild animal can result in injury or death. For example, in 2013, in Belarus, a man was killed by a beaver! Nor are wild animals found only in the wilderness. Even in urban areas in Canada, coyotes, raccoons, and skunks can be found, so caution is always advisable. However, for the purposes of this book, I have only listed wildlife as a hazard where larger and/or more aggressive species such as bears, bobcats, mountain lions, badgers, rattlesnakes, or wolves are known to commonly roam.

Permitted Uses: this table indicates what uses are permitted on all or part of the profiled route.

Finding the trailhead: information on roads to trails, parking areas, and trail signage.

Trailhead: the GPS coordinates of both the start and finish of each profiled route. In addition, the community or park name most closely associated with each is mentioned next to the coordinates. For routes where a return or loop distance is provided, coordinates are listed for the starting location.

Observations: very brief descriptions of my impressions of each particular route. I had never hiked or biked most of these trails before, and in many cases I had not even travelled to the part of the country where they are found. I hope that readers will find these brief comments about my own explorations interesting and informative.

Route description: a walk/bike-through of the route, relating what I found when I travelled it in 2016. Trails in urban areas are frequently rerouted – I have attempted to ensure that all information is accurate as of September 2018. In every case I describe junctions and landmarks from the perspective of someone following the trail in the direction I have indicated. If travelling in the opposite direction, remember to reverse my bearings.

Further information: links to pertinent websites, such as the local trail group, the area's tourism association, associated parks, or municipalities, or anything I thought useful

Sidebars: brief capsule descriptions of some of the plants, animals, geological features, and human history that you might encounter. These are intended to be brief samples to whet your curiosity about the terrain through which you are hiking/biking, and to encourage you to learn more.

Trails at a Glance

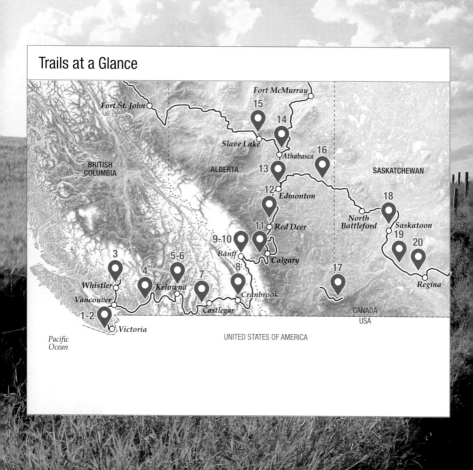

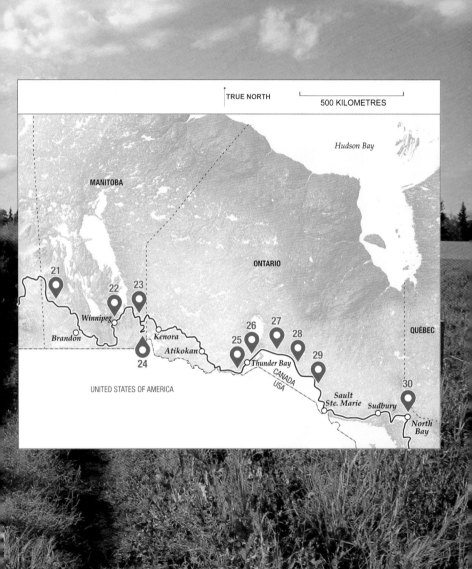

Trails at a Glance

Best of The Great Trail — Western Canada						
Trail Name	Length km (mi)	Permitted Uses (no snow)	Permitted Uses (snow)	Dogs	Fees	Page
Uses (no snow): W = Walk, B = Bike, H = Horseback Riding, I = Inline Skating, A = ATV Uses (snow): S = Snowshoe/Walk, X = Cross-Country Ski, Sm = Snowmobile Dogs: N = no dogs permitted, L = dogs permitted on leash, O = dogs permitted off-leash * = Permitted on some sections of the route, but not all						
British Columbia						
1. Galloping Goose Trail	18.3 (11.4)	W, B, I*	S, X	L	N/A	29
2. Cowichan Valley Trail	35.7 (22.2)	W, B, H	S, X	L*	N/A	39
3. Sea to Sky Trail	23.2 (14.4)	W, B, I*	S, X	L*	N/A	48
4. Othello Tunnels	4.9 (3)	W, B, H*	S*, X*	L*	N/A	61
5. Penticton KVR	24.6 (15.3)	W, B, H	S, X	L*	N/A	70
6. Myra Canyon	10.9 (6.8)	W, B, H	S, X, Sm	L	N/A	81
7. Columbia and Western Trail	50.2 (31.2)	W, B, H, A	S, X, Sm	O	N/A	90
8. North Star Trail	24.7 (15.4)	W, B, I	S, X	L	N/A	101
Alberta						
9. High Rockies Trail	24.8 (15.4)	W, B	S, X	L	N/A	113
10. Rocky Mountain Legacy Trail	20.2 (12.6)	W, B, H*, I	S, X	L*	N/A	123
11. Glenbow Ranch Provincial Park	26.5 (16.5) return	W, B, I*	S, X	L*	$	131
12. Lacombe County	15.2 (9.4)	W, B, I*	S, X*	L	N/A	141
13. Edmonton River Valley	27.3 (17)	W, B, I*	S, X*	L	N/A	150
14. Athabasca Landing Trail	13.2 (8.2)	W, B, H	S, X	O	N/A	162
15. Mirror Landing Trail	31.7 (19.7)	W, B	S, X	L	N/A	170
16. Iron Horse Trail	62.5 (38.8)	W, B, H, A	S, X, Sm	O	N/A	181

Saskatchewan						
17. Cypress Hills	17.1 (10.6)	W, B*, H	S, X	L*	$	194
18. Meewasin Trail	15.5 (9.6)	W, B, I*	S, X	L	N/A	205
19. Douglas Provincial Park	10.2 (6.3)	W, B	S, X	L	$	215
20. Saw Whet Trail	7.8 (4.8)	W	S, X	N	N/A	224
Manitoba						
21. Rossburn Subdivision	9.2 (5.7)	W, B, H	S, X, Sm	0	N/A	234
22. Winnipeg Forks	15.8 (9.8) return	W, B, I*	S, X*	L	N/A	243
23. Pinawa	28.6 (17.8) loop	W, B, H, A*	S, X, Sm*	L*	N/A	251
24. South Whiteshell Trail	37.4 (23.2)	W, B, H	S, X	L*	N/A	261
Northern Ontario						
25. Pigeon River Provincial Park	16.5 (10.3) return	W	S	L	$	271
26. Sleeping Giant Provincial Park	27.9 (17.3) loop	W, B*	S, X*	L	$	279
27. Mount Gwynne	7.2 (4.5)	W	S	0	N/A	289
28. Pukaskwa National Park	63.5 (39.5)	W	S	L	$	296
29. Lake Superior Provincial Park	10.1 (6.2)	W	S, X	L	$	320
30. Kate Pace Way	12.2 (7.6)	W, B, I	S, X	L	N/A	329

Signage for The Trans Canada Trail/The Great Trail:

original   c. 2010   c. 2016

Trail amenities:

 Bridge

 Camping

 Drinking water

 Ford

 Information

 Outhouse

P Parking

Rustic cabin

S Services (gas, $, etc.)

 Tunnel

 Washroom

7. Columbia and Western

1. Galloping Goose Trail

The Great Trail begins the long journey from its western terminus in the city of Victoria on Vancouver Island, following the famous Galloping Goose Trail. One of the very first major rail trail developments in Canada, in 1987, the Goose is a 55+ km (34.1+ mi) pathway that begins in the heart of downtown Victoria before ending on the Sooke River near the former community of Leechtown. For about 18 km (11.2 mi), The Great Trail follows the Goose before turning off to head toward Goldstream Provincial Park.

However, the route of The Great Trail changes continually as new and better off-road routes are developed. In 2016, it separated from the Galloping Goose at Glen Lake Road; in 2018 The Great Trail was rerouted onto Kelly Road, nearly 2 km (1.2 mi) closer to downtown.

Once the E&N Rail Trail is completed, the route of The Great Trail will change again, separating from the Galloping Goose at the Atkins Road Trailhead. It will follow this new off-road pathway (E&N) through the city of Langford.

I profiled this route on the Goose as far as the Glen Lake Road because it reaches Glen Lake, an attractive destination, and the parking area at Sooke Road, a convenient pickup or return point.

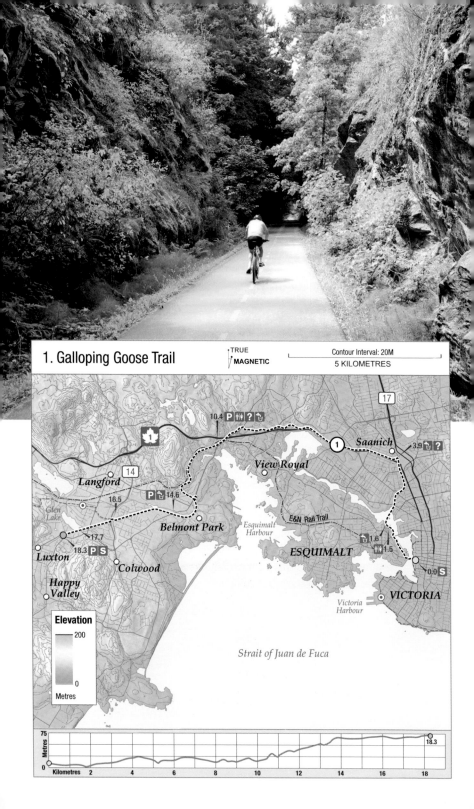

1. Galloping Goose Trail

TRUE
MAGNETIC

Contour Interval: 20M
5 KILOMETRES

1. Galloping Goose Trail

Distance: 18.3 km (11.4 mi), one way
Ascent: 164 m (538 ft)
Descent: 85 m (279 ft)

Trail conditions: asphalt, crushed stone
Cellphone coverage: yes
Hazards: high usage, road crossings, ticks

Permitted Uses							
Walking	Biking	Horseback Riding	Inline Skating	ATV	Snowshoeing	Cross-country Skiing	Snowmobiling
✔	✔	—	✔*	—	✔	✔	—

Finding the trailhead: Begin in downtown Victoria at the south end of the Johnson Street Bridge, at public parking parkades.

Trailhead: 48°25'40.1" N, 123°22'13.6" W (Start: Victoria)
48°26'01.0" N, 123°31'32.6" W (Finish: Glen Lake Road)

Observations: Ever since I started working in trail development, the Galloping Goose was seen as the standard to which all rail trails should aspire, so I was more than a little excited to be riding it for the first time. I was not disappointed. The pathway was in excellent condition, its signage accurate and clear, and its integration with roads and transit nearly seamless.

Best of all, it was well used. There were people on it everywhere, from the asphalt-surfaced downtown to the gravelled Glen Road section. In fact, between the Johnson Street Bridge and the Lochside Trail intersection there were so many cyclists that I almost felt like a motorist during rush hour. (It wasn't actually that busy, but compared to a wilderness path, it was pretty hectic.)

The Galloping Goose Trail is an amazing community resource and definitely a worthwhile trail to explore.

Route description: Begin at a small park in downtown Victoria, at the eastern end of the Johnson Street Bridge. I visited before the replacement bridge was completed, so my directions cannot be completely accurate, but it seems the best option is to use the crosswalks at the intersection of Wharf Street and

Johnson Street to reach the broad dedicated pedestrian/cycle lane on the north side of the bridge.

Take your time crossing, as the scenery is quite attractive. The new overpass is itself impressive, a stylish lift bridge with wide pedestrian/cycle paths on both sides. To the right is Victoria's Upper Harbour; to the left is the downtown, with its seaplanes, ferry terminal, and the dome of the provincial Parliament Buildings. On most days numerous kayaks can be seen dotting the bay.

On the far side of the bridge, turn right onto Harbour Road. Pedestrians have a sidewalk and cyclists a bike lane in the street. On the right is a shipyard where Canadian military coastal patrol vessels were being outfitted when I passed. To the left, rows of new condominiums line the street.

At about 900 m/yd, just where Harbour Road curves left, a paved off-road pathway branches off to the right. Take it. The pathway is well signed for Point Ellice Park, but there is also a tall totem pole marking the turnoff. Separate tracks are available for cyclists and pedestrians, and there was a cyclist counter there too. Across the street is a bicycle shop.

This is a busy bike commuting pathway, so be cautious when you stop. It tracks along in the small space between new housing and the Upper Harbour, passing underneath the Bay Street Bridge just 100 m/yd from Harbour Road. There is a public washroom about 600 m/yd, at 1.5 km (0.9 mi) and numerous connections are available from neighbouring streets. Expect lots of slow-moving pedestrian traffic.

1.6 km (1 mi) The trail arrives at a major trail intersection and a Great Trail Pavilion. This is a busy spot, with multiple paths converging. There are benches, interpretive panels, bike parking, and even a water fountain. To the left is Banfield Park; keep to the right.

Almost immediately the path reaches the Selkirk Trestle, a 300+ m/yd hemlock and fir restored railway bridge spanning a wide pool known as the Selkirk Water. This impressive structure is extra wide and has several viewing platforms at which to stop and enjoy the view. At its opposite end is a Discovery Panel on the bald eagle.

The pathway continues alongside a narrow inlet for a short distance, although you might not be able to see it through the thick vegetation. On the right are more new residences, but there are some interpretive displays that refer to the area's industrial past.

At 2.2 km (1.4 mi), the trail passes underneath Gorge Road and enters an interesting area known as Cecelia Ravine Park. Tiny Cecelia Creek runs on the right, and the narrow ravine is choked thickly with trees and scrubs. Although the city is all around us, this slender natural corridor is insulated by its dense foliage. There is even room for the Thomas Clive Arkell Trail beside the stream.

Mile Zero

The Great Trail, like the Trans-Canada Highway, has three beginnings — Arctic, Atlantic, and Pacific — but no end. On the Pacific Ocean, both Highway and Trail start at a monument on Douglas Street at its intersection with Dallas Road near Beacon Hill Park in Victoria. But both routes share more than just this marker; like the Highway, the trail is a massive project that will change and evolve in every year of its existence.

In "The Graceful End of the Trans-Canada Highway" (*Maclean's*, 9 August 2012), correspondent Mark Richardson perfectly captured the reality of both: "It would take another 50 years before the Trans-Canada Highway would be declared open, and another decade after that before it could really be considered finished.

"And it's still not finished, though it is complete. It will never be truly finished, because it's improved, widened, straightened, smoothed over with every year that passes. In another hundred years, who knows what the Trans-Canada will look like, or what route it will take? But it will be there, linking the provinces, lending its iconic route to the country, never to be taken away."

The trail climbs through this sylvan interlude, passing beneath another road and following the little ravine as it flattens out. Its separation from the urban environment lessens with every metre/yard, completely disappearing by the time it crosses Tolmie Lane at 2.9 km (1.8 mi).

These trail/street intersections are accommodating. Metal bollards sit in the trail on either side of the road, and a crosswalk spans the street. There are also several warning signs of the road crossing for trail users, and automobiles have a stop sign at the crossing.

More street crossings follow in rapid succession as the trail traverses an area of commercial properties. Employees from these businesses use the adjacent footpath to enjoy their lunch break, eating at one of the trail's benches. After crossing Culduthel Road, at 3.7 km (2.3 mi), the trail crosses above multi-lane Highway 1 on the Switch Bridge.

3.9 km (2.4 mi) Descending from the bridge, the pathway arrives at the junction of the Galloping Goose and Lochside Trails. A large trailhead kiosk, which features a good map, is found here, as well as garbage cans, a number of benches, and a side trail to a nearby road. Perhaps most important, there is a water fountain.

About 100 m/yd further the two trails connect in a triangular intersection; the Galloping Goose heads left, gently curving toward Highway 1, crossing a few small streets as it does. Be wary: trail users must now stop at these intersections, not cars. Once the trail crosses Harriet Road, less than 200 m/yd from the Goose/Lochside junction, it is running parallel and adjacent to the extremely busy Highway 1.

For the next 3 km (1.9 mi), trail and highway run beside each other, often with no vegetation buffer whatsoever. Frequent side trails connect to the neighbourhoods on the right. At 4.6 km (2.9 mi), the trail crosses beneath the highway in a short tunnel.

When the trail reaches major intersections with traffic signals, such as Tillicum Road 300 m/yd further, cross the entrance/exit ramps cautiously. After Tillicum, there is a little more separation from the road and some vegetation in between trail and road. Bus stops are right beside the pathway, and there is a small shelter. At 5.2 km (3.2 mi), the trail crosses Burnside Road and Colquitz River on a roughly surfaced bridge. Mckenzie Avenue, at 6 km (3.7 mi), is an especially busy crossing.

A small bridge crosses Belgrave Road at 7 km (4.3 mi), after which the trail moves further away from Highway 1 for a short time. Actually, the terrain is a little more uneven, so the pathway begins a series of curves to follow the undulations of the landscape. Sometimes there will be houses or small parks on the left, other times it will be Highway 1 again.

At 8.2 km (5.1 mi) there is a new tunnel, and one that is well lit, beneath Helmcken Road, followed immediately by another small one as the trail climbs up from the far side. A few hundred metres/yards later, the path moves into an area where tall trees cushion it on both sides. This is quite lovely, though fairly brief. At 9 km (5.6 mi) the trail crosses Talcott Road, then 400 m/yd further it climbs to a signalized intersection at Burnside Road. (On the positive side, there is a signed connector to The Nest Café just after crossing.)

The wooded passage resumes, but it is significantly narrower and soon a major road runs close on the left. At 10 km (6.2 mi) the trail crosses beneath the two bridges of Highway 1 and it gets very noisy!

10.4 km (6.5 mi) The Goose arrives at the Atkins Road Trailhead, a major facility with washrooms, information, maps, parking, benches, and drinking water. This is also a junction with the E&N Rail Trail, currently under development.

The section that follows next was my favourite, running through a deep rock cut topped by high trees. It is quite attractive and refreshingly cool on a hot summer day. It is short, however, crossing Six Mile Road on a bridge 500 m/yd from the trailhead, and Atkins Road 200 m/yd later. Another cozy section follows, until once again Atkins Road must be crossed, at 12 km (7.5 mi).

Returning to a forested passage, the Goose curves left, crossing Mill Stream 500 m/yd later and reaching Wale Road at 12.9 km (8 mi). A difficult area follows, where there has been considerable urban development in recent years. One option is to follow the crosswalks, turning left to cross Wilfert Road then right to cross Wale Road and resume on the pathway, now gravel surfaced. This ends at multi-lane Highway 1A, where there is no crosswalk. You must turn left and follow the sidewalk to the Wale Road/Highway 1A intersection.

The other option is to cross Wilfert and Wale, then follow Wale's sidewalk to the intersection with Highway 1A. Either option brings you to this very wide, extremely busy intersection. Use the crosswalk to traverse it; on the opposite side, at about 13.2 km (8.2 mi), turn right and continue alongside Highway 1A for about 150 m/yd to reconnect with the off-road pathway – next to a Denny's restaurant, which has a connecting path.

Turn left onto the now crushed-stone-surfaced trail. Instantly the urban chaos disappears, as the Goose moves into a sheltered and shaded area, a small wooded ravine. Belmont Road crosses overhead on a small bridge, and at 14.2 km (8.8 mi), an interpretive panel to the left describes the tall trees found in this pleasant refuge, which is also the edge of the Royal Roads University grounds.

14.6 km (9.1 mi) The path carves a wide, gentle arc to the right as it turns nearly 180° before reaching and crossing busy Sooke Road at a signalized crossing with crosswalks. There is a water fountain just before the road and a large trailhead parking area on the opposite side.

The gravel track continues through a wooded area, paralleling Aldeane Avenue. To the left, for more than 1 km (0.6 mi), the large Hatley Memorial Gardens graveyard provides a buffer from nearby housing. At 16.2 km (10.1 mi), the path crosses quiet Pickford Road, but 300 m/yd later it reaches the much busier Kelly Road.

Here the pathway curves right, following Kelly Road to its intersection with the Veterans Memorial Parkway. The Goose resumes after crossing both highways; there are numerous other connecting trails, so watch for signage.

The Goose curves right, then enters a long, wooded straight section where multiple side trails branch off on both sides. It crosses Brittany Drive at 16.9 km (10.5 mi) and Jacklin Road 500 m/yd later, with tiny Colwood Creek only 100 m/yd after that.

17.7 km (11 mi) Lovely Glen Lake appears on the right. There is a small municipal park here, and this is a popular swimming area. On a hot summer day, trail users might enjoy a quick dip! If you wish a short side trip, the Cy Jenkins Trail traces Glen Lake's southern shoreline.

18.3 km (11.4 mi) The trail emerges from its forested shelter, arriving at the intersection of Sooke Road and Glen Lake Road, and another trailhead parking area. A large Welcome to Langford sign also adorns this intersection. The Galloping Goose continues, but I recommend that you stop here. There are businesses to the left, should you wish to resupply, and a water fountain at the Luxton Fairground, only about 100 m/yd further.

Return via the Galloping Goose back to downtown Victoria.

Further Information:
City of Victoria: www.victoria.ca
Galloping Goose Regional Trail: www.crd.bc.ca/
    parks-recreation-culture/parks-trails/find-park-trail/galloping-goose
Tourism Victoria: www.tourismvictoria.com

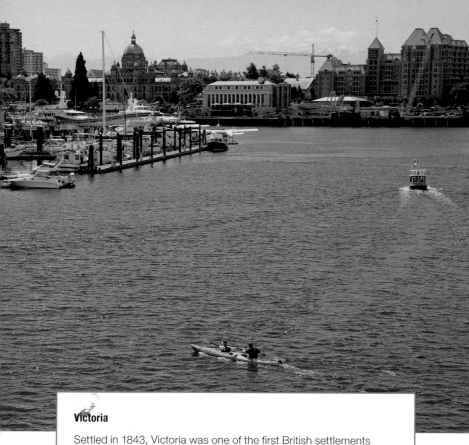

Victoria

Settled in 1843, Victoria was one of the first British settlements in the Pacific Northwest and the region's commercial centre until Vancouver became the terminus of the Canadian Pacific Railway. Victoria is British Columbia's capital, however, and with nearly 370,000 people, it's the second-largest metropolitan area in the province.

Victoria is famous for its "un-Canadian" mild winters, enjoying an annual snowfall of barely 25 cm (10 in). With its mild, warm Mediterranean summer climate and thick, fertile soil — which was farmland until urban growth claimed them — the city has become known as the Garden City.

Victoria is also well known for being one of Canada's most bicycle- and pedestrian-friendly cities, with some of the highest rates of active transportation. The city's adoption of cycling-friendly policies relates directly to the development of the Galloping Goose and other regional trails, and Victoria was one of the first cities in Canada to endorse first the Trans Canada Trail, then The Great Trail.

2. Cowichan Valley Trail

Flanked by hills reaching 1,000 m (3,280 ft) high, the Cowichan Valley is a fertile triangle of land extending from Lake Cowichan in the west to Cowichan Bay and the community of Duncan in the east. To better access Vancouver Island's rich forests, which were opening up to logging in the early 20th century, the Canadian National Railway, successor to the Canadian Northern Pacific Railway, built a long, nearly parallel, route that followed the base of the hills on both sides of the Cowichan Valley.

The valley gained its name from the Coast Salish word *Khowutzun* meaning "land warmed by the sun," and the area has been occupied by the Cowichan Peoples for many centuries. Cowichan is a collective name for a number of villages on eastern Vancouver Island, including Comiaken, Somenos, Koksilah, and Quamichan. Members of the Cowichan Tribes First Nation own and reside on much of the land surrounding Duncan and the Cowichan River. The trail passes next to and through several reserves.

Beginning in the town of Lake Cowichan, and continuing to the Kinsol Trestle, this route features excellent services and numerous options for side trips. It can also be easily broken into a two-day trip by choosing to end the first day, and begin the second, at the Glenora Trails Head Park.

2. Cowichan Valley Trail

TRUE
MAGNETIC

Contour Interval: 40M
5 KILOMETRES

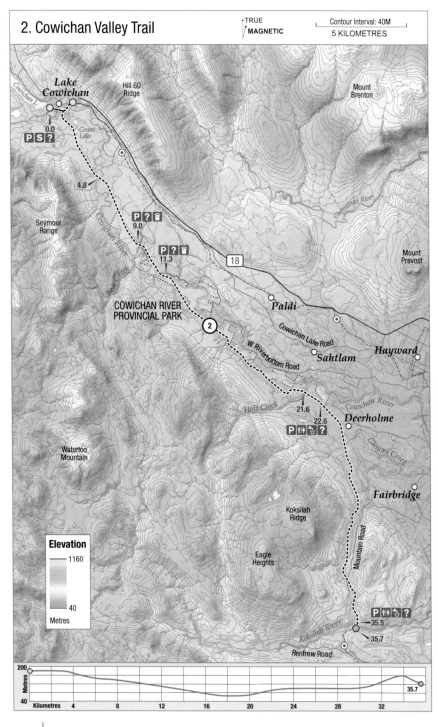

Lake Cowichan

Cowichan

Hill 60 Ridge

Mount Brenton

0.0

P S ?

Grant Lake

4.8

Chemainus River

Seymour Range

P ? 🚻
9.0

Cowichan River

P ? 🚻
11.3

18

Mount Prevost

COWICHAN RIVER PROVINCIAL PARK

2

Paldi

Cowichan Lake Road

W Riverbottom Road

Sahtlam

Hayward

Holt Creek

Cowichan River

21.6

22.6

Deerholme

P 🚻🚮 ?

Glenora Creek

Waterloo Mountain

Fairbridge

Koksilah Ridge

Mountain Road

Eagle Heights

Elevation

— 1160

— 40

Metres

P 🚻🚮 ?
35.5
35.7

Koksilah River

Renfrew Road

200
Metres
40
Kilometres   4   8   12   16   20   24   28   32

35.7

2. Cowichan Valley Trail

Distance: 35.7 km (22.2 mi), one way
Ascent: 324 m (1,063 ft)
Descent: 393 m (1,289 ft)

Trail conditions: compacted earth, crushed stone
Cellphone coverage: Partial
Hazards: giant hogweed, road crossings, ticks, wildlife

Permitted Uses							
Walking	Biking	Horseback Riding	Inline Skating	ATV	Snowshoeing	Cross-country Skiing	Snowmobiling
✔	✔	✔	—	—	✔	✔	—

Finding the trailhead: The route begins at the Trans Canada Trail Western Terminus pavilion at the junction of Wellington and Nelson Roads in the community of Lake Cowichan.

Trailhead: 48°49'23.2" N, 124°03'23.0" W (Start: Lake Cowichan)
48°40'18.7" N, 123°41' 46.5" W (Finish: Kinsol Trestle)

Observations: I thought that this was an absolutely outstanding route, from the compact, attractive village of Lake Cowichan all the way to the massive Kinsol Trestle. There are excellent services and facilities available at several locations in the provincial park, and the varied terrain – from the steep mountains flanking the valley to the farmlands near Duncan – provided constant visual stimulation.

The people are also marvellously friendly. While cycling this section I suffered a flat tire, and my patch would not hold. It was near sunset, and I was nearly 20 km (12.4 mi) from Lake Cowichan. An oncoming cyclist stopped to help and stayed with me while we walked to his car. Although he had to drive into Duncan to cross the Cowichan River, then back again to Lake Cowichan, despite residing about an hour and a half away in Victoria, he returned me to my car. It doesn't get friendlier than that.

Route description: The trailhead structure in Lake Cowichan is quite elaborate and features maps of the community as well as the trail. Picnic tables are nearby, and so are several stores and other businesses if you need any supplies before you depart. The trail is surfaced in excellent crushed stone, and it proceeds through the community, crossing a couple of streets and with roads and houses on both sides, until it reaches a junction at 575 m/yd.

This junction is with the main Cowichan Valley Trail, and there is another map here. Turn right, leaving the trail and continuing on a road, Pine Street. Continue straight for 300 m/yd, where Pine Street ends at Comiaken Avenue and the route returns to an off-road pathway. Less than 100 m/yd later, the path reaches another junction and map kiosk. Side trails branch to the right and straight ahead; turn right onto the former rail bed, about 1 km (0.6 mi) from the start.

The next section is interesting, with the surface quite rough and vegetation narrowing the treadway to one lane. After 300 m/yd the trail crosses Boundary Road, and the last of the community's houses, which are to the left, end by 1.9 km (1.2 mi). The treadway continues quite narrow and rough, with ATV tracks branching off both sides. (Watch out for ruts and potholes!)

The first bridge, crossing Fairservice Creek — which was completely dry when I travelled this — is at about 3.1 km (1.9 mi). Large trees shroud the pathway, but because a considerable amount of forest to the right has been recently cut, the steep slope of the Seymour Range is visible. Another range of hills flanks the valley on the left, but it is further away and can rarely be seen through the thick vegetation. Numerous ATV or logging vehicle tracks cross the trail through this section. At 4.5 km (2.8 mi), a sign announces your entry into the Cowichan River Provincial Park.

4.8 km (3 mi) About 300 m/yd later, the trail reaches the 70.2 Mile Trestle bridge and crosses the Cowichan River (for the first time). A set of stairs leads down to the water, and there is an interpretive panel at the bridge's far end. After the bridge, the trail makes a short curve right, then settles into an extended straightaway. Some unsigned paths occasionally branch off the rail trail, as does at least one vehicle track.

At 6.3 km (3.9 mi), a dirt road crosses the trail, and a park sign indicates that the Skutz Falls Day-Use Area is 2.8 km (1.7 mi) further ahead. The forest through here is quite luxuriant, with a canopy high overhead providing shade. Massive clumps of ferns spring from the ground, and many of the large tree trunks are covered with moss. It very much looks like the rain forest it is, though temperate, not tropical.

When another gravel track connects on the right, at 7.8 km (4.8 mi), there is another park sign providing direction. These signs are the only human structures since the trestle bridge. However, only 400 m/yd later houses and farms appear on the left.

9 km (5.6 mi) The trail reaches the Skutz Falls Day-Use Area, where there are picnic tables, outhouses, and a kiosk with maps. The falls are almost in sight

to the right; you can probably hear the cascading water. The trail also crosses the dirt Skutz Falls Road here, after which the roughest section of the pathway follows. It was nearly overgrown when I visited, narrowed to footpath width as it passes through the Skutz Reserve #8.

At 9.7 km (6 mi), the trail crosses Mayo Road. On the right is the Skutz Falls trailhead, start of an excellent hiking trail that follows the Cowichan River. Continue straight, in another 250 m/yd the pathway crosses Riverbottom Road, where there is another picnic area. On the opposite side a gate restricts vehicle access to the trail, and regulatory signage lists permitted and restricted uses.

From here the pathway widens and becomes smoother cycling. The river soon becomes visible to the right, and there are several connections to park footpaths.

11.3 km (7 mi) The trail arrives at the 66 Mile (Marie Canyon) Trestle Day-Use Area — and its impressive namesake bridge, which crosses high above the Cowichan River. The picnic ground, with outhouses, is to the left, and footpaths connect to the rail trail on both ends of the trestle. This bridge, made of steel, is not very long, but it sits quite high above the deep, narrow gorge.

The good surface disappears on the far side of the bridge, and once again vegetation crowds toward the centre, narrowing the trail considerably. Curving right, the path continues straight, with no views available through the dense tree cover. At 13.2 km (8.2 mi) it crosses a gravel road, after which grass covers almost the entire trail surface. About 800 m/yd later, the next small bridge traverses another dry creek bed.

At 14.2 km (8.8 mi), the Cowichan River Footpath, which began at the 66 Mile Trestle, reconnects with the rail trail. It will do so several times more over the next several kilometres/miles: always on the left, and always marked by a park sign – sometimes one that provides distances to picnic grounds along the Cowichan Valley Trail.

The river comes into view 200 m/yd later and is visible for the next several hundred metres/yards. At 14.7 km (9.1 mi), a deep ravine to the right is choked with moss-covered tree trunks, giving the impression of a jungle. Through this section, the thick vegetation is quite fascinating, especially to those unfamiliar with the Western rain forest.

Another deep ravine, created by a surprisingly small creek, opens on the right at 16.3 km (10.1 mi). Some 600 m/yd further the trail briefly touches the bank of the Cowichan River. This is almost the lowest point in the route, the trail having been almost continuously downhill since leaving Lake Cowichan. The trail will continue more or less at this level for the next 3 km (1.9 mi), then climb for most of its remaining distance.

21.6 km (13.4 mi) After a long trek through forest, which gradually shifts to being mostly softwoods, the trail gradually widens and arrives at the impressive 73 m/yd long Holt Trestle. This is a wooden bridge, and it crosses high above a deep ravine, not the Cowichan River, but Holt Creek. This structure was renovated in 2001, and again in 2017-18. There is no picnic ground near the bridge, but the park footpath connects just before reaching it.

The trail has returned to being very wide now, with almost a crushed-stone surface. The moss-covered forest has been replaced by towering pines and a smattering of hardwoods.

22.6 km (14 mi) The trail arrives at a wide connecting trail, lined with cedar rail fences, to the Glenora Trails Head Park, which is to the left. This community park features excellent facilities, including covered picnic tables, a year-round washroom, and drinking water. It is also an important trailhead for horseback riders, so be prepared to encounter them and be familiar with the proper trail etiquette: hikers and cyclists yield to them in all circumstances.

A sign at the junction indicates that it is 13 km (8.1 mi) further to the Kinsol Trestle. The trail is in good condition through here and continues straight, paralleled on the right for about 800 m/yd by Shawnigan Road. At 24 km (14.9 mi) it touches the end of Rowe Road, and after this it curves right and narrows. Several ATV or 4x4 tracks cross in the next few hundred metres/yards, before reaching and crossing Shawnigan Road 700 m/yd later and

Waters Road 150 m/yd after that. Concrete barriers lie across the trail at the latter.

Once across Waters Road the trail widens again, and for the first time moves into an area of cultivated land. There is a tiny creek to cross, and a few quiet roads, but by 26.6 km (16.5 mi) the pathway is once again bordered by thick forest. Less than 1 km (0.6 mi) later, a gas pipeline connects from the left, and parallels the trail for most of the remaining distance to the Kinsol.

For the next several kilometres/miles, the trail meanders through the thick forest, gradually climbing and accompanied by a grass-covered berm covering the pipeline. At 30.7 km (19.1 mi), there is another small bridge, after which there are warning signs about giant hogweed. It is clear from the tread marks in the trail that vehicles share the track, and some maps name this Hawthorne Road.

Shortly after the bridge is a cultivated area, but the path/road soon returns to forest, with frequent side roads, ATV tracks, and driveways branching off. It is only at 32.8 km (20.4 mi), after crossing Mountain Road and passing a gate, that the route returns to being solely a recreational pathway.

The path curves right, then begins to rapidly (for a rail trail) descend, crossing Humes Road at 34.2 km (21.3 mi). Just past it, on the left, is a small pond – the first one seen along this path. With only 500 m/yd remaining (a sign says so), there is a connecting path on the left, gated, and an information kiosk. The final few metres/yards are through a rock cut, and drop noticeably.

35.5 km (22.1 mi) The trail arrives at the north end of the Kinsol Trestle: an awe-inspiring sight. The high bridge appears to be an elaborate lattice of Popsicle sticks rather than an actual industrial structure. Fortunately, numerous interpretive panels are available to explain how and why it was built as it is. An entire park has been developed around this magnificent structure, with washrooms, picnic tables, and a number of viewing platforms providing different perspectives of this somewhat overwhelming edifice.

It is less than 200 m/yd across, but take the time to explore the footpaths that descend to the Koksilah River and run beneath the trestle. This is a fascinating perspective unavailable at most of these exceptional constructions. When you have rested and contemplated the Kinsol long enough, retrace the trail back to Lake Cowichan.

Further Information:

Canada's Historic Places — Kinsol Trestle: www.
    historicplaces.ca/en/rep-reg/place-lieu.aspx?id=18478

Cowichan River Provincial Park: http://www.env.gov.bc.ca/
    bcparks/explore/parkpgs/cowichan_rv/

Cowichan Valley Regional District : www.cvrd.bc.ca/1379/
    Kinsol-Trestle

Tourism Cowichan Valley: www.tourismcowichan.com

Kinsol Trestle

By 2008, only one piece of the puzzle to connect Victoria to Nanaimo remained: the former trestle bridge crossing the Koksilah River in the Cowichan Valley. The provincial government wanted to tear it down because of 30 years of decay and arson damage, but the local community demanded it be restored. By 2010 reconstruction began, and in July 2011, it was officially opened for use.

The Kinsol — named from the former King Solomon copper mine — is no ordinary trestle bridge: at 187 m/yd long and standing 44 m (144 ft) above the river, it is one of the tallest free-standing and timber rail trestle structures in the world. Originally completed in 1920, the gently curving structure is an elegant testament to the sophisticated engineering techniques of railway construction required in British Columbia's challenging topography.

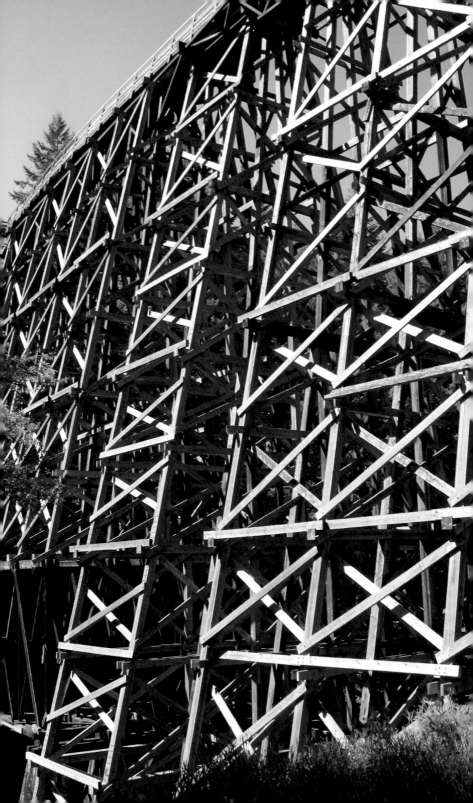

3. Sea to Sky Trail

Ultimately intended to run for 180 km (112 mi) through the mountainous terrain between Squamish and D'Arcy, the Sea to Sky Trail connects The Great Trail to one of Canada's premier resort communities: Whistler. Well known for its central role in the 2010 Winter Olympics, it is difficult to visit this bustling community of nearly 12,000 permanent residents – and throngs of seasonal workers and tourists – and consider that its celebrated ski hill only opened in 1966. Whistler Blackcomb has grown to become one of the largest ski resorts in North America. Its Peak 2 Peak Gondola attracts visitors year round.

Today, Whistler is one of the most dynamic outdoor communities in the nation, as famous for its mountain biking as its alpine skiing. Whistler Mountain Bike Park, first opened in 2008, now sees an estimated 100,000 visitors annually. Its advanced runs feature an impressive 1,100 m (3,609 ft) vertical descent.

In most places the Sea to Sky Trail is well signed and easy to follow. However, junctions with other sections of the extensive Valley Trail pathway system and informal side trails and footpaths are frequent. In addition, there are several places where the route follows a road, sometimes on a designated pathway, but sometimes not. In the residential area there are many opportunities to take a wrong turn, but it also should be easy to relocate. Once you are on the mountain bike section, following the correct trail is much simpler.

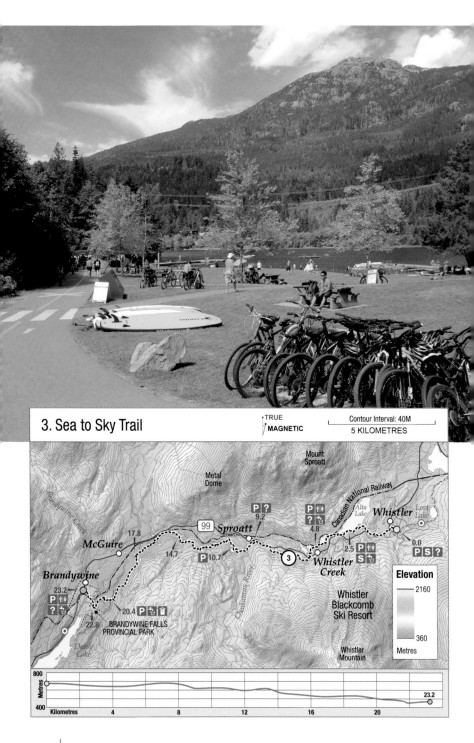

3. Sea to Sky Trail

TRUE
MAGNETIC

Contour Interval: 40M
5 KILOMETRES

Brandywine Creek

Mount
Sproatt

Metal
Dome

Canadian National Railway

Alta
Lake

Whistler

Lost
Lake

P ?
9.2

P
4.8

99 Sproatt

McGuire
17.8

14.7

P 10.7

3

2.5 P S

0.0
P S ?

Whistler
Creek

Brandywine

23.2
P

?

20.4 P

22.8 BRANDYWINE FALLS
PROVINCIAL PARK

Cheakamus River

Whistler
Blackcomb
Ski Resort

Elevation
— 2160

360
Metres

Daisy
Lake

Whistler
Mountain

800

Metres

400

Kilometres   4   8   12   16   20

23.2

3. Sea to Sky Trail

Distance: 23.2 km (14.4 mi), one way
Ascent: 468 m (1,535 ft)
Descent: 668 m (2,192 ft)

Trail conditions: asphalt, crushed stone, natural surface
Cellphone coverage: partial
Hazards: road crossings, rugged terrain, ticks, wildlife

					Permitted Uses			
Walking	Biking	Horseback Riding	Inline Skating	ATV	Snowshoeing	Cross-country Skiing	Snowmobiling
✔	✔	—	✔*	—	✔	✔	—

Finding the trailhead: Begin this route at the southwest corner of Village Gate Boulevard and Whistler Way in the community of Whistler. Start on the off-road pathway alongside the extra-large inukshuk.

Trailhead: 50°06'58.1" N, 122°57'27.1" W (Start: Whistler)
50°02'16.3" N, 123°02'16.6" W (Finish: Brandywine Falls Provincial Park)

Observations: This route is two distinct experiences. From its start to the site of the former Olympic Village, about 10.5 km (6.5 mi), the trail is paved and mostly passes through areas of housing, resorts, and golf clubs. It is an easy ride through what is often a nearly urban setting, although with phenomenal mountain scenery. Once it descends the hill from the hostel and enters the forest, the track becomes a rugged pathway through challenging terrain and remains that way until it reaches Brandywine Falls Provincial Park.

Although there are frequent small climbs and descents, overall this route descends toward Brandywine Falls Provincial Park, losing more than 200 m (655+ ft) of elevation. Except for one challenging hill, the first portion is suitable for novices and families using hybrid or even road bicycles. However, the second section definitely requires mountain bikes, as the terrain is rocky and hilly, negotiated on a narrow track, and heads into fairly remote countryside, where wildlife encounters are far more likely.

Put together, this route offers a wide range of experiences and should provide a complete and enjoyable day for anyone who undertakes it all.

Route description: From the inukshuk, follow the paved pathway toward Highway 99. It curves left and soon runs alongside Whistler Way. Turn right onto the first paved road, following the signs directing toward the Valley Trail. This road passes underneath Highway 99; at 350 m/yd, turn left onto an off-road pathway, just before you reach the Whistler Golf Club.

There are two large kiosks here with excellent maps, and directional signs indicate that this is the Sea to Sky and TCT (or Great Trail) route. Bear-proof garbage cans sit nearby, and there is an interpretive panel about the Sea to Sky Trail.

The asphalt-surfaced path follows an attractive, and rather hilly, route that is flanked and shaded by tall conifers. Light posts provide nighttime illumination, for this is a busy route, with cyclists and walkers, residents and visitors, tourists and staff all using this as a safe active transportation corridor. To the right is the golf course, framed by snow-tipped Mount Sproat and Rainbow Mountain. On the left is busy Highway 99, usually heard rather than seen.

After about 1 km (0.6 mi), this pleasant forested trail reaches Blueberry Drive and turns right, paralleling the road. Just 50 m/yd later, the Sea to Sky Trail heads left alongside St. Anton Way, crossing Blueberry Drive via a crosswalk, and at km 1.8 (1.1 mi) it turns left again at Archibald Way on a bidirectional cycling lane. Well marked, well signed, and with crosswalks at every intersection, the route turns right at Carleton Way then left once more at Lakeshore Road.

2.5 km (1.6 mi) The pathway enters Lakeside Park, a popular beach and picnic area, where there are barbeque pits, washrooms, drinking water, and a canteen. Canoe and bicycle rentals are available here as well. During the summer, expect to walk your bike through this busy area. Once past the beach, the trail climbs to Lakecrest Lane, where the trail ends and you must use the road.

But after barely 100 m/yd, the off-road pathway resumes and the trail re-enters the forest. At 3 km (1.9 mi), at a T-junction, turn right, and follow the winding trail as it drops down once more to Alta Lake and small Wayside Park, where there are washroom facilities and another trail map kiosk. The trail resumes winding through the gorgeous forest, emerging at a trail junction beside the railway tracks at 3.5 km (2.2 mi); keep left.

Reaching Nita Lake, the path curves left to follow its shoreline. At 4.1 km (2.5 mi), it crosses the small bridge over Whistler Creek. On the far side are a trail junction, a map kiosk, picnic tables, and several interpretive panels. Continue straight, passing in front of and around the Nita Lake Lodge. At 4.6 km (2.9 mi), the trail reaches the Whistler train station, where there is a water fountain.

4.8 km (3 mi) After touching briefly on Lake Placid Road, the pathway reaches Alpha Lake Park, a lovely picnic area and beach with washroom facilities. It also features a large off-leash beachfront dog park known as "Arfa Park." The pathway once again traces the lake's perimeter, before turning left, crossing a few quiet streets, and ending at Highway 99 at 5.5 km (3.4 mi).

There is a sign here that says Trail Ends. Turn right, walking or cycling on the paved shoulder for 100 m/yd to the signalized intersection with Bayshore Drive. Turn left and cross Highway 99. On the opposite side, a bidirectional pathway resumes on the left side of Bayshore. Follow this uphill, crossing Brandywine Way, after which Bayshore changes its name to Cheakamus Way.

For 600 m/yd from Highway 99, the pathway is on the left of Cheakamus. It then crosses that road – in mid-block – at a crosswalk, after which the trail wanders a short distance away from the road and very close to some houses. At 6.5 km (4 mi), the trail intersects Cheakamus Way again and ends with no sign. Continue straight on Cheakamus – there is a tennis court on the left – and turn left 60 m/yd later onto Millars Pond Crescent.

This road ends in less than 100 m/yd, after which the off-road path resumes – and climbs sharply! Some 300 m/yd later, it crosses Alpha Creek, and 100 m/yd further the trail connects to the end of Spring Creek Drive. For the next 1.1 km (0.7 mi), the pathway parallels this road, though separated by a vegetated buffer and sometimes a building. It is a quite pleasant descent, almost reaching Highway 99, passing behind the Spring Creek Community School, École la Passerelle, and the Whistler Community Services Society.

At 8.2 km (5.1 mi), the trail crosses Spring Creek Drive and re-enters a forested area. For the next 850 m/yd, the route meanders through the trees and underneath a large power line. There is even a hairpin 180° turn, just before the path drops down to the edge of the large parking area for the Whistler Interpretive Forest.

9.2 km (5.7 mi) The trail reaches Cheakamus Lake Road, where the Interpretive Forest has a large trailhead pavilion. Several footpaths branch off the asphalt-surfaced Sea to Sky Trail and head into the woodlands; your route curves left and follows the road uphill.

The path is separated from the road by a narrow buffer, at least until trail and road merge to cross the fast-flowing Cheakamus River, 550 m/yd later. The road changes name here, becoming Legacy Way, and the asphalt pathway continues alongside this road

The asphalt path ends at the Whistler International Hostel, site of the former Olympic Village, at 10.2 km (6.3 mi). There is a nice café in the hostel, and I advise refreshing your food and water before continuing further. Behind the hostel is Bayly Park, boasting a huge new playground and soccer field. Continue along Legacy Way for another 150 m/yd, then turn right into a parking lot. Follow the gravel path out of the lot and between the soccer field and an off-leash dog area. At the next junction turn left; the trail descends the hillside, runs beneath the power line, and briefly connects with the gravel Jane Lakes Road.

10.7 km (6.6 mi) Arrive at the start of the mountain bike section, where there is a Sea to Sky sign that states it is 12.3 km (7.6 mi) to Brandywine Falls Provincial Park. It also says that it is 1,000 m/yd to a side trail to the Train Wreck Site.

The experience changes completely from this point. Instead of a wide asphalt pathway, the track narrows to single-track width, and although the

Brandywine Falls

At 70 m (230 ft), Brandywine Falls is higher than Niagara Falls, though not even one of the ten highest in British Columbia. However, its setting, deep within a canyon carved into volcanic basalt cliffs, is dramatic and has been attracting visitors for more than 100 years. In the early 1900s, people travelled to Brandywine Falls by train, as there was no road until the 1950s. There was a station nearby, and log cabins housed visitors.

The origins of the name are uncertain, but the most popular story has it receiving its unusual appellation as a result of a wager over the height of the falls between two surveyors for the Howe Sound and Northern Railway. Whoever guessed closest would win a bottle of brandy(wine). Bob Mollison won the bottle of brandy; Jack Nelson named the falls Brandywine after the prize.

Train Wreck Site

In 1956, seven Canadian National boxcars derailed near Function Junction, a Whistler suburb. The train's owner, Pacific Great Eastern Railway, did not have the necessary equipment to move the wedged boxcars and hired local loggers to help extricate their wedged cars. The loggers did so, dragging them away from the tracks and into a wooded area, but the railway never retrieved them.

Over the years, the surrounding trees have thrived, creating the striking contrast of industrial detritus within a seemingly pristine natural setting. Further, well-known graffiti artists such as BC-born Chili Thom and Whistler street artist Kris Kupskay, among many others, have been visiting the wrecks for years and painting the boxcars.

The result has been the creation of one of the area's most popular — and certainly unique — artistic sites. With the construction of a suspension bridge over the Cheakamus River in 2016, the Train Wreck Site can easily be reached with only a short detour from the Sea to Sky Trail.

treadway is surfaced with crushed stone, the route becomes a twisting anaconda that is constantly changing elevation; it is rarely level for more than a few metres/yards. Either exposed rock or steep hillsides line the path, and there is no longer any expertly landscaped housing anywhere: you are in an area of forest and isolation.

For the next several kilometres/miles the trail cuts a narrow, challenging route through the rugged terrain. Frequent, tiny ravines and brooks are crossed on short unrailed bridges. And although tall fir and pine usually snuggly enfold the path, whenever there is a break in the vegetation the views of Mount Sproat and the Metal Dome (what a cool name!) are breathtaking. The Cheakamus River, though often quite close, will be heard but rarely seen.

At 14.5 km (9 mi), the trail connects to a gravel road; turn right and follow it downhill.

14.7 km (9.1 mi) You reach Cheakamus River Suspension Bridge, an impressive span across the wide and roiling river that was constructed in 2014. A sign indicates 6.3 km (3.9 mi) to Brandywine Falls Provincial Park. There are no picnic tables or other facilities nearby, but this is a lovely area for a short rest and a snack.

Once across the bridge, the single track returns, although it seems as if it might be using the route of a former forest road. In several places the treadway has been built up above its original level, its layers of large gravel topped by crushed stone quite apparent. About 1.1 km (0.7 mi) from the bridge, the path enters a clearing. To the right, the railway and Highway 99 are less than 100 m/ yd away; turn left.

Once past the clearing, the trail enters an area that had been quarried, but is now regenerating. Some of the remaining rocks appear almost sculpted at times, and there are even places where small boulders have been arranged in artistic designs.

Between 16.2 and 16.7 km (10.1 and 10.4 mi) is probably the most challenging section of this route, with the trail switching back and forth several times through tight corners. At 17.3 km (10.8 mi), the path reaches gravel Cal Cheak Road. Cross, and continue straight on the natural surfaced narrow track beneath towering pines, with views of Callaghan Creek.

17.8 km (11.1 mi) Arrive at the Cal-Cheak Suspension Bridge. Actually, this is a junction, where you turn left. The bridge is in sight to the right, but if you want to cross it that is a bonus walk. There are picnic tables in this area, and an outhouse, but the campground is closed. Less than 200 m/yd from the bridge, the trail reconnects with the Cal Cheak Road and ends.

Turn right, and follow the road. It crosses the Cheakamus River 200 m/yd farther, and continues through the fields and nearly abandoned community of McGuire. Although there is no signage in this section, continue until you reach the entrance to Whistler Bungee at 20.2 km (12.6 mi). Head left and climb uphill.

20.4 km (12.7 mi) You arrive at the Whistler Bungee Bridge, which spans the Cheakamus River more than 50 m (164 ft) above a deep, basalt cliff-lined gorge. If cycling, you will definitely need to dismount and walk the narrow bridge through the crowd if people are jumping.

Once across, you are in Brandywine Falls Provincial Park, where the bungee company has washrooms…and a bar! There are also some picnic tables in the surrounding area, close to nearby Pothole Lake. The Sea to Sky, once again with a crushed-stone surface, turns left and along the lip of the ravine to an excellent lookout, where you can view the jumpers.

The winding pathway enters a lovely area of jack pines and other conifers, passing several small ponds. It curves right until reaching a junction at 21 km (13 mi). From here it turns sharply left, crossing once again beneath a power line, then works its weaving way through the rocky terrain, always descending. Some of the best mountain views occur through here, when Castle Towers Mountain and The Black Tusk can be seen to the south.

After reaching the power line a second time, the trail almost turns back upon itself before dropping down to reach the railway tracks, and a trail junction, at 22.7 km (14.1 mi).

22.8 km (14.2 mi) Turn left onto the side trail to the lookout for Brandywine Falls, and arrive there 100 m/yd from the junction. There is an excellent viewing platform with interpretive panels, perched atop the sheer cliff walls overlooking the 70 m (230 ft) cascade.

Return to the main trail, and cross the railway tracks. After an easy 250 m/yd, much of it lined by wooden rail fences, the trail reaches a roofed bridge crossing Brandywine Creek. There is a mini waterfall here.

23.2 km (14.4 mi) Arrive at the parking area in Brandywine Falls Provincial Park, where there are washrooms, drinking water, picnic tables, and interpretive panels. This is often a busy spot. The off-road section of the Sea to Sky Trail ends here. To reach Squamish, walkers/cyclists must follow Highway 99. Rest a little, then retrace the route back to Whistler Village.

Further Information:
Brandywine Falls Provincial Park: www.env.gov.bc.ca/bcparks/explore/
    parkpgs/brandywine_falls
Sea to Sky Trail: www.slrd.bc.ca/recreation-culture/parks-trails/sea-sky-trail
Tourism Whistler: www.whistler.com
Trails BC (Updates and Closures): www.trailsbc.ca/closures

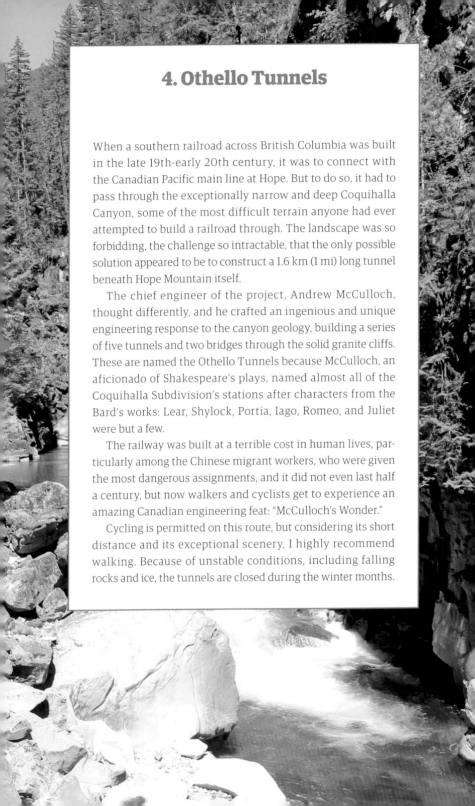

4. Othello Tunnels

When a southern railroad across British Columbia was built in the late 19th-early 20th century, it was to connect with the Canadian Pacific main line at Hope. But to do so, it had to pass through the exceptionally narrow and deep Coquihalla Canyon, some of the most difficult terrain anyone had ever attempted to build a railroad through. The landscape was so forbidding, the challenge so intractable, that the only possible solution appeared to be to construct a 1.6 km (1 mi) long tunnel beneath Hope Mountain itself.

The chief engineer of the project, Andrew McCulloch, thought differently, and he crafted an ingenious and unique engineering response to the canyon geology, building a series of five tunnels and two bridges through the solid granite cliffs. These are named the Othello Tunnels because McCulloch, an aficionado of Shakespeare's plays, named almost all of the Coquihalla Subdivision's stations after characters from the Bard's works: Lear, Shylock, Portia, Iago, Romeo, and Juliet were but a few.

The railway was built at a terrible cost in human lives, particularly among the Chinese migrant workers, who were given the most dangerous assignments, and it did not even last half a century, but now walkers and cyclists get to experience an amazing Canadian engineering feat: "McCulloch's Wonder."

Cycling is permitted on this route, but considering its short distance and its exceptional scenery, I highly recommend walking. Because of unstable conditions, including falling rocks and ice, the tunnels are closed during the winter months.

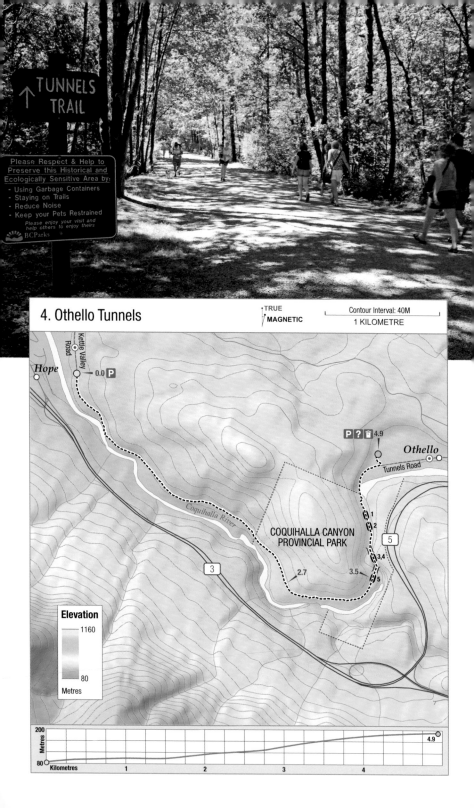

TUNNELS TRAIL

↑

4. Othello Tunnels

TRUE
MAGNETIC

Contour Interval: 40M
1 KILOMETRE

Hope

Kettle Valley Road

0.0 P

P ? 🚻 4.9

Othello

Tunnels Road

Coquihalla River

COQUIHALLA CANYON
PROVINCIAL PARK

3

5

1
2

3,4
5

2.7

3.5

Elevation

1160

80

Metres

200

Metres

80

Kilometres   1   2   3   4

4.9

4. Othello Tunnels

Distance: 4.9 km (3 mi), one way
Ascent: 184 m (604 ft)
Descent: 22 m (72 ft)

Trail conditions: compacted earth, crushed stone
Cellphone coverage: yes (but not in the tunnels)
Hazards: ticks, wildlife

Permitted Uses							
Walking	Biking	Horseback Riding	Inline Skating	ATV	Snowshoeing	Cross-country Skiing	Snowmobiling
✔	✔	✔*	—	—	✔*	✔*	—

Finding the trailhead: From Highway 1, exit onto Old Hope Princeton Way. Turn left onto 6 Avenue, about 900 m/yd. After 250 m/yd, turn right onto Kawkawa Lake Road. Turn right onto Kettle Valley Road in 1.8 km (1.1 mi). Continue to the end of the road in 750 m/yd.

Trailhead: 49°22'26.2" N, 121°24'23.0" W (Start: Kettle Valley Road)
49°22'40.7" N, 121°22'10.9" W (Finish: Coquihalla Canyon Provincial Park)

Observations: There is nothing else like this on any other trail in Canada: a series of tunnels and bridges, one immediately after the other, which spans a deep canyon. The impact of so impossible looking a landscape is breathtaking, particularly as it arrives so suddenly, and is so dramatic. While moving through the high arched passageways, or crossing the bridges beneath dizzying granite heights, it seems more like an amusement park than reality, or like a CGI illusion.

This route is very short compared to any other in either Volume 1 or Volume 2, but you have only to experience it yourself to understand why it could not be ignored. This is a trail where speed of travel is unimportant, and dawdling should be mandatory. I spent a considerable length of time standing on those bridges, looking into the tunnels at either end, and attempting to imagine the engineers dangling in wicker chairs from the heights above.

Route description: Kettle Valley Road is built on what was once a railway line. A metal gate restricts further travel by vehicles, and the only sign that this is

a trail is a TCT marker on the gate. A garbage can is the only facility, although there is plenty of room for parking.

The setting is lovely. To the right the Coquihalla River bubbles away jauntily, barely seen but certainly heard. Trees tower overhead and provide welcome protection from sun and wind. The pathway itself is wide and in excellent condition, a compacted earth surface sprinkled over with pine needles. Oak and maple are mixed in with the pine, but softwoods dominate. Only an errant power line clashes with the natural backdrop.

Side paths depart to the right, heading toward the nearby river. By 300 m/yd there are rocky embankments to the left, though moss covers them and softens their normally rugged appearance. By 350 m/yd the river is already 10-15 m (33-49 ft) lower than the trail. Some 50 m/yd later the power line exits right, crossing the Coquihalla.

This river is a magnificent mountain stream, rapidly flowing over and around a rock-strewn bed, the water cold and clear, sparkling in the sunlight. At 550 m/yd, at a gap in the vegetation to the right, the 1,844 m (6,050 ft) Hope Mountain dominates the skyline, though other jagged peaks are nearby. Even in July, patches of snow can be seen in north-facing ravines near their summits.

Huge trees rear out of the river valley, towering above the trail, especially by the 700 m/yd mark. These fir and pine trees also grow on the slope above. The trail is easy walking, wide and level, and seems incongruous in this rugged landscape. But the adjacent vegetation is so thick that it isn't until 950 m/yd that another good view of the river can be obtained.

At 1.2 km (0.8 mi) a wide track branches right and lower into the river valley; keep straight. As you continue, you will notice that the lower branches of many trees are thickly coated in green moss and that huge ferns grow alongside the pathway. At the western end of the Fraser Valley, and at the edge of the temperate coastal rain forest, Hope enjoys cool summers and mild winters, and quite a bit of rain.

At 1.6 km (1 mi) the trees give way on the right for a short time, and there are excellent views up and across the narrow valley and into the mountains. In any railway cuts – vertically edged defiles carved through the rocks – the vegetation is especially thick and almost jungle-like. A rocky knoll on the right at 2.3 km (1.4 mi) sits high above the river; the water below looks inviting, but it is at the bottom of a cliff. Soon afterwards, the trail returns to its sylvan shade.

2.7 km (1.7 mi) When you reach the junction with the Hope-Nicola Valley Trail you are already inside the Coquihalla Canyon Provincial Park, but there has been no signage of any type thus far except for a single TCT marker at the gate. This intersection is well signed, and you will note that horses may use the Hope-Nicola Valley, as well as what you have walked on so far. They may not continue further on the rail trail, however.

Before the railroad, mule trains and pack horses used to climb to Coquihalla Valley, and a trail was cut over these hills to enable passage. The Hope-Nicola Valley Trail follows that historic route in a difficult grunt that ends at the parking area of the provincial park. Ordinarily, I would have recommended doing this route as a loop including the Hope-Nicola Valley, but the tunnels are so exceptional that I did not.

About 100 m/yd later there is a gate across the rail trail, with a park map affixed. Immediately afterwards, the path enters a rail cut over which several large tree trunks lie. Once past this gate, you are likely to encounter a fair number of people who have entered the park from the other direction. As the trail moves toward the tunnels, it leaves the cut. To the right is a steep embankment down to the river, and at 3.4 km (2.1 mi) there is a prominent sign warning of rock falls. Beyond it is a chain-link fence on the river side and a concrete retaining wall to the left. The trail surface is crushed stone.

3.5 km (2.2 mi) The trail enters the first tunnel; the park maps label it as Tunnel #5 and it bears the date 1951 above the arch. The tunnel curves left, so you cannot see the exit initially. When it does emerge, at a bridge over the Coquihalla River, the park's first interpretive panel is visible: Conquering the Canyon.

Nation-Building Railway 2.0

With the discovery of silver in the southern interior of British Columbia in 1887, thousands of American prospectors and businessmen moved into the area. As supplies were available more quickly and cheaply via the Northern Pacific Railway through Spokane, the area was essentially occupied by the United States.

Critics had long complained that the Canadian Pacific Railway's original cross-Canada route was too far north, and this "invasion" seemed to support that view. To reclaim BC's south for Canada, the Kettle Valley Railway (KVR) was hastily commissioned to connect Vancouver with Calgary and was dubbed the "Coast-to-Kootenay" route.

Because of the extraordinarily difficult terrain, the railroad took twenty years to complete and was phenomenally expensive. One mile of track near the Othello Tunnels was the most costly single mile of rail line built anywhere in the world to that date.

By the time the KVR opened in 1915, BC's southern interior was firmly Canadian once again. But the line did not last long. With its steep grades though mountainous terrain, it was always dangerous to operate and difficult to maintain. A large washout in 1959 near Hope led to the Coquihalla Subdivision being abandoned; the remainder died piece by piece over the next two decades.

The trail crosses this bridge and immediately enters Tunnels #4 and #3. Take some time here to marvel at the vertical canyon walls, the raging river, and the amazing tunnels engineered through a mountain of granite. Between #4 and #3 is a section where the right side is open and supported with concrete pillars. I thought that this entire length was all one long tunnel, not two.

The next bridge is shorter but no less impressive. If you look carefully, you should be able to see through to the far side of both remaining tunnels, #1 and #2, which is so cool! Voices and footsteps echo in the enclosed spaces – somewhat spooky when you are alone – but it is pretty noisy when there are lots of people.

You emerge from the final, longest tunnel, #1, at 4.3 km (2.7 mi). Another interpretive panel, titled McCulloch's Wonder, stands to the right. After what you just experienced, you can probably accept that this is not an overstatement.

The pathway is much wider here, and the river runs beside it, almost at the same level and rather sedately compared to its seething passage through the canyon. The first benches and picnic tables make their appearance, and within 200 m/yd there is access to the water. You might wish to dip your feet, but swimming is not recommended. Looking upstream, you can see Ogilvie Peak, which forms a northern mountain rampart to the Coquihalla Valley.

The trail now is almost twice as wide as when you started, but there is still a high rock face to the left. The path curves right, following the river's course, until 4.8 km (3 mi). The route of the former rail line continues a short distance until it reaches and is covered over by Tunnels Road. The trail turns left.

4.9 km (3 mi) The trail ends at the parking lot for Coquihalla Canyon Provincial Park. There are outhouses here and more picnic tables, as well as garbage cans and additional interpretive panels.

From here you may return via the Hope-Nicola Valley Trail, if you really need to add some challenge and effort, or return through the tunnels and marvel once again at McCulloch's Wonder.

Further Information:
Coquihalla Canyon Provincial Park: www.env.gov.bc.ca/bcparks/explore/
    parkpgs/coquihalla_cyn
District of Hope: www.hope.ca
Hope Tourism: www.hopebc.ca

Steller's Jay

Common to western forests, the Steller's jay resembles its eastern cousin, the blue jay, sporting a large crest. It even shares a raucous, abrasive call. The Steller's jay has a black head, however, and its dark colours allow it to hide in the dense coniferous forests it prefers.

Most of the time it forages high in trees for its food, preferring pine seeds and acorns. It also tends to nest high in trees, at least 3 m (10 ft) off the ground. However, it will look for nourishment at ground level, and though not as bold as its boreal forest cousin, the grey jay, the Steller's jay will eat table scraps, or some of your picnic lunch, if offered.

Though preferring the coniferous forest, Steller's jays will range into other varieties of woodland and orchards, and even into well-wooded suburbs.

5. Penticton KVR

Railway construction in British Columbia's mountains required perseverance, creativity, engineering excellence, and lots of money. Nowhere was that more true than on the Kettle Valley Railway, connecting Midway to Hope through the southern BC interior. To reach Penticton, at the bottom of Okanagan Lake, the best solution available was to complete the longest stretch of 2.2% grade in Canada: more than 40 km (25 mi). At a 1% grade, train engines can move half of the load that they can on a level track; grades steeper than 2.2% were not considered economically feasible except for very short stretches.

For a trail, this characteristic makes this route virtually unique: it is entirely uphill in one direction and, for a considerable distance, down in the other. As a hiker this will not be particularly helpful, but cyclists will love it. I selected to end this route at the Adra, or Big, Tunnel, as the distance worked well for completing it as a two-day hike. Those wishing a two-day bike ride should consider continuing to Chute Lake, where there is a Regional Park campsite and the Chute Lake Lodge.

Trail users should be mindful that there is little or no water available along this trail, and they should expect to experience extremely hot and dry conditions. Bring sufficient water supplies, and be prepared for long periods of sun exposure. Keep in mind also that as much of the trail surface is loose gravel, the long uphill trip will seem even longer.

5. Penticton KVR

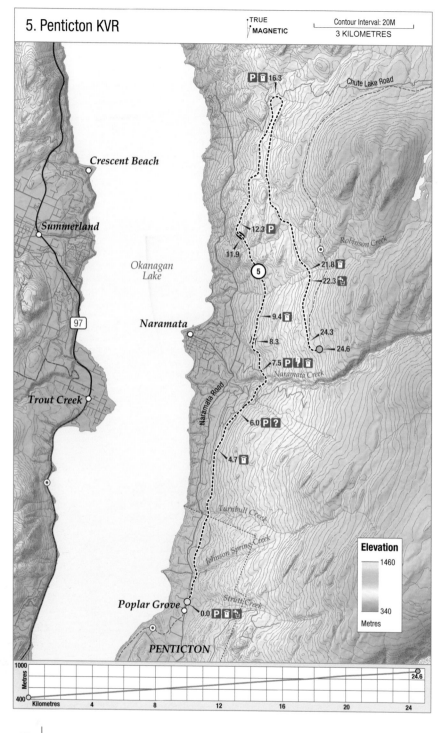

TRUE
MAGNETIC

Contour Interval: 20M
3 KILOMETRES

Crescent Beach

Summerland

Okanagan
Lake

Naramata

Trout Creek

Chute Lake Road

Robinson Creek

Naramata Road

Naramata Creek

Turnbull Creek

Johnson Spring Creek

Poplar Grove

Stratti Creek

PENTICTON

16.3
12.3
11.9
5
9.4
8.3
7.5
6.0
4.7
0.0
21.8
22.3
24.3
24.6

Elevation
1460

340

Metres

5. Penticton KVR

Distance: 24.6 km (15.3 mi), one way
Ascent: 559 m (1,834 ft)
Descent: 51 m (167 ft)

Trail conditions: asphalt, compacted earth, crushed stone
Cellphone coverage: partial
Hazards: cliffs, road crossings, ticks, wildlife

Permitted Uses								
Walking	Biking	Horseback Riding	Inline Skating	ATV	Snowshoeing	Cross-country Skiing	Snowmobiling
✔	✔	✔	—	—	✔	✔	—

Finding the trailhead: From Highway 97, turn onto Eckhardt Avenue W. In 1.7 km (1.1 mi), turn left onto Haven Hill Road. Follow it for 300 m/yd, then turn right onto Johnston Road. In 1 km (0.6 mi), turn left onto Upper Bench Road S (it turns into Upper Bench Road). Continue 1.8 km (1.1 mi) and turn right onto McMillan Avenue. In 300 m/yd turn left onto Naramata Road. Park on the left in 2.5 km (1.6 mi), at the intersection with Poplar Grove Road.

Trailhead: 49°31'59.8" N, 119°33'44.0" W (Start: Poplar Grove)
49°36'26.5" N, 119°33'00.4" W (Finish: Adra Tunnel)

Observations: This route contains some outstanding scenery, especially in the section between Naramata and Little Tunnel. It also is quite challenging, despite the relatively gentle incline. Combined with the soft trail surface after Little Tunnel, the ascent to Adra Tunnel can feel like a long session on an exercise bike. The reward, of course, is in the return, when it is quite possible to slowly coast without pedalling for almost the entire distance.

I was not at all surprised that I saw few people beyond Little Tunnel and that those I did were riding one way, from Chute Lake to Penticton. The remaining distance contains fewer services and enjoys less panoramic vistas. However, I found the Rock Ovens Park quite fascinating, and a worthwhile addition. From there, the short extra 2+ km (1.2+ mi) to the tunnel mouth seemed essential.

Route description: The Bike Park trailhead is large and well provisioned, with an outhouse, picnic tables, garbage cans, a water fountain, and a bike repair

station. It also sits in an appealing location, surrounded by vineyards. The trail crosses Naramata Road on a distinct crosswalk; gates, a garbage can, and more regulatory signage sit on the opposite side.

The path begins its climb immediately, moving past more vineyards and orchards. Wonderful views of Okanagan Lake are available from the start. At 400 m/yd, a side path left leads to the Hillside Winery and Bistro (very tempting), and at 800 m/yd the trail crosses Riddle Road, where there is another small parking area on the right. Another winery is just up the hill. (I like this trail!)

The ground near the trail looks dry and sandy, and vegetation is a little sparse containing lots of sage and pine. Benches can frequently be found along the trail, always positioned to facilitate panoramic views of the valley. Soon rock outcroppings intrude, usually on the right. There are distance markers as well, but these are calculated from downtown Penticton. The km 5.5 marker is situated just before Sutherland Road crosses the trail, 1.6 km (1 mi) from your Bike Park start.

The houses in this area are quite impressive, as are the vineyards. Very few trees block your view, but the scattered pines that border the pathway are often quite tall. At about 2.6 km (1.6 mi), there is a cluster of signs as the trail crosses a community boundary line. Welcome to Penticton faces back in the direction you have travelled; two interpretive panels are on the right, describing the vegetation and the soils of this arid landscape.

The next sign, encountered almost immediately beside a bench, warns of rattlesnakes. This captured my full attention.

The first covered picnic shelter is on the right, with a great view, at 3.7 km (2.3 mi). About 1 km (0.6 mi) later, Ben's Biffy, an outhouse, is tucked away under some trees on the right. A scree slope sits behind it. More and more

Rattlesnakes

British Columbia's interior dry southern valleys are home to significant numbers of the northern Pacific rattlesnake (*crotalis oregonus*), one of three species native to Canada. Though usually non-aggressive, rattlesnakes will strike if threatened. When hiking in rattlesnake territory, wear long pants and high-ankled leather boots. Should you see or hear a snake, stop immediately and remain still until it backs away. Once it is distant from you the length of its body, step backwards from it and go around it — or wait until it leaves.

Rattlesnake bites are rare and almost never fatal, but in the event of a snakebite, head to the nearest hospital immediately. Do not kill the snake, and never ice the wound, attempt to suck out the venom, or apply a tourniquet.

houses line the downslope on the left, and you can see that the community of Naramata is quite close.

6 km (3.7 mi) The trail crosses Arawana Forestry Road at a very bad angle; there is no crosswalk, so be especially cautious. On the other side is a Naramata trailhead, but its parking area is 100 m/yd down the trail, a section you share with automobiles. There are oodles of signs — including the first TCT marker I noticed — and an excellent map. Picnic tables, sheltered tables, and benches are scattered ahead beneath the pines on the trail, all on the left.

About 500 m/yd from the trailhead, the trail crosses a small creek, and 150 m/yd beyond that another paved road. Houses and roads are close at hand on both sides. After another 400 m/yd, the trail route appears to have been moved off its original alignment, because there is a very un-rail trail descent to Naramata Creek, at 7 km (4.3 mi), and an even steeper ascent on the far side. A connecting footpath descends the hillside to the Naramata Waterfall.

7.5 km (4.7 mi) Arrive at the Smethurst Trailhead, with its large parking area, benches, outhouse, map, and interpretive panels. On the far side of the road is a gate, another large map, regulatory signage, and distance measurements: Little Tunnel 4.4 km (2.7 mi), and Adra Tunnel 17.6 km (10.9 mi).

From here, the trail soon leaves the houses of Naramata behind. The views keep getting better and better as you climb, with benches positioned to take advantage of the expansive vistas. A lone outhouse sits at 9.4 km (5.8 mi), and 500 m/yd later the trail spans Robinson Creek.

The hillside vegetation seems to be little more than scattered pine growing out of bare rock, so there is no shade. At 11.4 km (7.1 mi), the Horseshoe Trail, a footpath, branches to the right. This climbs the hillside alongside trickling Trust Creek, and leads to several of the campsites used by rail workers. Some of their lodgings, such as the "Stone Ovens," remain, and this trail leads you to a few of those.

From here, the route appears to be heading directly toward a massive rock face; to the left, the slope resembles a cliff face.

11.9 km (7.4 mi) The trail arrives at the entrance to the Little Tunnel, and the most splendid view on this route. Look back in the direction of Penticton: the southern end of Okanagan Lake and the city are framed splendidly by the mountains east and west. An interpretive panel explains that even before the railway was complete, excursion trains would climb to this spot so that towns-folk could marvel at the view. There is a bench here too.

The treadway inside Little Tunnel is actually asphalted, and this surface continues for 400 m/yd to a gate, on the other side of which is a parking area. There are no facilities here other than a garbage can.

Beyond the asphalt, the ground is sandier and softer. Anyone cycling, as I was, will find it more challenging as their tires sink into the yielding surface. And the trail continues to climb. In addition, automobiles may use this section, so you might encounter oncoming vehicular traffic. With the limited space available, walkers and cyclists will be required to move out of the way. The view also changes, becoming less powerful, though still scenic. Okanagan Mountain, directly ahead, increasingly dominates the skyline as you move toward it.

About 1.3 km (0.8 mi) from the end of the asphalt, a sign marks a heritage structure. All the stonework on the KVR was done by Italian craftsmen. The dry stack wall on the left, with a bench atop it and a set of stairs leading to its base, is one of these special constructions. The trail curves more now, and sometimes trees and embankments on the left even block the view.

Nearly 800 m/yd from the heritage structure, a decrepit Texas gate (a lattice of metal bars across a road spaced to prevent wildlife from walking across it) crosses the pathway, with modest barbed-wire fencing on either side of it. Beyond it, I saw no cattle, nor much evidence of anything for them to eat on the dry hillsides. The sandy track continues through a rocky landscape sprinkled with a scrubby covering of ponderosa pine.

16.3 km (10.1 mi) Curving right, the trail reaches the Glenfir Trailhead. A few picnic tables and an outhouse are visible to the right before the vehicle entrance from the Chute Lake Road, where there is another Texas gate. Houses can be seen to the left.

The trail describes a massive curve here, turning through nearly 180°. Its surface becomes rougher again, deeply rutted with vehicle tracks, and with the higher ground on the left and tall pine to the right there is no view. Cell reception is regained at about 18 km (11.2 mi).

The first views occur around 18.2 km (11.3 mi), where you will notice that you have climbed almost as high as the mountains on the far side of Okanagan Lake. About 300 m/yd further there is another Texas gate; when I was there more than a dozen scrawny cattle were on the trail on the other side. Some 200 m/yd beyond that is a bench, positioned to provide a most impressive view.

But the path soon turns back behind a couple of intervening knolls, and the vista disappears. At 20.3 km (12.6 mi), a power line, with its own ATV track, crosses the trail. There are numerous signs, including a TCT marker, to indicate the correct route.

On the other side of the power lines, signs announce your arrival in Rock Ovens Park, which is for day use only. Numerous side trails exit the rail trail to reach the historical stone structures left behind by railway construction workers. About 500 m/yd later the Tote Road Trail, which connects to the main trail just before the Little Tunnel, reconnects. Several rock ovens can be reached on it. An outhouse and the first picnic table as well as another side trail are reached at 21.8 km (13.5 mi). Other tables follow, and the path crosses little Robinson Creek,

22.3 km (13.9 mi) At this point on the trail there is a signed source of drinking water, Adra Springs. There is also a bench, picnic table, interpretive panel, map, and bike parking. One marker for points of interest indicates a small garden of Adra irises. These were planted by the station mistress in 1920 and transplanted to this location in 2010.

This is a good place to stop and relax, but only a few kilometres/miles remains to the tunnel. About 2 km (1.2 mi) later the trail reaches the junction with the Adra Bypass. The main trail leaves the rail bed to the left and reconnects just beyond the tunnel. It is well signed and includes a map; continue straight.

This section of the rail trail shows evidence of heavy use, and there are numerous signs of camping as you get closer to the tunnel mouth. The path curves left, and a dirt vehicle track connects on the right, just before a line of boulders blocks the pathway. From here, you must dismount your bicycle and continue on foot.

24.6 km (15.3 mi) The trail arrives at the tunnel mouth, which opens into a vertical rock face. Entrance is impeded by concrete blocks and a wire fence. Unfortunately, its roof has collapsed in several places and some of the wooden support timbers burned. Signs warn that access is prohibited and that falling rock and poor air quality should be expected inside. At 489 m (1,604 ft), the U-shaped tunnel is the longest on the entire Kettle Valley Rail Trail, but it is closed and extremely dangerous to enter – so do not. It might be restored in the future.

As the many nearby firepits attest, the tunnel mouth is a popular camping location. Should you decide to stay overnight, do not light a fire, as this is an area with an extremely high fire hazard. However, if you decide instead to return to Penticton, the good news is that the entire return trip is downhill.

Further Information:
City of Penticton: www.penticton.ca
Regional District of Okanagan-Similkameen: www.rdos.bc.ca/departments/
    community-services/regional-trails
Rock Ovens Regional Park: www.rdos.bc.ca/departments/community-
    services/regional-parks/rock-ovens-park
Tourism Penticton: www.visitpenticton.com

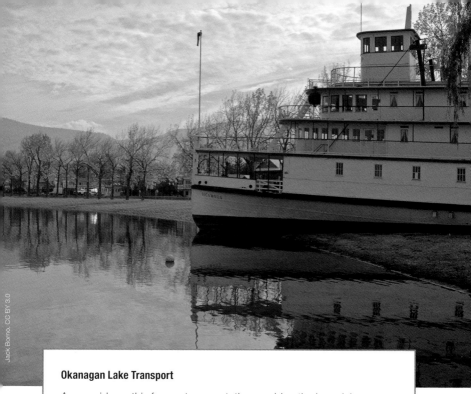

Okanagan Lake Transport

As you ride on this former transportation corridor, the large lake on your left was the means of travel the railway replaced. Okanagan Lake is 135 km (83.9 mi) long, and for the first settlers it was far easier to use than the rudimentary roads through the mountains. Several steamboat services soon began operating, but these were eventually consolidated into the Canadian Pacific Railway Lake and River Service.

Even when railways began to be developed, the mountainous terrain left gaps. Freight and passengers were carried over the lake between the CPR mainline at Sicamous to the Kettle Valley Railway at Penticton. The KVR's first engines had to be shipped by boat to Penticton, prompting a civic celebration when they were delivered.

After the railways became established, transport on the lake declined, but it continued for a number of years. The SS *Naramata* began work in 1914 and was not decommissioned until 1967. It is now on permanent display in Penticton with the larger luxury stern-wheeler SS *Sicamous* (above).

6. Myra Canyon

Few photographs of the entire Great Trail evoke such awe as do those taken at Myra Canyon. And deservedly so, because it is genuinely spectacular: massive trestle bridges perched high in the mountains, traversing rocky cliffs and spanning deep gorges. Nowhere else in the country has so many bridges in such a short distance, and from each there is a stunning view of the deep Myra Canyon.

Canadian Pacific Railway abandoned the Midway-Penticton branch line in 1978, removing the rails in 1980. The trestles soon became a popular, if unofficial, trail. However, as they were unmaintained, accidents occurred, and in 1993 the Myra Canyon Trestle Restoration Society was formed to restore them.

As the trail improved, visits soared, and in 2001 the province created Myra-Bellevue Provincial Park to help protect the area. In 2002, a 9.6 km (6 mi) section was recognized as a National Historic Site of Canada. After the devastating fire of 2003, the damaged bridges were replaced thanks to funding from the Federal/Provincial Disaster Financial Assistance Agreement. Improvements to the trail surface were undertaken by Reconstruction Society volunteers.

This route is ideal for both walking and cycling and is also used by horseback riders. Expect large numbers of people and families with young children near the Myra Station trailhead, especially in afternoons and on weekends. Cyclists will need to exercise caution and reduce speed; walkers and cyclists must yield to horseback riders.

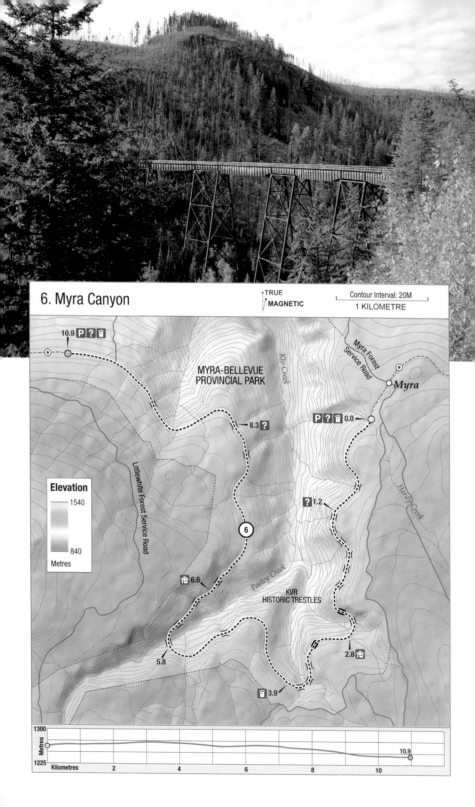

6. Myra Canyon

TRUE
MAGNETIC

Contour Interval: 20M
1 KILOMETRE

MYRA-BELLEVUE
PROVINCIAL PARK

Klo Creek

Myra Forest Service Road

Myra

10.9 P ? 🚻

8.3 ?

P ? 🚻 0.0

? 1.2

Hardy Creek

Littlewhite Forest Service Road

Elevation
1540

840
Metres

6

6.6 🏠

Pooley Creek

KVR
HISTORIC TRESTLES

5.8

2.8 🏠

3.9 🚻

Metres					
1300					
1225					10.9

Kilometres   2   4   6   8   10

6. Myra Canyon

Distance: 10.9 km (6.8 mi), one way
Ascent: 75 m (246 ft)
Descent: 102 m (335 ft)

Trail conditions: crushed stone
Cellphone coverage: yes
Hazards: cliffs, hunting, mountain weather, ticks, wildlife

Permitted Uses								
Walking	Biking	Horseback Riding	Inline Skating	ATV	Snowshoeing	Cross-country Skiing	Snowmobiling
✔	✔	✔	—	—	✔	✔	✔

Finding the trailhead: From Highway 97, turn west onto Dilworth Drive. In 500 m/yd, this becomes Benvoulin Road. After 2.4 km (1.5 mi), turn left onto KLO Road. Follow it for 2.6 km (1.6 mi), then turn right onto McCulloch Road. Continue on McCulloch for 7.8 km (4.8 m), turning right onto Myra Forest Service Road. Drive 8.8 km (5.5 mi), keeping right, to the end of the road at the trailhead parking lot.

Trailhead: 49°48'00.7" N, 119°18'44.7" W (Start: Myra Station)
49°47'40.7" N, 119°21'29.9" W (Finish: Ruth Station)

Observations: Myra Canyon is a trail that you should not be in a hurry to complete. Although it is ideal for cycling, there are so many locations where you will wish to stop that you may spend almost as much time off your bicycle as riding it.

There are so many bridges, crossing such rugged landscape, that by the time you reach the last few your response to them may be somewhat blasé, and you might not give them the attention they deserve. It will only be after you return to a more ordinary section of trail, during the final kilometre to Ruth Station, that you begin to appreciate how exceptional the canyon truly is.

This is the only route of all those profiled in both volumes that I returned to and visited a second time. I cannot emphasize how overwhelming this landscape is and these bridges are. I started at sunrise, when there were few people. Even so, by the time I returned to Myra Station the lot was nearly full and the first kilometre from it packed with walkers.

Route description: There is a very large parking area at Myra Station, with out-houses and picnic tables. A gate blocks further vehicle access along the Kettle Valley Rail (KVR) Trail. Next to this gate is a variety of regulatory signage, an excellent map of the Myra Canyon section, and a zero-kilometre marker.

The track is wide and well surfaced, and very quickly views to the right toward Kelowna and Okanagan Lake open up. Evidence of the 2003 fire is all around, with hundreds of slender dead tree trunks climbing above the low, thick, regenerating foliage.

The ruggedness of the terrain is also quickly apparent, with the pathway in a rock cut one moment then with a slope steeply banking away from the trail only a few metres/yards later. The mouth of Myra Canyon is soon visible, and at 400 m/yd you can actually see one of the bridges – Trestle #2 – on the opposite side of the canyon wall.

At 500 m/yd, the first bench and interpretive panel are on the right, where they sit on the lip of a sheer hillside. There are no protective fences, and it is a long way to the bottom. From here you can see Kelowna and West Kelowna, 910 m (2,985 ft) below; they look very far away. Passengers from Kelowna had to ride a stagecoach up the mountain to Myra Station to use the Kettle Valley Railway; not an easy trip.

At the next bench a little more than 100 m/yd further, four of the trestles are visible. It is quite an impressive view. More benches and interpretive panels decorate the trail before reaching the first bridge, the 55 m (180 ft) Trestle #18 at 1.1 km (0.7 mi). A detour path of crushed stone goes around it on the slope side.

Barely 100 m/yd later, the trail arrives at a large pavilion, on the right in a wider large open area. This is a place you must stop, because there are many panels of railroad and natural history information, photographs of both the original construction and the reconstruction after the 2003 fire, maps, and more. Several benches provide superb panoramas, and there is a bronze plaque from the National Historic Sites and Monuments Board affixed to a nearby rock.

The next bridge (#17) is reached at 1.6 km (1 mi), and from there the next four follow almost immediately afterwards; they are all in sight from Trestle #17. There are more benches and additional interpretive panels and another bronze plaque – provincial this time – dedicated to those who rebuilt the trestles lost in the 2003 fire. The plaque looks directly at Trestle #6, the longest, which spans the Pooley Creek ravine.

By the time you cross Trestle #13, you have barely travelled 2 km (1.2 mi). It is quite phenomenal, and difficult to believe that railway engineers thought that they could construct this railway, using hand tools, and that this was their easiest option!

Summer Wildfires

In recent years, the number and severity of wildfires in British Columbia's forest have increased. In 2003, wildfires ravaged Myra Canyon, razing twelve of the wooden trestles and damaging two of the steel bridges, as well as destroying almost all the facilities along the route. The canyon route was closed until repairs were completed in 2008.

In 2017-18, more than 25,000 km² (9,650 mi²) of woodland was destroyed. Summer wildfires now regularly threaten trails all over the province, and it appears as if they will only become more common in the future. Two of the routes in this volume were closed because of nearby forest fires in 2018.

Before setting out on any isolated section of The Great Trail in British Columbia, consult the Recreation Sites and Trails BC website for closures and warnings. You can also consult the British Columbia Wildfire Service website.

Trestle #12 rapidly follows, and at 2.2 km (1.4 mi) the trail enters a curving 114 m/yd tunnel. At the start of Trestle #11 is a plaque stating that this is the highest point of the KVR Trail: 1,274 m (4,178 ft).

2.8 km (1.7 mi) On the far side of the curving 132 m/yd #11 is a bright red storm shelter, provided by the Myra Canyon Trestle Restoration Society volunteers. Distances to washrooms are thoughtfully indicated on its exterior. A long deep cut follows, the bordering rock walls high above the trail. At 3.3 km (2.1 mi), the pathway enters the second, and last, tunnel, which is 84 m/yd long.

Trestle #10 is immediately on the far side, another short curving bridge with a bench on its far side. Trestle #9 is the first steel bridge and is much higher than most of the others, standing 48 m (157 ft) above KLO Creek. The next bridge follows immediately, and on its far side, at 3.9 km (2.4 mi), is an outhouse.

The next section is the longest so far without a bridge, as the trail heads through some rock cuts. About 300 m/yd from #8 is a water tower and an interpretive panel, followed by a talus slope. For the first time there are almost no views – although when there are they are pretty fantastic.

Trestle #7 (shown above) is special: it is S-shaped, the only rail bridge like this in Canada. It is followed by yet another deep cut and another talus slope, which talks about an alpine rodent, the pika.

5.8 km (3.6 mi) The trail arrives at the longest and highest bridge in Myra Canyon, Trestle #6. This 220 m/yd long structure towers 55 m (180 ft) above the deep gorge cut by Pooley Creek. Originally constructed by thirteen decks of wooden trestles, in 1930-31 it was replaced by the current steel bridge. Trestle #6 is so long that there is more than one viewing platform built into its deck.

The km 6 marker is on the far side, in the small space between Trestles #6 and #5. After the long curving #6, #5 seems barely noticeable. The deepest ravines have been crossed, and the trail now is almost straight at times. Trestle #4, at 131 m (430 ft), is actually the third longest in Myra Canyon, yet somehow seems quite modest. Another emergency shelter is found on its far side, at about 6.6 km (4.1 mi).

The hillsides show tremendous scarring from forest fires, with dead, half-burnt trees everywhere. Once past Trestle #3, new growth actually appears on both sides of the treadway. There is a lovely stopping area, with a bench, on the far side of #3, but there are many benches along this route.

The trail moves away from the edge of the canyon, and views become less frequent. Thicker vegetation grows here, including some areas that have not been burnt. For the first time on this path, the trail seems almost ordinary, with a thick buffer of fir and spruce between you and the canyon. That being said, at 8 km (5 mi) there is an excellent view of the ravine opposite that includes several of the trestles.

8.3 km (5.2 mi) The trail arrives at Trestle #2 and some quite remarkable views. Not only is the opposite side of the canyon visible, but you should actually be able to see the parking area. Just beyond it is another short rock cut, then a large trail pavilion, with more benches and another historical plaque.

From here the pathway begins curving left, and the views are fleeting. Enjoy the scenery visible from Trestle #1, at 9.8 km (6.1 mi), even though it is of a different ravine, as this is the last dramatic lookout on this route. Shortly after crossing the bridge, there is an outhouse and a side trail connecting with a map posted of the Crawford Trail system. A sign here identifies the location as Myra Bailout.

10.9 km (6.8 mi) The end comes rather quickly, with a gate blocking the pathway and the trail beyond it turned into a parking lot. There are his and hers outhouses and a trailhead kiosk with a good map. Take a moment to look at the remains of Ruth Station, and the nearby rock ovens built and used by railway workers. An interpretive panel explains their use.

Beyond Ruth Station, the trail is open for motorized vehicle use, so retracing your route back to Myra Station should be welcome. Take time on the return trip, if you did not on the approach, to read every interpretive panel. This was a remarkable railroad; it is now an outstanding trail. Learn the story of both.

Further Information:
Myra-Bellevue Provincial Park and Protected Area: www.env.gov.bc.ca/
    bcparks/explore/parkpgs/myra
Myra Canyon Trestle Restoration Society: www.myratrestles.com
Tourism Kelowna: www.tourismkelowna.com

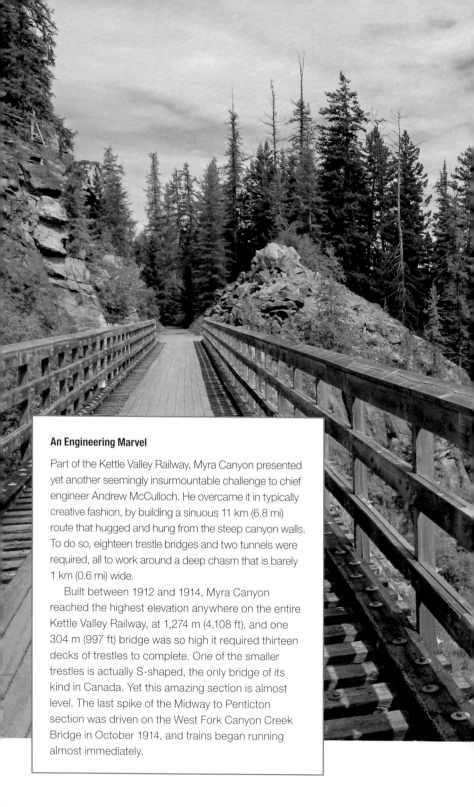

An Engineering Marvel

Part of the Kettle Valley Railway, Myra Canyon presented yet another seemingly insurmountable challenge to chief engineer Andrew McCulloch. He overcame it in typically creative fashion, by building a sinuous 11 km (6.8 mi) route that hugged and hung from the steep canyon walls. To do so, eighteen trestle bridges and two tunnels were required, all to work around a deep chasm that is barely 1 km (0.6 mi) wide.

Built between 1912 and 1914, Myra Canyon reached the highest elevation anywhere on the entire Kettle Valley Railway, at 1,274 m (4,108 ft), and one 304 m (997 ft) bridge was so high it required thirteen decks of trestles to complete. One of the smaller trestles is actually S-shaped, the only bridge of its kind in Canada. Yet this amazing section is almost level. The last spike of the Midway to Penticton section was driven on the West Fork Canyon Creek Bridge in October 1914, and trains began running almost immediately.

7. Columbia and Western Trail

Extending from Midway, where it connects to the Kettle Valley Rail (KVR) Trail, to Castlegar on the banks of the Columbia River, the Columbia and Western Trail is 160+ km (100+ mi) of exceptional scenery. Less well known than its western neighbour, the KVR Trail, the Columbia and Western is for those who like the trail less travelled.

I have profiled the section between Castlegar and Paulson, found in the West Kootenay Region, and it comprises some of the most remote and scenic pathways on the Columbia and Western. The West Kootenays are a mountainous southeastern region of British Columbia and home to several different mountain ranges: the Selkirks, Valhallas, Purcells, and Monashees.

Trail conditions along the Columbia and Western are constantly changing and hard to predict, particularly in the spring and fall; snow can linger at the highest elevations until early June or arrive unexpectedly in September or October. Because of the extremely steep slopes above the trail, avalanches occur every winter, and users early in the year might encounter unexpected obstacles.

Hikers and cyclists should be prepared for travelling for extended distances without access to services or many easy options to bail if they run into difficulties. However, significant improvements to the Columbia and Western around Grand Forks and Christina Lake have contributed to an increased popularity for this section, and there are more cyclists every year.

There is heavy motorized use on this part of the Columbia and Western, not just ATVs but dirt bikes and even 4x4 trucks. This has degraded the treadway enough that cycling can sometimes be difficult. Using a sturdy bicycle with suspension is recommended.

In August 2018 there was a major forest fire on Bulldog Mountain; the damage caused to the trail was not clear at the time of writing.

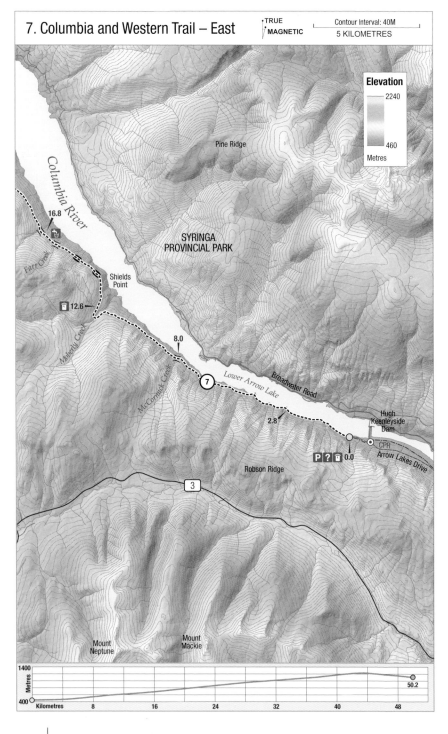

7. Columbia and Western Trail – East

TRUE
MAGNETIC

Contour Interval: 40M
5 KILOMETRES

Elevation
2240
460
Metres

Pine Ridge

Columbia River

16.8

Farr Creek

Shields Point

12.6

Moberly Creek

8.0

McCormick Creek

7

Lower Arrow Lake

Broadwater Road

SYRINGA PROVINCIAL PARK

Hugh Keenleyside Dam

2.8

0.0

CPR

Arrow Lakes Drive

P ?

Robson Ridge

3

Mount Neptune

Mount Mackie

1400
Metres
400

Kilometres   8   16   24   32   40   48

50.2

7. Columbia and Western Trail

Distance: 50.2 km (31.2 mi), one way
Ascent: 1,257 m (4,124 ft)
Descent: 669 m (2,195 ft)

Trail conditions: compacted earth, crushed stone, natural surface
Cellphone coverage: no
Hazards: cliffs, isolated, mountain weather, wildlife

Permitted Uses							
Walking	Biking	Horseback Riding	Inline Skating	ATV	Snowshoeing	Cross-country Skiing	Snowmobiling
✔	✔	✔	—	✔	✔	✔	✔

Finding the trailhead: Exit from the Crowsnest Highway (Highway 3) onto Columbia Avenue. Follow it through Castlegar city centre for about 3.5 km (2.2 mi). Continue toward Hugh Keenleyside Dam. Columbia Avenue merges with and becomes Arrow Lakes Drive. Continue on Arrow Lakes for 6.8 km (4.2 mi) until it reaches the dam. Turn left; the trailhead is at end of road in 800 m/yd.

Trailhead: 49°20'04.7" N, 117°46'56.7" W (Start: Lower Arrow Lake)
49°12'23.9" N, 118°07'02.0" W (Finish: Paulson)

Observations: The Columbia and Western is one of the most isolated sections of trail in this volume, and one of the most scenic. Much of its distance, it seems to be perched on the side of a cliff or requires a passageway through a wall of sheer rock. And then there is the Bulldog Tunnel, long and curved, so that when you enter, it is literally not possible to "see the light at the end of the tunnel." Headlamps are required, cyclists must dismount, and the eerie journey through the long darkness is punctuated only by the dripping of water from the ceiling.

This is only for the most confident and prepared hikers/bikers. There are no services, no cell reception, and no easy exit options once you begin. I found this remoteness quite exhilarating and only wished that I could have spent more time on this route.

Route description: The start of the trail is actually at 14.2 km (8.8 mi) of the former railway division. An excellent trailhead kiosk sits beside the parking area, as do picnic tables, an outhouse, and a garbage can. Gates are set across the

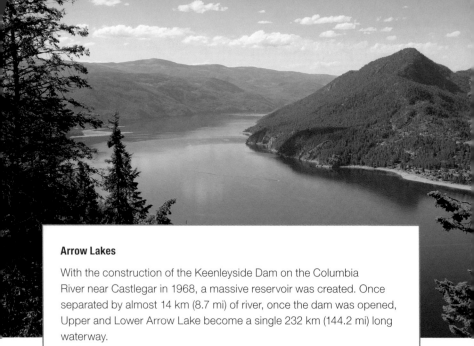

Arrow Lakes

With the construction of the Keenleyside Dam on the Columbia River near Castlegar in 1968, a massive reservoir was created. Once separated by almost 14 km (8.7 mi) of river, once the dam was opened, Upper and Lower Arrow Lake become a single 232 km (144.2 mi) long waterway.

The water level of Lower Arrow Lake was raised more than 12 m (39.4 ft) when the dam was created, forcing the relocation of several communities and flooding most of the region's arable land. The resulting lake is now bounded east and west by the Selkirk and Monashee Mountains. Lower Arrow Lake features steep cliffs, rocky headlands, and forested slopes springing directly from the waterline.

Popular with recreational boaters, the Arrow Lakes — really only one lake now — are also extensively used to move lumber to the large Interfor Mills below Keenleyside Dam. Huge rafts of logs are slowly towed down the lakes, where they remain in the water waiting their turn in the sawmill.

pathway. When I travelled it in 2016, rails were still in the corridor for 1,400 m/yd, but in 2018 the first 6 km (3.7 mi) was resurfaced with crushed stone, covering the rails. More of the trail will receive a crushed-stone treadway in future years.

The pathway begins almost at lake level but immediately begins to climb. Within 500 m/yd, vertical rock faces line the left, and there was evidence of a rock fall before the first kilometre. Side trails occasionally branch right, leading to the lake.

At 2.8 km (1.7 mi) there is an excellent view of the flooded Labarthe Tunnel. When the dam was built in 1968 the rising lake flooded the original route of the railway. It was relocated to its current location; when water levels on the Arrow Lakes are low, you can see the Labarthe Tunnel.

As the trail continues, there are frequent long vistas looking far up the lake. The scenery is exceptional, with steep-sided, thickly wooded hillsides lining the water. At 3.5 km (2.2 mi), there is a picnic table and an interpretive panel on the mountain pine beetle. The trail passes through multiple vertical cuts through the rocky hills. The surrounding forest is almost completely made up of softwoods.

Every time there is a break in either the terrain or the vegetation, the panorama that opens up is magnificent. At 6 km (3.7 mi), a fence sits atop a concrete retaining wall, to the right, where the trail crosses another vertical rock face. A slight curving detour bypasses a bad washout 300 m/yd later, and the next part of the trail is somewhat rougher.

8 km (5 mi) Any challenge is swiftly forgotten when the path reaches the McCormack Trestle at 8 km (5 mi). Spanning the deep McCormack Creek ravine, this metal bridge provides impressive views out across the lake but mostly directly below.

The path continues, contouring along the steep slope of the Robson Ridge, with views north up the length of the narrow Lower Arrow Lake. Huge rafts of logs, usually being towed by a tiny speck of a tug, can be seen on their way to the large sawmill at Castlegar.

At about 11.6 km (7.2 mi), the path turns sharply right and heads into a ravine. Some 500 m/yd later it crosses an embankment high above Shields Creek. This was once also a trestle bridge, but the railway carted in earthen fill and completely buried the wooden bridge that once spanned this gorge. At the bottom of this embankment the culvert draining Shields Creek is large enough to walk through, but the climb down to it is quite steep.

12.6 km (7.8 mi) The trail arrives at the Shields rest area, which is situated on the site of a former water stop for steam locomotives, although nothing of the former structure remains but a tree-covered foundation. There is an outhouse and picnic table here, and a dirt road that connects to Highway 3 to the left – though it is a long way away – and to some lakeside cottages to the right. Camping is permitted and there is a trailhead kiosk.

The trail reaches the first tunnel at 14 km (8.7 mi), and the next is 1 km (0.6 mi) after that. Both are quite short but breach impressively solid-looking stone ramparts. The slope is deeply etched and steeply sloped toward the lake, so the trail hugs it closely.

The Farr Creek Trestle is crossed at 16 km (10 mi), and 800 m/yd later you reach the largest and most picturesque bridge on this trail, the Cub Creek Trestle. Just past Farr Creek is a spring where you can refill your water bottles.

Often in the next several kilometres/miles, there is no fence on the right, but a very, very long drop to the bottom of the hill. This is also one of the rougher parts of the route. Cyclists should be particularly attentive.

18.9 km (11.7 mi) At 89 m/yd, the Coykendahl Tunnel is the longest thus far. It curves left, is dark in the middle, and water drips from the ceiling and walls. Impressive! After the tunnel, the trails swings left into the Grassy Creek Canyon, where it crosses the creek on another culvert.

Little remains of the former Coykendahl Station, at 19.9 km (12.4 mi), except for a small railway cart mounted on a short piece of rail. Look on the left just past this, and you might find a tiny emergency shelter for railway workers built into the hillside.

At 20.2 km (12.6 mi), a very steep vehicle track branches right from the trail and descends – plummets, really – down the slope. Apparently it leads to several lakeside cottages. And at 22.7 km (14.1 mi), there is a picnic table at a particularly good lookout: George's Viewpoint. There is a wonderful vista that includes the tiny community of Deer Park, on the opposite side of the lake, and Deer Park Mountain rising behind it.

About 300 m/yd later the trail turns away from Lower Arrow Lake for the final time, and heads into the Pup Creek ravine. It continues inland for 3.3 km (2.1 mi) before it crosses the creek and curves right again. The trail works around a few gullies and small creeks; in front and to the right the imposing bulk of Bulldog Mountain rises ever higher.

29.6 km (18.4 mi) The entrance to Bulldog Tunnel is at the end of a railway cut, so there are vertical rock walls on either side as you approach it: think *Lord of*

Bulldog Tunnel

One of the greatest challenges facing the builders of the Columbia and Western was traversing Bulldog Mountain. At first, the rail line went over the top through a narrow pass. However, this required six switchbacks on each side, with grades as steep as 6% — this when the standard maximum grade in the 19th century was 2.2%! This meant that trains had to be disassembled and slowly eased over the mountain a few cars at a time, then reassembled on the other side, a time-consuming, dangerous, and expensive operation.

In 1899, work began on the Bulldog Tunnel, the first time that the technique of air drilling was used on a railway in Canada. Even though tunnelling was started on both sides of the mountain, it took two years before the new passage was open for use.

At 912 m (2,992 ft), the Bulldog Tunnel is the longest found on The Great Trail. At 15 m (49.2 ft) high, it is also quite spacious. One interesting feature is that it curves, so the end cannot be seen once inside. Hikers and cyclists must carry their own light, and it is best if you don't suffer from claustrophobia. These original switchbacks are being restored by the trail group and may soon offer an exciting footpath up and over the top of Bulldog Mountain.

---

the Rings. Inside it is completely dark, and as it curves you cannot see its end, so you must have a light to traverse it. At 912 m/yd long, it will probably take at least 15 minutes to pick your way through. Expect it to be cool, regardless of the exterior temperature. When I walked it, it was at least 30°C (86°F) outside, but in the tunnel I could see my breath. For me, the Bulldog Tunnel is the high point of this route.

When you emerge, it is at the site of Tunnel Station, where you will find the foundation. This is a lovely spot to camp; there is a wide space, an outhouse, and a picnic table. The view now overlooks the Dog Creek Valley and the tree-covered mountains of the Christina Range.

The trail is heading south now, but still climbing; you are already more than 500 m (1,640 ft) above the start trailhead. At 32.3 km (20.1 mi) a high embankment spans Quinn Creek; it is steep-sided on both directions, and there is no railing. About 1.1 km (0.7 mi) later, a forestry road crosses; this eventually leads to the summit of Bulldog Mountain, should you desire a challenging side trip.

The slopes on this canyon are not as steep as they were facing Lower Arrow Lake, so this is easier travelling, and straighter. One exception is at 37.6 km (23.4 mi), when the trail curves into a ravine and uses an embankment to cross Porcupine Creek. A side trail to the left leads to a secluded picnic area at the mouth of the stone culvert that is large enough to walk through.

42.8 mi (26.6 mi) Just after crossing a forestry road, the trail arrives at the site of the former Farron Station and the high point of this route. The railway positioned a turning point for the helper locomotives that were necessary to lift trains up the long grade. Today little remains except foundations, though the trailhead kiosk contains excellent historical notes and old photographs of when the railroad operated. There is plenty of room to camp here, and there is a picnic table, an outhouse, and a firepit.

It is all downhill now, into the McRae Creek Valley. The forest on the hills opposite belongs to Gladstone Provincial Park. Several more interpretive panels talk about the Doukhobor history of the region, including the death of Peter Verigin in a 1924 train explosion near here, which may have been Canada's first recorded terrorist act.

At about 46 km (28.6 mi), a footbridge crosses McRae Creek and heads into the park. This is the start of the difficult Mount Gladstone Trail, a 6 km (3.7 mi) hike to its 2,256 m (7,401 ft) peak. Cyclists who worked so hard on the climb up will probably be gently coasting now, enjoying the descent. Hikers must continue their trudge.

At 49.1 km (30.5 mi), the trail reaches the Paulson Trailhead, where there is a kiosk. A road crosses the pathway; heading left leads up to Highway 3.

50.2 km (31.2 mi) End your trek at the site of the former Paulson Station, which is now a campsite, ideally positioned close to McRae Creek. When I visited, it was the evening abode for several groups of cyclists and hikers, which made for a lively evening. The good news: when you return to Castlegar, the trip will be almost all downhill!

Further Information:
Columbia and Western Trail Society: www.columbiaandwestern.com
Destination Castlegar: www.destinationcastlegar.com
Gladstone Provincial Park: http://www.env.gov.bc.ca/bcparks/explore/parkpgs/gladstone
Trails BC: http://trailsbc.ca/tct/west-kootenay/paulson

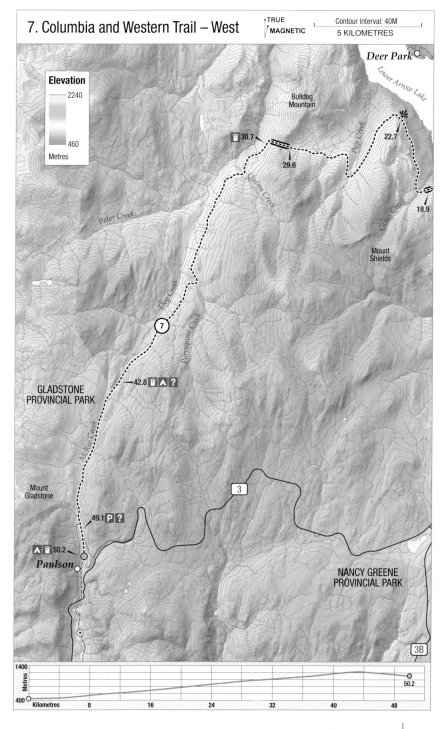

7. Columbia and Western Trail – West

TRUE
MAGNETIC

Contour Interval: 40M
5 KILOMETRES

Elevation
2240
460
Metres

Deer Park

Lower Arrow Lake

Bulldog
Mountain

Pup Creek

22.7

30.7

29.6

Quinn Creek

Grass Creek

18.9

Mount
Shields

Peter Creek

Dog Creek

7

Porcupine Creek

42.8 ⬆ ▲ ?

GLADSTONE
PROVINCIAL PARK

McRae Creek

Mount
Gladstone

3

49.1 P ?

▲ ⬆ 50.2

Paulson

NANCY GREENE
PROVINCIAL PARK

3B

1400
Metres
400
Kilometres   8   16   24   32   40   48

50.2

8. North Star Trail

Kimberley is a city that was built on the mining industry. Discovered in 1892, a massive deposit composed primarily of lead, zinc, silver, and tin led to the founding of the community and its being named after the famous South African mining city. By 1899, the Canadian Pacific (CP) Railway completed a spur line to connect the mines to the main line at Cranbrook and the smelter at Trail.

The Sullivan Mine in Kimberley ultimately became the largest producer of lead and zinc in the world, operated for 92 years, and produced more than 15 million tonnes (16.5 million tons) of ore. It closed in 2001, and CP abandoned the line almost immediately afterwards.

Development of the North Star Trail, following the route of the abandoned railway, began in 2009 and was completed in 2010, when it officially became part of the Trans Canada Trail, then The Great Trail. It is virtually the only asphalt-surfaced trail between Banff in Alberta and Kelowna. (In 2018 part of the Columbia and Western between Grand Gulf and Christina Lake was paved.)

Cranbrook is the largest community in the Regional District of East Kootenay. The town prospered as a rail and trade centre for all the neighbouring mining communities, such as Kimberley and Fort Steele. Today Cranbrook has a population of just under 20,000. It also boasts having the most hours of sunshine of any city in British Columbia – so expect good weather when you trek the North Star.

8. North Star Trail

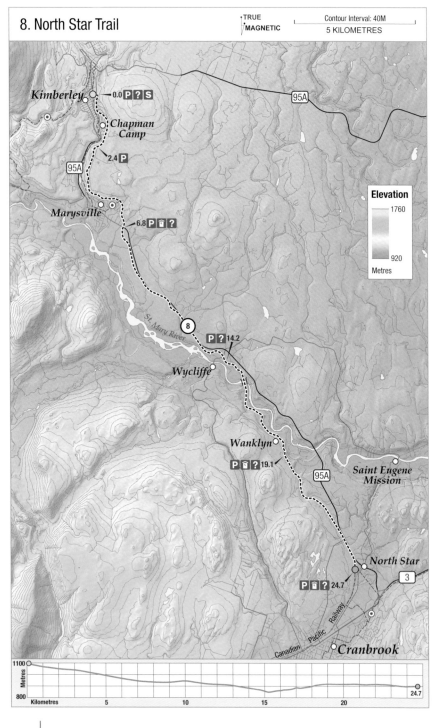

TRUE
MAGNETIC

Contour Interval: 40M
5 KILOMETRES

Kimberley — 0.0 P ? S

Chapman Camp

2.4 P

95A

Marysville — 6.8 P 🚻 ?

St. Mary River

8

P ? 14.2

Wycliffe

Wanklyn

P 🚻 ? 19.1

95A

Saint Eugene Mission

North Star

3

P 🚻 ? 24.7

Canadian Pacific Railway

Cranbrook

Elevation
1760
920
Metres

1100
Metres
800
Kilometres   5   10   15   20   24.7

8. North Star Trail

Distance: 24.7 km (15.4 mi), one way
Ascent: 169 m (554 ft)
Descent: 331 m (1,086 ft)

Trail conditions: asphalt
Cellphone coverage: yes
Hazards: poison ivy, road crossings, ticks, wildlife

Permitted Uses							
Walking	Biking	Horseback Riding	Inline Skating	ATV	Snowshoeing	Cross-country Skiing	Snowmobiling
✔	✔	—	✔	—	✔	✔	—

Finding the trailhead: From the intersection of the Crowsnest Highway and Highway 95A, take the 95A north toward Kimberley. After 24 km (14.9 mi), turn right onto Rotary Drive. Continue 1.9 km (1.2 mi) to Archibald Street. The trailhead is on the left.

Trailhead: 49°40'31.3" N, 115°58'37.7" W (Start: Kimberley)
49°32'51.2" N, 115°45'21.4" W (Finish: Cranbrook)

Observations: How can one not enjoy a trail that is almost all downhill? This is, of course, unless you need to return along the uphill path. As a mining railway line, the one between Cranbrook and Kimberley had a steeper grade than that of any main line. For a railroad, it was expensive and dangerous; for a trail, it is wonderful.

The paved pathway is ideal for cyclists, while walkers will find the asphalt surface less appealing. However, the terrain through which it passes is magnificent, and that should moderate any minor quibble about the treadway.

There are also good facilities along the route : several washrooms, numerous benches, and a good variety of interpretive panels. Water sources are few, however, so walkers should be well-provisioned before undertaking this route. Take advantage of opportunities to restock when the trail passes through communities.

Route description: A trailhead kiosk sits in the Civic Centre parking lot, at the corner of Archibald Street and Rotary Drive. The kiosk contains the usual regulatory and information postings, and it includes an excellent map of the path to

Cranbrook. Cross Rotary Drive on the crosswalk, and continue down a paved alley for 50 m/yd to reach the off-road pathway.

Another kiosk is posted here; it also features a map, and a TCT marker and arrow point to the right. A garbage can sits next to the kiosk, also a bike repair station, and a bench is in sight a few metres/yards down the path. Follow the paved pathway, which passes behind the houses facing Rotary Drive.

Almost immediately the downhill grade becomes sufficient so that, if you are cycling, pedalling becomes optional. The asphalt track is smooth and wide, and I found no foot traffic to impede travelling at whatever speed I wished. The ground looks arid and is slightly higher to the left, and there is considerable tree cover there as well. Numerous footpaths connect from the nearby homes.

At 1.5 km (0.9 mi), the trail crosses Knighton Road at a crosswalk. Concrete jersey barriers narrow the passage, encouraging trail users to obey their stop sign. Next to the road are two picnic tables and interpretive panels. The path soon moves away from houses, although occasional residences are still seen, as are benches.

The next road crossing, Jim Ogilvie Way at 2.4 km (1.5 mi), also uses jersey barriers to slow trail traffic. On the far side sits another round concrete picnic table — unshaded, so brutal in the summer sun — and to the right a gated path that is signed the Volksmarch Trail. There is a parking area for both trails.

Past here, houses are few, and the gently curving pathway moves through the peaceful arid landscape. You can often see the road to the left, but it was not very busy when I was there. At 3.6 km (2.2 mi), a bench is nicely positioned on the right to overlook the small Mark Creek Valley. Fine views of the hills to the west are also obtained from this spot, and the Volksmarch Trail appears to reconnect here.

The trail curves left, and a low ridge climbs on that side of the trail, blocking the road from sight. The ground slopes down on the right, providing frequent views of the mountains. By the time you reach the next benches, 400 m/yd later at about 4.4 km (2.7 mi), the community of Marysville is visible below.

The ridge is sandy and rocky, with pines the dominant vegetation and only occasional tufts of grass stabilizing the slope. The descent is quite pronounced, dropping toward Marysville quickly. The next road crossing is once again Jim Ogilvie Way, at 5.7 km (3.5 mi). Metal gates now impede the trail at the intersection.

The pathway continues on a wide curve right, with most of Marysville's houses some distance away. Lovely tall pines are to the right. At about 6.4 km (4 mi), the trail passes one of its least scenic spots: a recycling facility with a fair amount of debris littered around its property.

6.8 km (4.2 mi) The trail crosses Highway 95A, which is a very busy road. There is a crosswalk, warning signs have been placed on the road, and the speed limit is only 50 kph (31 mph), but exercise particular caution when crossing. Just before the road there is a trailhead kiosk, and on the far side is a solid-looking stone and concrete outhouse. A bike rack and garbage can sit beside it. On the left, shaded by pines, is a trailhead parking area.

Now curving left, the trail passes a golf course, which is to the right. By 7.6 km (4.7 mi) trail and Highway 95A are close together and run parallel. There is an informal parking area where a dirt road connects them. A thick row of pine provides a buffer with the highway. If you haven't noticed earlier, kilometre lines are painted on the treadway. As you pass through this forested stretch, watch for the 8 km (5 mi) line.

Almost exactly at 9 km (5.6 mi), the trail shifts left and moves to within 5 m/yd of the highway. The border of trees disappears. For the next 3.7 km (2.3 mi), except for one place where the trail curves around a private property, road and trail remain close. However, for the first time you gain unobstructed views of the Rocky Mountains on the left, which are far more rugged than those visible to the right, and are snow-tipped. This is wonderful scenery.

By 12.7 km (7.9 mi), the right side of the trail becomes a high vertical bluff overlooking the broad St. Mary River far below, which begins in the Purcell Mountains and empties into the Kootenay River. Once heavily polluted by mine tailings from Kimberley, it has been restored to near pristine condition and is a prime sport fishing stream.

At a bench about 200 m/yd later, the view of the river, valley, and mountains is quite wonderful: pause for a few minutes and appreciate it. The trail continues to descend, and because there is now slightly higher ground to the left, you will not notice that it has separated from Highway 95A.

The trail makes a couple of tight curves before reaching Wycliffe Park Road at 13.9 km (8.6 mi). The pathway drops down into the small community, running between some houses. A couple of driveways cross it. About 300 m/yd from Wycliffe Park Road, there is a trailhead kiosk, although I did not see a designated parking area. The trail curves right, edging into the first rock face of this route.

15.3 km (9.5 mi) There is quite a long bridge over the St. Mary River. Just before it, two interpretive panels recount the history of Wycliffe. The bridge's deck is concrete, with high chain-link fences making up both sides. The view from it is bracing, as the river sits at the bottom of a gully.

On the far bank something unusual begins – an extended stretch of several kilometres/miles of mostly uphill. This probably should not come as a surprise, but after the easy ride since leaving Kimberley, it is mildly irksome.

The pathway enters a thickly wooded area, with quite high ground to the right. The path ascends the slope, contouring along the hillside. At two locations, large concrete blocks line the upslope side of the trail, acting as rock slide barriers. This is the most remote section of this trail, which works through the forest with only occasional views of the river or the bluffs on its opposite bank.

19.1 km (11.9 mi) The path arrives at a trailhead parking area, where it reconnects to the Wycliffe Park Road. Another sturdy stone outhouse is here, and a trailhead kiosk, a garbage can, and bike parking. A bench just before the outhouse is positioned to overlook Highway 95A's bridge crossing the St. Mary River.

Road and pathway follow each other, and some houses are once again evident. About 700 m/yd from the outhouse, there are two new benches and another interpretive panel, facing the river. At 20.2 km (12.6 mi), Wycliffe Park Road turns left and crosses the trail.

The route once again is separated from roads and housing, as it curves into another narrow ravine and begins to descend. Except for occasional glimpses of houses – and mountains – through fairly thick tree cover, until it crosses a

Mule Deer

British Columbia is home to three deer species, but it is the mule deer that prefers the dry valleys and plateaus of the southern interior. Mule deer are relatively large, with adult males, or bucks, averaging 70-115 kg (154-254 lb). Bucks in peak physical condition, however, may be as large as 180 kg (397 lb). Females, or does, are much smaller: 50-75 kg (110-165 lb).

Mule deer have a reddish-brown coat that changes from tawny in summer to dark in winter. They have a dark brown forehead, a whitish face with a black muzzle, and a white throat patch. Unlike the eastern white-tailed deer, mule deer have a large white rump patch with a narrow black-tipped tail.

What really distinguishes this species from its cousins, and gives it its name, are its large ears, which reminded trappers of a mule's ears. Estimates put the number of mule deer in the interior of the province at about 165,000.

driveway at about 22.4 km (13.9 mi), the trail feels fairly secluded. Actually, the best view of the eastern mountains to this point occurs shortly afterwards.

By 23.1 km (14.4 mi), trail and Highway 95A have reconnected, without any vegetation buffer between them. Busy Echo Field Road is crossed 400 m/yd later, and the appearance of commercial properties nearby indicates that we have reached the outskirts of Cranbrook.

The trail remains paired with the highway almost to its finish, but as consolation there are splendid vistas available east and south. At 24.4 km (15.2 mi), the trail begins to curve to the right, while Highway 95A bends left.

24.7 km (15.4 mi) Rather abruptly the trail arrives at the Cranbrook Trailhead, where another outhouse and garbage can are located. Parking lot and pathway are blended together, and only the yellow centre line of the bike path, located at the extreme right side of the parking area, marks the trail route.

This is the official end of the North Star Trail, but an extension continues an additional 1.6 km (1 mi) to McPhee Road, where the off-road pathway ends.

If you must retrace the North Star back to Kimberly, remember that it is mostly uphill. Make sure that you restock your water supplies, and allow plenty of time for the longer return trip.

Further Information:
Cranbrook Tourism: www.cranbrooktourism.com
North Star Rails to Trails Society: www.northstarrailtrail.com
Tourism Kimberley: www.tourismkimberley.com

Rocky Mountain Trench

Cranbrook and Kimberley are the largest communities in a distinct geological area that extends more than 1,500 km (932 mi) from northwest Montana to the Yukon Territory: the Rocky Mountain Trench. This is a broad, flat valley, situated along a major fault line, which separates the western range of the Rocky Mountains from the eastern range of the Columbia Mountains, known as the Purcells. It is primarily an arid zone made up of grasslands and semi-open forests of ponderosa pine and fir.

These towering peaks bordering the trench, sharply divided by the level valley and rising up precipitously on either side, give it its nickname, Valley of 1,000 Peaks. As you travel the North Star Trail, you will undoubtedly see why.

10. Rocky Mountain Legacy Trail

9. High Rockies Trail

The High Rockies Trail, connecting Banff National Park to the Elk Pass in British Columbia, officially opened in 2017 and filled a long gap between the Alberta and British Columbia sections of The Great Trail. The full length of this challenging mountain track is more than 80 km (50 mi), and there are no services along its route. However, there are frequent connector paths to the Smith-Dorrian Trail (road) which parallels the trail's route, permitting it to be explored in manageable sections.

Alberta TrailNet, the provincial body coordinating the development of The Great Trail, made the High Rockies Trail a priority in recent years and committed considerable resources to its development. For many, the High Rockies Trail is the pinnacle achievement in the twenty-five-year effort to connect The Great Trail across Alberta. Its opening was eagerly anticipated, and even before it officially opened – the first 40 km (25 mi) in 2016, the remainder in 2017 – usage was high.

Users should be aware that there is no cell reception on most of this route, and it is quite remote. Cyclists definitely should pack a repair kit. In addition, this is prime wildlife habitat, so carrying bear spray is a wise precaution.

Winter has its own unique issues: between Goat Creek and Three Sisters Dam, commercial sled-dog operators share the trail. One of the reasons I ended my profile at this spot is because between the Spray Lakes Day-Use Area and Buller Pass Trail junction the trail is closed for avalanche control from November 1 to May 1.

9. High Rockies Trail

TRUE
MAGNETIC

Contour Interval: 40M
3 KILOMETRES

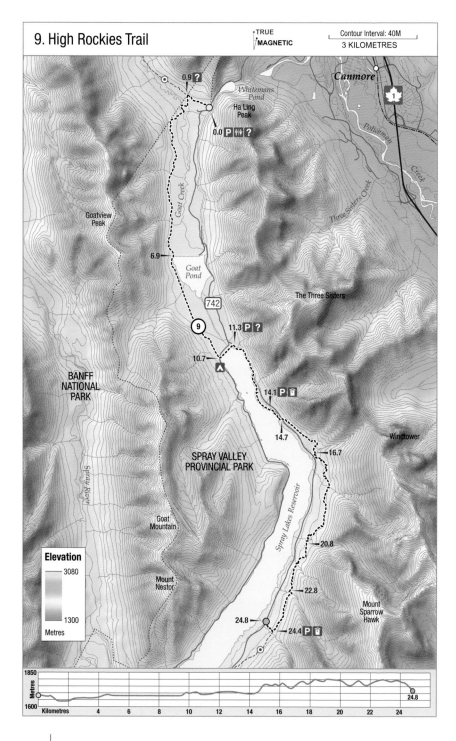

9. High Rockies Trail

Distance: 24.8 km (15.4 mi), one way
Ascent: 607 m (1,991 ft)
Descent: 567 m (1,860 ft)

Trail conditions: crushed stone, natural surface
Cellphone coverage: partial
Hazards: cliffs, isolated, mountain weather, road crossings, rugged terrain, wildlife

Permitted Uses							
Walking	Biking	Horseback Riding	Inline Skating	ATV	Snowshoeing	Cross-country Skiing	Snowmobiling
✔	✔	—	—	—	✔	✔	—

Finding the trailhead: From Bridge Road in Canmore, continue 500 m/yd on Rundle Drive. Turn left onto Three Sisters Drive, and in 650 m/yd turn right onto Highway 742. Follow for 7.3 km (4.5 mi); note that it will change to gravel surface. The parking area is on the right.

Trailhead: 51°03'42.2" N, 115°25'06.5" W (Start: Goat Creek Trailhead)
50°55'36.3" N, 115°19'06.8" W (Finish: Spray Lake Day-Use Area)

Observations: I love this trail! It is isolated, difficult, and in the mountains: everything I like (except oceans). It even has a large lake nearby. I cycled rather than hike it, although by riding a hybrid instead of a mountain bike I ended up spending almost as much time carrying my bike up hills as I did riding it.

Though described as "hiker-friendly," the High Rockies Trail is heavily used by mountain bikers. Indeed, it is ideal for them. But with its hilly, winding, tree-lined route, sudden, surprise encounters of hikers and bikers are likely. Walkers need to be especially attentive when using this trail and should be prepared to move out of the way very quickly. This contradicts normal trail etiquette of "wheels yield to heels," but with the steep hillsides it is safer for all if walkers take the initiative to move out of the path for the few seconds that it will take a mountain biker to pass. And remember, there probably will be more than one.

Route description: Begin at the Goat Creek Trailhead, in a rather large parking lot. But get there early, because this lot fills up, particularly on weekends,

because it is also a trailhead for the popular Ha Ling Peak hike. There are picnic tables, garbage cans, and washrooms on site, but no water source. A map of the trail is mounted on a trailhead kiosk, and TCT markers are posted as well. The sign states that the Banff National Park boundary is 1.7 km (1.1 mi) distant; nothing mentions that you enter Spray Valley Provincial Park almost as soon as you leave the parking area.

For the first 900 m/yd, follow the Goat Creek Trail in the direction of Banff. This wide path meanders through the softwood forest, providing magnificent mountain views that are a foretaste of what you will experience on this route. The junction with the High Rockies Trail is well marked, with a kiosk where there is another map and an arrow directing you to the left.

The path descends steadily, reaching a small pond 300 m/yd from the junction — where there are superb views of Ha Ling to the left — and making a sharp right turn 100 m/yd later. At 1.7 km (1.1 mi), the trail crosses the first of many bridges, over Goat Creek. Nearby is a water control station where there is an amazing view of the surrounding mountains.

From here, the trail follows a former road, which is wide and mostly grass covered. This is the easiest portion of this route, as it follows this clearly defined track along the base of a mountainous wall of rock, Goatview Peak. Views of the surrounding mountains are excellent, as well as the Smith-Dorrian Trail (gravel road) on the opposite side of the valley. Except for a few short rough and rocky patches where washouts have occurred, this should be a pleasant few kilometres/miles.

6.9 km (4.3 mi) The path reaches Goat Pond, at the end of a dirt road. This crosses the earthen dam that created the pond; it is 860 m/yd to a parking lot at its far end. This is another phenomenal view, with the imposing Three Sisters Peaks dominating the eastern skyline.

The TCT/Great Trail markers direct you straight, where the trail soon reaches a power line corridor, which it follows for a considerable distance. While doing so, it crosses several bridges and a very long boardwalk. At 9.8 km (6.1 mi), the path, which is like a forestry road, turns left off the power line corridor. It continues for another 800 m/yd, where it reaches a set of gates.

10.7 km (6.6 mi) The trail arrives at the Three Sisters Dam, which creates the long Spray Lakes Reservoir. Directly ahead is the Spray Lakes West Campground, but the path's route turns left and crosses the wide open earthen dam. As you might expect, the scenery is stunning. However, by now you probably will no longer have cell reception – those Instagram shots will have to wait to be posted.

After 600 m/yd, this road reaches the Smith-Dorrian Trail (road). Turn right, and almost immediately TCT signs direct you right and onto a side road, which ends in a parking lot. At the far end of the lot are a mounted trail map and a very rough and rocky single track heading into the trees: the easy part of this route is over!

Cut into the hillside and wedged into the narrow space between the road and the lake, the slender track contours along the lakeshore. The slope both above and below the trail is often fairly steep, although it never climbs very high above the lake. This is probably the roughest portion of the route, but there is no risk here of getting lost, and the views up the reservoir toward Mount Lougheed and Goat Mountain remain impressive.

At 13.1 km (8.1 mi) there is a particularly bad spot, where the trail is entirely loose rocks and appears to be at a junction. This is the High Water Overpass. The usual route is to the right, but when the reservoir levels are high, this is flooded and trail users must take the left fork. Furthermore, a mountain stream empties here and has scoured a section of the trail into a talus track. (I had to walk my bike through here.)

After a bumpy 100 m/yd or so, the treadway improves, but it is still rough. About 900 m/yd later, the trail reaches the Driftwood Day-Use area. There are several picnic tables, an outhouse, and a boat launch. A map has been mounted where the trail crosses the boat launch access road.

The next section is somewhat easier, with the picnic tables extending for a considerable distance along the shoreline. Quite a few people seem to fish from this park. Watch for fishers using the trail. After 400 m/yd from the boat launch, the trail turns away from the lake and begins to climb the hillside.

14.7 km (9.1 mi) The trail reaches and crosses the Smith-Dorrian Trail, where there is another map post. It climbs the hillside, the steepest and highest ascent in the entire route. It also moves into a thickly forested area, where views are rare, and the narrow single-track is closely bordered by tall conifers.

From this point, the trail seems designed for mountain bikers. It is winding and undulating, and even many of its tight corners are banked to permit cyclists to whip around them. But it is also great for hikers, working along the slope and crossing some excellent new bridges. It remains rough, sometimes including significant stretches of loose rock, especially when it intersects the hiking trail at Spurling Creek.

16.7 km (10.4 mi) The road is quite close, to the right, before the trail turns left and crosses the creek. There is one map posted at the junction, another down by the road. This is also the only access to the highway for an extended and difficult stretch of trail, so assess your energy level carefully before you continue.

What follows next is, in the words of a young mountain biker I spoke with, "a nice flowy trail." (Of course, another called it "a gnarly ride.") After leaving Spurling Creek, the trail climbs back up the hillside, but in a twisting path featuring numerous tight corners. Small but sturdy bridges span rock-littered creek beds, which are mostly dry in the summer. Meanwhile, the rugged, undulating terrain prevents the trail from remaining level for more than 5 m (16 ft) at a time. Most of this section is shrouded by tall, dense vegetation,

Mountain Wildflowers

Surrounded by the overpowering peaks of the Rocky Mountains, it can be easy to overlook the scenery at your feet. Almost as soon as the snows melt, flowering plants appear on alpine meadows, but the peak is mid-July to mid-August.

The wide range of elevations and environmental conditions means that the variety of species is larger than expected. At lower elevations, one can see Montane Zone species growing in the foothills or prairies, such as early blue violet, prairie crocus, and yellow lady's slipper. In the Subalpine Zone, the higher ground up to the treeline, expect bunchberry, bronze bell, and white-flowered rhododendron. Above the treeline, glacier lily, alpine forget-me-not, and mountain sorrel can create carpets of colour.

So even when you find yourself surrounded by the majestic summits of the Rocky Mountains, take a moment occasionally to look down. You might be just as captivated by what you see growing at your feet.

with no views of the mountains except at rare gaps in the brush, the bordering slopes thickly matted with bright green sphagnum moss.

Yet it is intensely enjoyable, both gnarly and flowy at the same time. The irregular terrain demands attention, the frequent bumps and curves ready to punish anyone whose attention strays from the path. This section is both physically and mentally . . . fun. By mountain standards, the trail actually isn't that tough, but compared to most of The Great Trail, it definitely is.

At 20.8 km (12.9 mi), the trail reaches a junction at the bridge crossing Spencer Creek, where a map is posted. The road is only 350 m/yd to the right, but this is not bikeable, and neither is the path that works upstream. Little more than 1 km (0.6 mi) later, another excellent bridge crosses Forbes Creek; a short footpath leads upstream to the grotto.

At 22.8 km (14.2 mi), the trail arrives at the exit path to the Sparrowhawk picnic area, which is pretty much 750 m/yd straight downhill. There is an excellent view at this intersection, the first in many kilometres/miles, where a pair of rough-hewn benches looks out onto the reservoir and Mount Nestor on its far side.

The main trail swings left and crosses Sparrowhawk Creek above a small waterfall. Except for one or two rough spots, this is the easiest section on the hillside, with the trail remaining at nearly the same elevation, and the downslope noticeably less steep.

24.4 km (15.2 mi) The trail arrives at the junction to the Spray Lakes Day-Use Area. There is a map here, bolted to a tree, and the footpath down the hillside is distinct. It is 400 m/yd to the Smith-Dorrian Trail, and another 100 m/yd to the picnic area, where there are outhouses, tables, garbage cans, access to the lake, and really excellent scenery.

From here, your options are to retrace the trail back to the Goat Creek Trailhead or follow the Smith-Dorrian Trail — a gravel road. The Smith-Dorrian Trail can be very busy, and extremely dusty; it might be shorter than the trail, but it is probably less enjoyable.

Further Information:
Alberta TrailNet: www.albertatrailnet.com
Kananaskis Trails: www.kananaskistrails.com/high-rockies-trail
Tourism Canmore Kananaskis: www.tourismcanmore.com

Grizzly

Also known as the North American brown bear, the grizzly is one of Alberta's two bear species — and the one considered most dangerous to encounter. Best distinguished by their large shoulder hump and flat faces, grizzlies can grow up to 325 kg (715+ lb). They are omnivorous, with plants making up the majority of their diet. For social and dietary reasons, these bears require a home range of 500-5,000 km² (190-1,900 mi²). Although they once ranged widely throughout Western Canada, today their range is restricted to the mountains, foothills, and northern boreal forest. Adults are active from spring to late autumn.

Most outdoor people consider the grizzly to be the perfect symbol of Canada's wilderness and think themselves lucky to see one. However, up-close encounters can be uncertain, especially if it is with a mother and cubs. In such a circumstance, you should back away slowly, avoiding eye contact. If the bear approaches within 5 m (16 ft), use bear spray.

For more information about hiking in bear country consult the Parks Canada website, www.pc.gc.ca.

10. Rocky Mountain Legacy Trail

Built in honour of Banff National Park's 125th anniversary, few trails have been as enthusiastically embraced by the public as the Rocky Mountain Legacy Trail. Connecting Canmore and Banff, two of the most popular tourism communities in the Rocky Mountains, this asphalt-surfaced pathway became heavily used from the day it opened. And why wouldn't it be? Superbly constructed and ideal for fast cycling, running, and inline skating, it runs between communities full of some of the most enthusiastic and active outdoor populations in the country.

But what makes this trail uniquely appealing is its visually stunning surroundings. High peaked, deliciously serrated mountains line both sides of the pathway for its entire distance, with some summits, such as Cascade Mountain, casting an overpowering presence for considerable portions of this route. Alpine wildlife, including elk, mountain sheep, and mountain goats, might be sighted. Grizzly bears and wolves, which also live in the Bow River Valley, are safely restricted to the opposite side of a wildlife fence.

This is an excellent route for anyone, whether families, casual tourists, or fitness enthusiasts, and it provides a gentle gateway into the landscape of Banff, one of Canada's most-visited national parks.

Should you wish a relaxed return, buses with bike racks travel between Canmore and Banff every hour during the summer, less frequently in other seasons.

Dogs are permitted on the Legacy Trail, but opportunities for wildlife encounters are high, and dogs must be on-leash at all times.

10. Rocky Mountain Legacy Trail

TRUE
MAGNETIC

Contour Interval: 40M

3 KILOMETRES

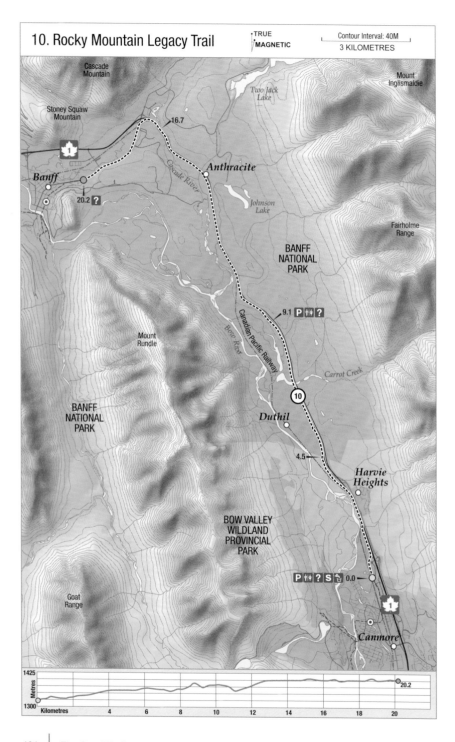

10. Rocky Mountain Legacy Trail

Distance: 20.2 km (12.6 mi), one way
Ascent: 171 m (561 ft)
Descent: 89 m (292 ft)

Trail conditions: asphalt
Cellphone coverage: yes
Hazards: mountain weather, road crossings, wildlife

Permitted Uses							
Walking	Biking	Horseback Riding	Inline Skating	ATV	Snowshoeing	Cross-country Skiing	Snowmobiling
✔	✔	✔*	✔	—	✔	✔	—

Finding the trailhead: Begin this route from the parking lot of the Travel Alberta Canmore Visitor Information Centre, 2801 Bow Valley Trail, Canmore.

Trailhead: 51°06'18.8" N, 115°22'02.0" W (Start: Canmore)
51°11'11.6" N, 115°33'11.9" W (Finish: Banff)

Observations: Ever since I first heard of this trail being opened, I had wanted to travel it. The Bow River Valley between Canmore and Banff is bordered by some of the most spectacular mountain scenery in North America, and both communities are renowned as meccas for outdoor enthusiasts. It was in this area that I began hiking many years ago, and I have been drawn back there many times since.

Because it is asphalt-surfaced and runs alongside the busy multi-lane Icefields Parkway, this route is sometimes overlooked by hard-core outdoors types. But while it is true that you rarely escape the sights or sounds of vehicle traffic, this is a superbly constructed trail passing through a stunning landscape. This is one route that I recommend for everyone – even the hard core.

Route description: Start at the Visitor Centre, which is very convenient as this large tourism area has washrooms, drinking water, vending machines, picnic tables, and other facilities on the grounds. To reach the trail, return to Highway 1A (Bow Valley Trail) by the entrance road; a crosswalk delivers you to a large signpost for the Legacy Trail. There is also a bike repair station beside it, so you may as well check the air pressure in your tires before you start.

The signpost actually counts trail users: daily, annually, and in total. (I was #260 that day.) The paved bidirectional pathway runs alongside the road initially, with the Canadian Pacific Railway nearby on the left. There is even a gas pipeline running parallel; the Bow Valley is a narrow and crowded transportation corridor.

There is a set of gates at 250 m/yd so that the trail can be closed against wildlife if necessary, but initially the pathway runs beside the Bow Valley Trail, almost like a sidewalk. Flat, nearly level – though it is effectively all uphill to Banff – and in excellent condition, the path invites fast cycling. In fact, significant numbers of speedy cyclists use this trail, so be mindful when riding recreationally that you will probably be overtaken. Be cautious dismounting; racing cyclists can be almost as dangerous as speeding cars.

By 750 m/yd, the trail reaches the junction of Highway 1 and the Bow Valley Trail, and now parallels the busy highway. Fortunately, it soon moves into a forested section, which provides a little buffer from the noise. But at 1.7 km (1.1 mi), the terrain squeezes river, rail, road, and trail together. Fortunately, this open area also means that views of the mountains are unimpeded, and this is more than adequate compensation for a little traffic racket.

At about 3 km (1.9 mi), the pathway moves away from the road, heading into a gorgeous stand of lodgepole pine and around another traffic interchange, this one for the community of Harvie Heights. The next 1.5 km (0.9 mi) is among the most insulated from traffic of the entire route, as the trail winds through the forest.

4.5 km (2.8 mi) The pathway reconnects with the highway as it enters Banff National Park; no park entry fee is required to use this trail. For the next 800 m/yd, the pathway is so close to the highway that it is separated only by concrete jersey barriers. The first small bridge is in this section.

About 5.3 km (3.3 mi), the trail curves left to climb a small knoll, providing a lovely informal lookout toward the mountains to the left. When it returns to running alongside the highway, there is a little distance between the two, a grass-covered buffer. The wildlife fence is immediately to the left now and massive Cascade Mountain towers directly ahead.

I found the greatest challenge on this route was my constant urge to stare at the surrounding scenery instead of concentrating on the trail. Talk about distracted driving! At 6.9 km (4.3 mi), there is a bridge crossing Carrot Creek, and about 1.5 km (0.9 mi) later, the first animal crossing culvert runs beneath the trail. It might also provide water drainage, and it looked as if it could do both.

9.1 km (5.7 mi) After passing a set of gates, the trail arrives in the Valley View Day-Use Area, which can be a busy spot, and where path and parking lot are the same for about 200 m/yd. This is a great place to take a break; there are picnic tables, a washroom, interpretive panels, and magnificent views of Mount

Mount Rundle

Marginally the tallest peak of the mountains that lie between Canmore and Banff on the south side of the Bow River, Mount Rundle is 2,979 m (9,771 ft) high. Forming this 12 km (7.5 mi) range are seven distinct peaks, presenting an impressive wall of jagged rock between the two communities.

The Cree called it *Waskahigan Watchi*, meaning "House Mountain." It was renamed in 1858 for the Reverend Robert Rundle, who introduced a written language for the Cree Peoples. Because of its proximity to Banff, Mount Rundle has been described as one of Canada's most recognized mountains. The famous view of the mountain from the Vermilion Lakes has appeared in many photographs and paintings.

From the Legacy Trail, Mount Rundle is barely recognizable, just another of the imposing mountain peaks towering above your route and just one tiny portion of the exceptional scenery.

Rundle and the Bow Valley. As you leave, there is a trailhead kiosk with park announcements posted.

The trail continues, staying quite close to the highway and crossing more culverts that allow animal movement, with nothing distinctive — except the phenomenal landscape, of course. At 14.7 km (9.1 mi), the trail squeezes next to the highway to cross the Cascade River on a narrow bridge. On the opposite side of the highway is TransAlta's Cascade hydro power plant, the only power development in a Canadian national park. A road sign states that Banff is 2 km

(1.2 mi) distant; in fact, although the highway exit is that far, the town is considerably further.

At 16.1 km (10 mi), the trail passes through an electrified gate. This includes a mat that carries a light charge, which permits the gate to remain open. Avoid stopping and stepping on the mat if you don't want to experience a mild electric shock. Cascade Mountain lies directly ahead, and its imposing bulk, rising ever higher as you approach, appears to create an impassible barrier.

16.7 km (10.4 mi) The trail arrives at its first junction, located where it dips below a road bridge. Signage appears to direct cyclists straight, while arrows point pedestrians, dogs, and horseback riders right, diverting them onto the Cascade Ponds Trail. In fact, this is a passageway for equestrians from Banff to access the backcountry, and this is the only place on the Legacy Trail they are permitted. Pedestrians and dog walkers are not required to exit right – they may continue straight into Banff – but cyclists may not ride on the Cascade Ponds Trail.

There is another electrified gate just beyond this junction, as the trail climbs back up to highway level. From here, the trail curves left, skirting a road interchange and turning away from both Highway 1 and the imposing Cascade Mountain. This is another extended stretch where jersey barriers are the only buffer between path and road.

At 17.5 km (10.9 mi), the trail has turned 90° and passes underneath the railway line. About 400 m/yd further there is another gate; cyclists cross the electrified mat, while pedestrians, dogs, and horseback riders use a manually operated gate next to it. (Important: always close the gate behind you.)

The two-lane road on the right is now Banff Avenue, and the first buildings of Banff come into view, with several resorts visible through the trees on the left. At 18.3 km (11.4 mi), the trail crosses Tunnel Mountain Road, where there is a stop sign for trail users and a crosswalk on the street. About 150 m/yd later a large stone cairn sits on the left, but most of this next section is lined by tall conifers. Higher ground on the left blocks any view.

📍**20.2 km (12.6 mi)** The off-road pathway ends at a driveway crossing with the bustling town of Banff visible ahead. A small set of gates narrows the path, and a large trailhead kiosk marks the spot. From here a sidewalk continues into the community and cyclists must take to the road. There is a very large sign next to the kiosk, facing Canmore, warning motorists that the next 3 km (1.9 mi) are a crossing zone for bear, wolf, and elk.

Officially, the Legacy Trail continues through the village using the road, but for trekkers, this is where I suggest you end your trip, unless you wish to continue into the town for refreshment. Retrace the route to return to Canmore. In this case, I expect the return trip will offer as dramatic a viewing experience as the journey out.

Further Information:
Banff National Park: www.pc.gc.ca/en/pn-np/ab/banff
Town of Banff: www.banff.ca
Town of Canmore: www.canmore.ca

11. Glenbow Ranch Provincial Park

One of the newer provincial parks in Alberta, Glenbow Ranch was opened in 2011 and sits on the north bank of the Bow River between Calgary and the town of Cochrane. Most of this 1,314 ha (3,247 ac) park is made up of the former ranch of Neil Harvie, which his family sold to the government of Alberta for conservation purposes and to protect it from the exploding urban development that has absorbed so many other ranching properties near Calgary. An extra 21 ha (52 ac) was added to bring the park to its current size. The Harvie family also created the Glenbow Ranch Park Foundation, which conducts research, monitors the biodiversity of the park, offers school and other educational programs, and generally promotes and develops Glenbow Ranch Park.

The park's trail system is extensive and in excellent condition, particularly the asphalt-surfaced sections. There are numerous washrooms, interpretive panels, and picnic tables, and the views are superb everywhere throughout the park. Former ranch buildings and other structures have been left in place, providing some sense of what life might have been like when this area was far from the rapidly expanding city.

Some sections of the pathway are occasionally restricted to prevent conflict with grazing cattle. Check the park website for closures.

11. Glenbow Ranch Provincial Park

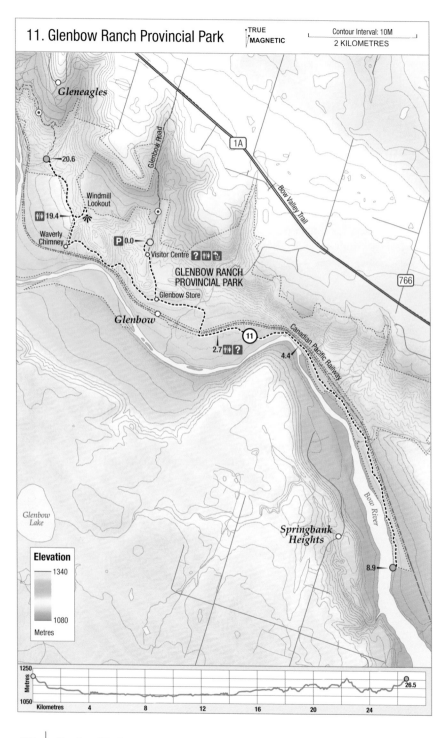

TRUE
MAGNETIC

Contour Interval: 10M

2 KILOMETRES

Gleneagles

20.6

Windmill
Lookout

19.4

Waverly
Chimney

Glenbow Road

1A

Bow Valley Trail

766

P 0.0

Visitor Centre

GLENBOW RANCH
PROVINCIAL PARK

Glenbow Store

Glenbow

11

2.7

4.4

Canadian Pacific Railway

Springbank
Heights

Bow River

8.9

Glenbow
Lake

Elevation

1340

1080

Metres

1250
1050

Metres

Kilometres   4   8   12   16   20   24

26.5

11. Glenbow Ranch Provincial Park

Distance: 26.5 km (16.5 mi) — return
Ascent: 488 m (1,601 ft)
Descent: 608 m (1,995 ft)

Trail conditions: asphalt
Cellphone coverage: yes
Hazards: ticks

Permitted Uses							
Walking	Biking	Horseback Riding	Inline Skating	ATV	Snowshoeing	Cross-country Skiing	Snowmobiling
✔	✔	—	✔*	—	✔	✔	—

Finding the trailhead: From Stoney Trail NW (Highway 201), turn onto Bow Valley Trail (Highway 1A) toward Cochrane. In 14 km (8.7 mi), turn left onto Glenbow Road. The parking area is on the right in 2.7 km (1.7 mi).

Trailhead: 51°10'5.9" N, 114°23'35.3" W (Start/Finish: Glenbow Road Trailhead)

Observations: Beginning in the parking lot, you will be impressed with this trail. The views everywhere are magnificent, and its facilities are superb. As most of the route lies at the bottom of the Bow River Valley, bounded by high bluffs on both sides, the rapidly expanding urban development of Calgary and Cochrane is largely hidden from view, giving the experience a much more isolated feel than its proximity to the city would suggest.

This is a fascinating area, with broad pastures lying at the base of steep, grass-sided bluffs. I biked this route, and the kilometres seemed to flash by on the mostly level asphalt-surfaced Glenbow, Narrows, and Bearspaw Trails. Yet the opposite side of the park along the Bowbend Trail, much hillier and more challenging, was no less enjoyable. This is an ideal park for family cycling, with quite a few additional options for exploration on side trails.

Route description: As soon as you arrive at the trailhead, you can tell that this will be an exceptionally scenic experience. Looking to the west you can see beyond the Bow Valley and to the mountains. Grass-covered bluffs slope away to the north. The vista is instantly arresting.

The facilities are impressive as well. A kiosk featuring an excellent map sits at the start of the path. Picnic tables, boasting a grand view, are positioned on the grass just behind it. Several interpretive panels line the trail and two large bear-proof garbage containers – one a blue recycling bin – are beside the parking area.

Follow the winding paved pathway downhill, where it reaches the Visitor Centre about 200 m/yd later. Washrooms and drinking water are available here, and there are more interpretive displays and another large map. You might also notice the first TCT marker and arrow, and an information panel about it. The view here is magnificent, with the Bow River visible below as well as an operating Canadian Pacific train track.

Follow the paved pathway, the Glenbow Trail, as it passes Coyote Junction – with a crushed stone surfaced path – and drops rapidly down the hillside. At 800 m/yd there is a nice little picnic area to the left, at the junction with the Yodel Loop. There are no trees to provide shade. Continue straight, another 300 m/yd, to a major junction, where there is a garbage can and three kiosks with interpretive panels and another map.

This is a T-junction. Directly ahead, the Canadian Pacific Railway line blocks further progress toward the Bow River, which lies just beyond the tracks.

Turn left, continuing along the Glenbow Trail. The view is quite impressive; bluffs line the left skyline, while directly ahead a thin ribbon of asphalt bisects the grass-covered valley floor. After an easy 900 m/yd, passing some livestock corrals along the way, the trail intersects the Scott Trail; turn right, and head to a crossing of the CP Railway.

Interpretive panels are everywhere, really slowing you down if you are cycling. There is a bench just before the trail crosses the railway tracks at 2.4 km (1.5 mi). Once across, the Glenbow Trail turns left and moves alongside the rails. Ahead and to the right, crushed-stone pathways meander toward the Bow River.

About 300 m/yd further, the trail reaches another junction, where there are washrooms, a kiosk with a map, and garbage cans. Fences line the fields, and there is a gate to restrict trail use when cattle are grazing. There is another sign indicating that winter maintenance ends here.

The Great Trail continues straight for another 500 m/yd, then curves right and descends to river level. For the first time you have unobstructed views of the water, and there are even groves of aspens nearby. At 4 km (2.5 mi), the trail reaches an area where river, bluffs, and railroad converge. For the next 500 m/yd, the route scrambles up and down constricted and uneven ground.

4.4 km (2.7 mi) Once again level with the railway tracks, the trail reaches a large fenced-in area overlooking a bend in the Bow River. There are benches and interpretive panels, and a sign that identifies this area as a Protected Site under the Alberta Historical Resources Act. The best view of the river is along this section of trail, and it is also a pleasant spot to stop.

Bow River

Beginning inside Banff National Park, the Bow River flows past Lake Louise, Banff, and Canmore — all names familiar to even the most casual outdoor enthusiast — before descending toward Calgary. The Bow River passes through the most heavily populated part of Alberta. Waters from the Bow feed into the South Saskatchewan River, Lake Winnipeg, and ultimately Hudson Bay.

In recent years, the Bow River is best known for the Calgary Flood of 2013. More than 100,000 people were evacuated, five died, and property damage exceeded $6 billion. Although one of the most intensively managed rivers in Alberta, with numerous dams and reservoirs providing water for irrigation, hydroelectricity, and industrial uses, the exceptionally quick melting of winter snows far exceeded their capacity.

Ironically, because Rocky Mountain snowfall supplies most of the Bow River's water, annual variations mean it is frequently subject to drought.

From here, the pathway soon after descends into a lovely wooded area, where there is significant shade for the first time. The meandering track passes through this lovely sylvan area for about 800 m/yd before emerging once again into open grassland. The narrow passage is long past, with the bluffs receding and a broad valley opening ahead. The Bow River widens considerably as well.

The trail wanders through fields, crossing Michael's Creek at 6.5 km (4 mi) and 200 m/yd later reaching the end of the Narrows Trail at another kiosk with interpretive panels. A small cluster of buildings sits on the right, beside the river, and their access road crosses the pathway.

The next section is named the Bearspaw Trail, after the ranch that once occupied this area. Many more houses are visible from the path, both on the left toward Calgary and across the river. The trail is level and views are completely unobstructed in every direction, except by the higher ground edging the valley. The railway track is quite close, on the left, and trains use it frequently.

8.9 km (5.5 mi) The paved pathway ends. Literally. It reaches a barbed-wire fence with a sign that says Private Property and simply goes no further. To the right, a distinct track in the grass leads to the bank of the Bow River, where there is a nice view. On the left, there are pastures and a cattle pen, but no access elsewhere.

Turn around at this spot, and retrace your route back to the T-junction with three kiosks at the bottom of the hill below the Visitor Centre. When you reach this spot, which is known as Glenbow Store, you will have travelled 16.7 km

(10.4 mi). The old store building is visible to the left, next to the railway tracks.

Continue straight, now on the Bowbend Trail. On this side of the park the terrain is much more rolling, and the bluffs are steeper-sided, exposing more bare earth. About 900 m/yd from Glenbow Store, there is another junction, this one with a crushed-stone path that descends the slope from the right. A map, a garbage can, and bike parking can all be found here.

There is a small pool of water as well, with another pathway on the far side of it 100 m/yd further. For a short distance the Bowbend is almost on top of the railway tracks before it moves away and descends. At 18.8 km (11.7 mi), the route turns almost 180° and begins to climb again. At this corner, on the left, is the Waverley Chimney, another former ranch site, where there are several interpretive panels and benches.

19.4 km (12.1 mi) After a long, winding climb, the trail reaches an important junction, and another washroom facility. The asphalt trail turns right and continues up the hill; The Great Trail continues straight on the crushed-stone pathway. I suggest you try both.

Continue straight to start; the wide pathway works easily over the hillside, with the houses of Cochrane visible on the bluff ahead. After about 700 m/yd, the path descends into a ravine, passing through a stand of gorgeous white birch. At 20.6 km (12.8 mi), it crosses a small rivulet and reaches a junction, with a kiosk and map. Turn back here and return to the asphalt trail.

At the washroom junction, turn left and climb the hill. This is a steep little climb, more than 35 m (115 ft) in 300 m/yd. If you look to the right, you should see the Visitor Centre in the distance. Where the asphalt ends, turn right onto a crushed-stone path.

22.2 km (13.8 mi) The path curves right and drops down to a fenced lookout, where there is a bench and an interpretive panel. This is a panoramic view, worth the effort to reach, and a particularly scenic location to enjoy a snack.

To return to the Glenbow Road Trailhead, go back down to the washroom, turn left, and retrace your route to the Glenbow Store junction. Then turn left and ascend the final 1.1 km (0.7 mi).

Further Information:
Glenbow Ranch Park Foundation: www.grpf.ca
Glenbow Ranch Provincial Park: www.albertaparks.ca/parks/kananaskis/
    glenbow-ranch-pp
Tourism Calgary: www.visitcalgary.com

Wild Rose

Alberta's quintessential symbol, the wild rose is more correctly known as *Rosa acicularis*, or wild prickly rose, and was adopted as the provincial flower in 1930. This attractive and fragrant flower grows almost everywhere throughout the province and blossoms between May and August. Its hardy scrubs can actually grow more than 1.5 m (5 ft) tall and create a dense, thorny hedge.

Though better known for its flowers, the wild rose's seed container, known as rosehips, is high in vitamin C and can be used in jams and marmalades. Rosehip oil is a popular skin-care product. Rosehips are also a food source for birds and mammals, including coyotes and bears.

Elk

If you are likely to sight any wildlife near Banff, it will be elk, the most numerous large mammal in the national park. More than 200 live in the lower Bow Valley, where they are constantly moving around to find the best feeding locations. An adult bull elk can weigh as much as 450 kg (990 lb), and such a size requires a lot of food to maintain.

Elk are browsers like most deer, eating twigs, bark, and leaves, but they are also grazers, eating the long grasses in the river valley. Light brown in colour, though with a darker face and lighter-coloured rump, elk are often difficult to see. However, elk are also extremely vocal, constantly keeping contact with barks and squeals. In the fall, during mating season, bull elk loudly proclaim their presence and power with eerie bugling.

Though herbivores, elk can be aggressive, and like all wild animals, unpredictable. Parks Canada recommends maintaining a distance of 30 m (98 ft).

12. Lacombe County

Every trail can claim some special characteristic: exceptional scenery, an endangered plant or bird, historical significance. However, few actually possess something unique, a feature that no other trail has. Such is the case of the Lacombe County/Blackfalds section of The Great Trail; it is the only place where the trail passes through the interior of a building.

In the Abbey Centre in Blackfalds, a 3,800+ m² (40,900+ ft²) recreation centre, the trail enters the facility, climbs to a higher level, then passes a series of displays, interpretive panels, artwork, and sculptures before exiting the building. Nowhere else in the 24,000+ km (14,900+ mi) Great Trail will you find anything quite like this.

The pathway from Lacombe to the Blindman River is paved throughout its entire length, although there are a few short portions where it uses quiet residential streets. It is generally in excellent condition, with a number of rest areas with washrooms. This makes it ideal for families, and provides easy benchmarks at which to reassess, especially if walking/cycling with children or novices.

The Lacombe County/Blackfalds trails are one of the few longer off-road pathways of The Great Trail between Calgary and Edmonton, and they highlight the agricultural richness of the province that attracted so many settlers in the late 19th and early 20th centuries.

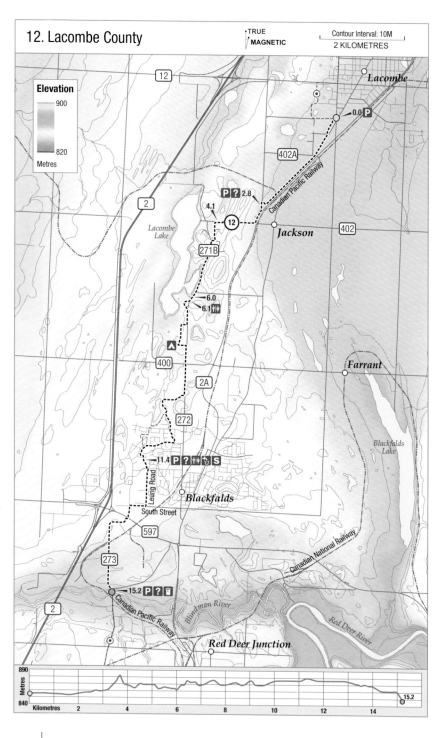

12. Lacombe County

TRUE
MAGNETIC

Contour Interval: 10M
2 KILOMETRES

Elevation
900
820
Metres

Lacombe

0.0 P

402A

P ? 2.8

4.1

2

12

271B

Lacombe Lake

Jackson

402

6.0
6.1

400

2A

272

Farrant

Blackfalds Lake

11.4 P ? S

Leung Road

Blackfalds

South Street

597

273

15.2 P ?

Canadian Pacific Railway

Canadian National Railway

Bindman River

Red Deer River

Red Deer Junction

890
Metres
840
Kilometres   2   4   6   8   10   12   14

15.2

12. Lacombe County

Distance: 15.2 km (9.4 mi), one way
Ascent: 86 m (282 ft)
Descent: 92 m (302 ft)

Trail conditions: asphalt
Cellphone coverage: yes
Hazards: road crossings, ticks

Permitted Uses							
Walking	Biking	Horseback Riding	Inline Skating	ATV	Snowshoeing	Cross-country Skiing	Snowmobiling
✔	✔	—	✔*	—	✔	✔*	—

Finding the trailhead: From Exit 422 on Highway 2, take Highway 12 into Lacombe. In 2 km (1.2 mi), turn right onto 58 Street. Continue for 800 m/yd to the entrance for the Central Alberta Agricultural Society, 4210 58 Street. Park on 58 Street; the off-road path begins on the left 25 m/yd up from the entrance road.

Trailhead: 52°27'21.4" N, 113°44'50.9" W (Start: Lacombe)
52°21'29.7" N, 113°49'04.2" W (Finish: Blindman River)

Observations: This is a route with a complementary collection of experiences: urban, suburban, and rural. Situated in Central Alberta between Edmonton and Calgary, in one of the most settled areas of the province, the Lacombe County Trail provides a different experience from the wilderness of the Rockies and the boreal forest and the hectic pace in the metropolitan areas of the major cities.

The agricultural richness of the region is apparent from the very start of this route, and I greatly enjoyed travelling past vast pastures populated by large herds of cattle. The fencing makes it possible to have close views of both cows and horses.

The excellent condition of this trail makes it a very smooth walk/cycle, and the indoor section in Blackfalds' Abbey Centre is impressive. It is also well signed, which is very helpful when it works through some suburban neighbourhoods in Blackfalds. This is a good route for a family.

Route description: From 58 Street, head up the entrance road to the Central Alberta Agricultural Society. In about 20 m/yd, a paved pathway links on the left, marked prominently by a TCT sign and another for Lacombe County.

The trail starts attractively, meandering through the grounds of Agriculture Canada's Lacombe Research and Development Centre. Well-kept lawns, towering trees, benches, garbage cans, and interpretive panels border the paved pathway.

After crossing a few of the Research Centre's entrance roads, at 450 m/yd the trail leaves the facility's grounds. It settles into a long straight stretch, lined on the right by a barbed-wire fence and on the left by the Calgary-Edmonton Trail (road). Stately tall trees provide some buffer between road and trail, and the fields to the right are cultivated.

At 1 km (0.6 mi), a crosswalk extends over Township Road 402A. On the opposite side, there is more signage, a bench, and another interpretive panel. This attractive pastoral passage continues, with more benches and interpretive panels to tempt you. The trail remains straight, now paralleling Highway 2A, until 2.3 km (1.4 mi), when it crosses a railway track; gates across the trail are on both sides. About 300 m/yd later, the trail turns sharply right, then left again to cross a small bridge.

The paved trail crosses dirt-covered Range Road 271, which looks a little odd. Once over the road, the trail turns 90° left and follows the road 200 m/yd to Highway 2A. There is a hill to the right, a cattle-filled pasture with a barbed-wire fence to keep trail users and livestock separate. Just before reaching the highway is a trailhead parking area among the trees on the left.

At Highway 2A, the trail curves right, following that road for another 300 m/yd until it reaches Township Road 402. Here it makes another right turn and begins the steepest climb of this route. The next 500 m/yd are uphill – you will probably be watched by curious bovines – but this is followed by a fun (if you are cycling) 200 m/yd downhill.

The trail crosses Township Road 402 at 4 km (2.5 mi) at another well-marked crosswalk. A fence and garbage can have been placed there. Once across, the trail continues downhill for less than 200 m/yd, where the off-road pathway ends.

4.1 km (2.5 mi) Turn left and use the road – there is no sidewalk – to continue your travel. This residential area is part of Lacombe Lake Estates, which features large homes on very big lots. Continue on this road for 400 m/yd, turning right at the next opportunity. (There is a TCT marker and arrow on the yield sign.) About 100 m/yd later, at the intersection with dirt-surfaced Range Road 271B, the paved pathway resumes on the left.

The large houses and fields are on the left now, while to the right it is thick forest. Less than 500 m/yd further, the trail crosses the range road, with an asphalt strip crossing the dirt roadway, where there is another Lacombe County interpretive panel. For the next 900 m/yd, the trail follows Range Road 271B with the forest on the right. Within 200 m/yd, you will have your first

views of Lacombe Lake, which was teeming with waterfowl, particularly red-necked grebes, when I was there.

6 km (3.7 mi) The trail arrives at a floating boardwalk and viewing platform overlooking Lacombe Lake. Grebes, coots, and other waterfowl dot the water and cruise among the nearby cattails looking for food. Two interpretive panels talk about the lake and its ecosystem.

About 100 m/yd further, the path turns right to work around a house. There is a gate across the trail, after which it arrives at the Lacombe Lake Day-Use Area, where there are sheltered picnic tables, washrooms, benches, and garbage cans. This area is wooded and feels secluded, even though there are houses to the left. But by 6.5 km (4 mi), the path has returned to running alongside the range road.

It looks very rural now, with a large pasture on the left and forest on the right. After 300 m/yd, the trail makes another 90° turn away from the road, once again working around several properties. In this section tall fences line both sides of the pathway, and there are several pastures populated by friendly horses.

After another couple of sharp corners, the trail returns to Range Road 272 (it changed its name) at 7.6 km (4.7 mi) and resumes running alongside it. Some 75 m/yd later, the trail crosses the entrance to the Watipi Campground. The trail ahead is slightly rolling, bordered by fields on both sides.

At 8 km (5 mi), the trail reaches the town limits of Blackfalds when it crosses Township Road 400. Once across, it continues straight, through fields and pasture for another 700 m/yd before it once again turns right and separates from the road. This is probably to avoid the small lake directly ahead.

The path curves around this before climbing a small hill and descending to another lake. Here it makes a sharp left and works along the lakeshore. Some lovely aspen provide shade, and there are a few benches as well. At 9.6 km (6 mi), the trail reaches the first houses of what appears to be a fairly new subdivision and a junction.

A TCT marker directs you straight (left), following the path running behind the houses, and away from the water. Crossing Aspen Lakes Boulevard 300 m/ yd later, the trail resembles a neighbourhood pathway and heads into a grass-covered park with a large playground. Slow for parents and children.

At 10.2 km (6.3 mi), the separated path ends beside a parking lot. A TCT maker and directional arrow direct you right, along Willow Road. At the next intersection, with Westbrooke Road, turn right again; watch for the TCT makers. Follow this residential street – walkers on the sidewalk, cyclists in the road – until you reach a large park at 11 km (6.8 mi). Opposite the intersection with Valley Crescent, an off-road path resumes on the left.

Follow this pathway around a large low area, which is a playing field. There are benches, garbage cans, and connector paths to the street. The path runs behind houses, crossing Vintage Close 400 m/yd later. Passing through a set of gates, the trail arrives somewhere unique.

11.4 km (7.1 mi) There is a junction at the edge of the parking lot for the Abbey Centre, Blackfalds' premier recreation centre. If you go left, the trail works around the Abbey Centre and arrives at Womacks Road 200 m/yd later. But if you cross the parking lot and go to the main entrance of the Abbey Centre, you can experience the only indoor portion of the entire 24,000+ km (14,900+ mi) Great Trail.

To see this, enter the building and follow the signs upstairs. There is a defined pathway on the floor, and there are interpretive displays, murals, sculptures, and all manner of special displays. You can even watch activity in the main gym a level below. The route describes an L, or two sides of a triangle, and exits the building by a different door. This delivers you on the bypassing trail just before it reaches Womacks Road, which is to the right.

The trail appears to end at this road, but turn left and follow the sidewalk to the nearest crosswalk, and the intersection of Womacks Road and Leung Road. Cross Womacks, then cross Leung; the trail resumes on the left side of Leung Road. There should be signs that indicate this route.

From here the paved pathway, somewhat rougher and narrower now but still asphalt surfaced, follows Leung Road. To the left is an older residential area, on the left are fields and one large public school, the Iron Ridge Elementary Campus. The trail crosses several streets, all at crosswalks, before moving into a completely open area.

Alberta Agriculture

Though better known today for its oil production, Alberta's agricultural industry is massive. More than 73,000 work in the agri-food sector. In 2016, there were 40,638 farms in the province with an average size of 500+ ha (1,236+ ac). Farm land area in Alberta encompassed 20,335,545 ha (50,249,131 ac), or nearly 32% of the entire province.

As you might guess from what you see travelling the Lacombe County Trail, cattle and other livestock make up a large percentage of Alberta's agriculture — more than 46%. In fact, there are 5,375,000 cattle and calves in the province, outnumbering the human population.

Alberta's agriculture is big business, with cash receipts in 2016 totalling just under $13.5 billion. Most agricultural products are exported, earning $10 billion that year. The largest markets were the United States (40.5%), China (13.8%), and Japan (12.3%).

At 12.3 km (7.6 mi), a side trail crosses Leung Road and provides access into All Star Park, a large area hosting multiple sports fields. The main path continues to the end of Leung Road at South Street, 200 m/yd further, where it turns right and crosses Leung. It then follows South Street to the next intersection, with multi-lane Vista Trail (road), in 375 m/yd.

This is a busy intersection with only a four-way stop sign – and traffic seemed disinclined to let me cross. The route turns left, crossing South Street, then parallels Vista Trail to an even busier intersection in 275 m/yd. The buildings in this area are all commercial/industrial, except for the large RCMP building to your left on South and Vista.

The intersection of Vista Trail and Highway 597 has traffic lights. The trail crosses Highway 597, then immediately crosses Vista. It turns left here and resumes following Vista Trail, which is now dirt-surfaced, but on the opposite side. This is also where the Blackfalds maintained pathway ends, and the Lacombe County Trail resumes.

Traffic is much lighter from this point, as the trail curves around more commercial/industrial businesses. There is even a bench and garbage can located just after Highway 597, although there is not much of a scenic view. The paved pathway runs alongside the dirt road until 14.1 km (8.8 mi), when it reaches the Canadian Pacific Railway tracks.

On the far side of the tracks, the road is paved and the off-road track ends, replaced by a paved shoulder. The highway is now Range Road 273, and the area appears completely rural again, with sizeable fields on both sides. Continue on this straight route for another 1.1 km (0.7 mi), descending gently, until the road curves left and the pavement ends.

15.2 km (9.4 mi) On the right is the Blindman River Day-Use Area, where there are outhouses, picnic tables, benches, and a new pedestrian bridge crossing the river. This is an excellent spot to relax and have a snack before you return along your route to Lacombe.

Further Information:
Central Alberta Regional Trails Authority: www.centralalbertatrails.org
City of Lacombe: www.lacombe.ca
Lacombe Tourism: www.lacombetourism.com
Town of Blackfalds: www.blackfalds.com

Red-Necked Grebes

Common waterfowl found in the shallow lakes and ponds of western Canada are members of a freshwater diving bird family named grebes. One of the largest of these is the red-necked grebe, so named because during breeding season its long neck turns bright red, and it develops a black head cap. During the winter, it is just another bird coloured light grey.

A good swimmer and fast diver, the red-necked grebe avoids danger by submerging rather than flying away. And with its feet positioned so far back along its body, the red-necked grebe is an awkward walker and is rarely spotted on land. It evens builds its nest in the water, on a floating mass of vegetation. Newborn grebes can swim almost as soon as they are born, but they enjoy hitching a ride on their parents' backs.

Grebes breed in freshwater ponds then migrate to the oceans to overwinter. But do not expect to see them in flight; they prefer to travel at night.

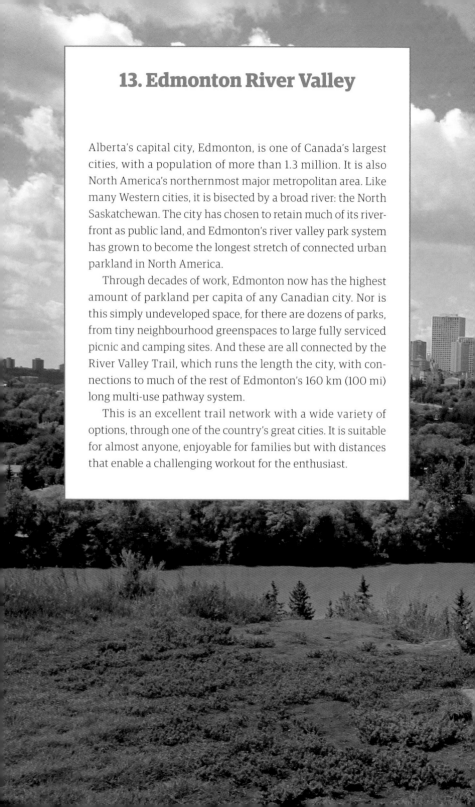

13. Edmonton River Valley

Alberta's capital city, Edmonton, is one of Canada's largest cities, with a population of more than 1.3 million. It is also North America's northernmost major metropolitan area. Like many Western cities, it is bisected by a broad river: the North Saskatchewan. The city has chosen to retain much of its river-front as public land, and Edmonton's river valley park system has grown to become the longest stretch of connected urban parkland in North America.

Through decades of work, Edmonton now has the highest amount of parkland per capita of any Canadian city. Nor is this simply undeveloped space, for there are dozens of parks, from tiny neighbourhood greenspaces to large fully serviced picnic and camping sites. And these are all connected by the River Valley Trail, which runs the length the city, with connections to much of the rest of Edmonton's 160 km (100 mi) long multi-use pathway system.

This is an excellent trail network with a wide variety of options, through one of the country's great cities. It is suitable for almost anyone, enjoyable for families but with distances that enable a challenging workout for the enthusiast.

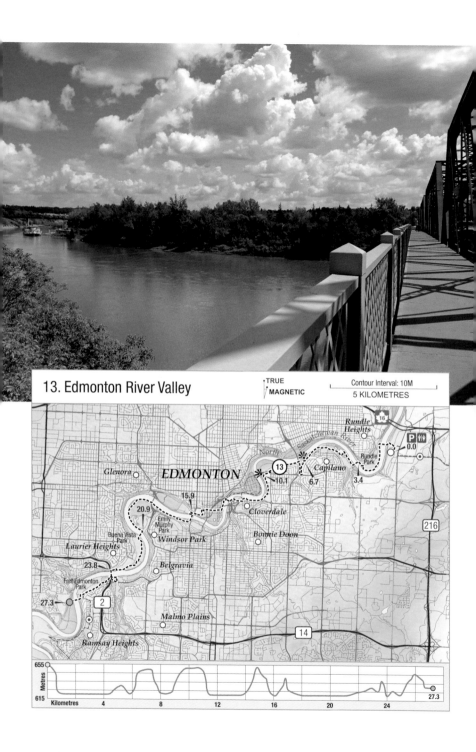

13. Edmonton River Valley

TRUE
MAGNETIC

Contour Interval: 10M
5 KILOMETRES

13. Edmonton River Valley

Distance: 27.3 km (17 mi), one way
Ascent: 252 m (827 ft)
Descent: 230 m (755 ft)

Trail conditions: asphalt, compacted earth, crushed stone
Cellphone coverage: yes
Hazards: high usage, road crossings, ticks

Permitted Uses							

Walking	Biking	Horseback Riding	Inline Skating	ATV	Snowshoeing	Cross-country Skiing	Snowmobiling
✔	✔	—	✔*	—	✔	✔*	—

Finding the trailhead: From the west, follow Highway 16 to Exit 216; keep right, toward 17 Street NW. Turn right onto 114 Avenue, which becomes 11 Street after about 250 m/yd when it curves right. In 300 m/yd, turn left onto 116 Avenue. Turn left on 17 Street NW 400 m/yd later. Follow 17 St. NW for 750 m/yd, then turn right into the park (unsigned on road). Keep left; the day-use picnic area is on the right in 400 m/yd.

From the east, take Exit 398. At an intersection about 900 m/yd later, turn left onto Hayter Road NW. After 450 m/yd, this becomes 17 Street NW. Follow it for another 750 m/yd, then turn right into the park (unsigned on road). Keep left; the day-use picnic area is on the right in 400 m/yd.

Trailhead: 53°33'36.5" N, 113°22'23.5" W (Start: Strathcona Science Provincial Park)
53°29'42.1" N, 113°35'32.6" W (Finish: Fort Edmonton Footbridge)

Observations: This was such a pleasant experience. The river valley trail and park system is superb, and there were countless beautiful spots where it would have been worthwhile to stop and spend a few hours enjoying a snack and the view. This is one of the country's premier urban pathway networks, and it should only continue to improve as the city and province invest in developing it further.

The only challenge was that there were insufficient TCT/Great Trail signs at junctions, and on several occasions I took wrong turns. In most cases this was only a minor inconvenience, but twice I unnecessarily climbed out of the valley, which was tiring.

However, it is impossible to be misplaced for long, and with the many facilities available, there are plenty of pleasant places to regroup. I would have enjoyed continuing further, but the Fort Edmonton Footbridge makes an excellent stopping point.

Route description: This route begins in the park's day-use area, where there is a large parking area, picnic tables, garbage cans – they are bear proof – and washrooms. Starting from the washrooms, follow the asphalt path running parallel to the entrance road back in the direction of 17 Street. At the second junction, about 300 m/yd, turn left and head downhill toward the North Saskatchewan River.

Be cautious; the asphalt is often broken and has deep cracks. If cycling, there are several spots where a wheel can get stuck and cause you to crash. After about 150 m/yd, the trail intersects a park road; turn left and continue downhill. Turn left at the next junction, 150 m/yd further, and continue on this path until you reach the end of the Rundle Park Footbridge, 750 m/yd from the start. This wide, high bridge is impressive, nearly 400 m/yd long and with expansive views up and down the river, and it features several observation decks. Footpaths in the sandy soil can be seen on both banks.

Once across, you have entered Rundle Park. The asphalt pathway continues in both directions, but turn left. Rundle Park is quite busy and consists mostly of large grass-covered fields with a scattering of hardwoods for shade. There are many picnic tables and other amenities, including a washroom about 500 m/yd from the bridge. The river is quite close to the left, although a footpath runs through the tree buffer near the waterline. Tennis courts, a football field, and baseball diamonds are passed, and there are water fountains near them but off the trail. There are even occasional interpretive panels.

At 2.2 km (1.4 mi), the trail curves around a pond, which is to the right. A small building across this modest body of water is the Rundle Paddling Centre. After 700 m/yd alongside this little lake, the trail curves away from the river and passes the parking lot for the Rundle Park Disc Golf Course. (Clearly, on this trail you are probably going to see a little bit of everything.)

3.4 km (2.1 mi) The trail reaches another impressive recreational bridge, the Ainsworth Dyer Memorial. I should mention that there are many directional and distance signs, but very few identify your route as being part of The Great Trail. Cross the North Saskatchewan once again, maybe spending a few moments on the bridge's observation deck benches to enjoy the placidly moving river.

On the far side turn right; the trail almost immediately heads into Gold Bar Park. At 3.8 km (2.4 mi), there is a multiple path junction; keep on the path marked Primary Trail heading toward Capilano Park. The river is to the right now, somewhat hidden by a thick buffer of trees. Numerous side trails branch into the woods. Gold Bar Park is mostly lawn, sprinkled with benches, picnic tables, and the usual facilities. There is also overhead lighting, and there are washrooms and a drinking fountain at a junction at 4.1 km (2.5 mi); keep right.

About 250 m/yd further, the pathway turns sharply left, passes next to a large parking area, then turns right again 200 m/yd later. Then for the next 750 m/yd, the trail runs alongside the massive, and occasionally malodorous, Gold Bar Wastewater Treatment Plant. There is even an interpretive panel explaining its capacity and coverage area.

At 5.4 km (3.4 mi), the path crosses 50 Street NW, entering Capilano Park and leaving the "aromatic" section behind. Keep left at the next junction, but keep in mind that washrooms and drinking water are available downhill when the trail emerges from the trees. For the next 1 km (0.6 mi), the path casually wends through lawns, housing, and residential streets just to the left.

6.7 km (4.2 mi) The trail arrives at a wonderful viewing platform, perched on a bluff high above the river, that provides excellent views of the river valley, and the first glimpse of downtown Edmonton. This is definitely a spot to stop and admire the surroundings.

From here, the pathway parallels Hardisty Drive NW for a further 650 m/yd until reaching the extremely busy 106 Avenue NW. The trail turns 180° right then descends sharply to river level, where it turns left and passes underneath Wayne Gretzky Drive at 8.1 km (5 mi). For the next 700 m/yd the path remains close to the river, moving through dense forest.

Turning away from the river, it climbs steeply and soon the Riverside Golf Course is visible to the right. There is one fairly large unnamed bridge that crosses a deep, narrow ravine about 9.4 km (5.8 mi). Just 200 m/yd later, the trail reaches a T-junction at Rowland Road NW; keep left, and climb. Your route passes underneath a pedestrian bridge, then circles left through a tiny parkette and uses the pedestrian bridge to traverse Rowland Road. From here it enters Forest Heights Park and curves left around McNally School.

10.1 km (6.3 mi) At the edge of the bluff may be the best view on this entire route, where a couple of benches face the river and toward downtown. Few trees are nearby, so a wide-angle view is available. The path works around more sports fields, hugging the edge of a forested area, and reaches a parking area 350 m/yd later; keep right.

The path continues hugging the forest/field edge, with more sports fields and lawn to the left, until it connects to the end of 101 Avenue NW at 11 km (6.8 mi). It turns right, enters the forest, and drops down the bluff and to the river. I found this to be a particularly enjoyable section, fairly isolated from housing as it works down the hillside, although cautionary signs for cyclists remind them to watch for pedestrians. Busy 98 Avenue NW is nearby, to the left, as river and road narrow the natural corridor.

At 12 km (7.5 mi), the path connects to George Hustler Memorial Plaza, where side trails lead to 98 Avenue NW and nearby shops. Keep right, working around the lawn until reaching a construction detour 300 m/yd later. Normally, the route for The Great Trail is to cross the river on the bridge at the end of 96a Street NW, reaching a pavilion on the opposite bank, then turning left and following a pathway near the riverbank.

However, from mid-2016 through late 2019 construction of the new Tawatinâ Bridge (LRT/pedestrian) has caused the route to make a significant detour, following alongside 98 Avenue NW and over the North Saskatchewan on the nearby Connors Road bridge. You arrive on the opposite bank at 13.3 km (8.3 mi). Once across, turn right to reconnect with the riverbank pathway and head underneath the road bridge.

Turn left at the first junction past the bridge, then continue straight, underneath the wide James MacDonald Bridge and into the lovely and peaceful Irene Parlby Park. This is a charming area, with beautifully kept grounds and clean benches, and in a sheltered residential enclave. Unfortunately, when you reach the intersection with 97 Avenue NW, at 13.9 km (8.6 mi), you must leave this attractive park.

Turn right onto a quiet residential stub of 97 Avenue NW, either walking on the sidewalk or cycling on the road the 200 m/yd to the intersection with 101 Street NW. On the far side a narrow asphalt bike track begins. Continue straight, almost immediately paralleling the now multi-lane 97 Avenue NW. Your route climbs a gentle hill and requires crossing – and probably dismounting – at several signalized and busy intersections. After crossing 106 Street NW, at 14.7 km (9.1 mi), the trail enters the grounds of the Alberta Legislature, where there are wide lawns, benches, and excellent views of the stately legislative building.

The trail continues only to just before 107 Street NW. Turn left, and follow the trail downhill to the intersection of 96 Avenue NW and 107 Street, which changes name to Fortway Drive NW. Use the crosswalks to traverse 96 Avenue and Fortway Drive, and follow the pathway as it curves around the legislative

grounds. There is much to see: public art, a bandshell, benches, picnic tables, drinking fountain, and much more.

At the Royal Lawn Bowling Club, the trail changes to the opposite side of the road via a crosswalk. Follow Fortway downhill, away from the legislature, underneath two bridges, and past the massive Royal Glenora Club, to its end at River Valley Road NW at 15.8 km (9.8 mi). Cross River Valley, and turn left on the asphalt bidirectional pathway.

15.9 km (9.9 mi) Arrive at the coolest bridge for walking or cycling, the Dudley B. Menzies, which has an LRT line on the top level and a pedestrian/cycling lane beneath it. A curving ramp leads up from the road to the walkway, and the views, as you cross the North Saskatchewan River once again, are interesting. Once across, 300 m/yd later, turn right and take the path running parallel to the river, past picnic tables and benches.

For the first time, the pathway surface is crushed stone, changing to compacted earth when very close to the river. The trail mostly follows the shoreline, although there is one small detour up the hillside around a University of Alberta site about 500 m/yd from the bridge. The path soon returns to the water's edge.

This is a thickly wooded area and somewhat isolated from the urban core; I saw a deer as I passed through. At 17.8 km (11.1 mi), the trail enters Emily Murphy Park, where there are benches, picnic tables, washrooms, water fountain, interpretive panels, and a very large parking lot. The crushed stone returns, while the path tracks alongside the lot. About 500 m/yd later, it passes underneath the Groat Road Bridge then splits into two distinct paths separated by trees.

Pedestrians use the right track, closer to the water, while cyclists ride the inner path, adjacent to the golf course. The trail describes a long gentle arc, as the river curves almost 180° in a giant oxbow. At 19.9 km (12.4 mi), the trail emerges from the forest into the lawns of Hawrelak Park, and all its facilities.

20.9 km (13 mi) Coming close to the park road, and the large pond used for winter skating, the trail meanders through the common until it reaches the Buena Vista/Hawrelak Park Footbridge. The asphalt pathway resumes, and for the fifth time you cross the broad river. Almost no buildings can be seen along the riverbank from the bridge.

Once across, turn left, and follow the asphalt pathway – although now there is a crushed-stone track running beside it – at least until it crosses a dirt road 1.1 km (0.7 mi) later. From there, the single paved pathway continues through the forest to the entrance road to the Edmonton Rowing Club, at 22.2 km (13.8 mi).

From here it is a crushed-stone path, and it narrows. Weaving through the forest, it reaches Buena Vista Road NW 250 m/yd later, and Sir Wilfred Laurier Park Road 275 m/yd after that. From here, turn left: cyclists ride on the narrow road, walkers on a natural surface footpath alongside.

The road ends at 23.5 km (14.6 mi), with an asphalt pathway continuing and climbing the hill, fairly steeply. At the next junction, just before Whitemud Drive NW (Highway 2), keep left.

23.8 km (14.8 mi) Arrive at the Quesnell Bridge, a multi-lane road bridge with one bike/pedestrian lane. Once across the river, the trail curves left beside Fox Drive NW. To the left is the unique *Talus Dome*, one of Edmonton's more controversial public art pieces. You are in the open, a busy road to the right and a field on the left. When the trail reaches the Fort Edmonton Park Road, cross it and turn left. Head back toward the river, keeping left and following the trail underneath the Quesnell Bridge.

Just beyond the bridge, your route crosses Fort Edmonton Park Road, then works alongside the huge parking lot. At 25.5 km (15.8 mi), it reaches a stop sign, where the trail temporarily ends. Turn left onto the wide walkway/park vehicle road and continue past the John Janzen Nature Centre, where there are washrooms and drinking water.

About 150 m/yd later the River Trail resumes, just before reaching the railway tracks for the Fort Edmonton steam engine. It curves slightly left, then works along the edge of Fort Edmonton Park and up and down the bluff slope until it reaches a quiet section of Whitemud Road NW at 26.6 km (16.5 mi).

The off-road pathway ends here, and The Great Trail heads left on Whitemud Road. Instead, turn right; in 100 m/yd the pathway resumes, on the left. Follow it for another 200 m/yd to the Fort Edmonton Footbridge – and your final crossing of the North Saskatchewan River. Benches line the bank overlooking this tranquil area, and there are massive shaded observation platforms in the middle of this relatively new pedestrian bridge.

27.3 km (17 mi) Arrive on the far side, where there are benches. The paved pathway continues, but turn back here; many parks and scenic spots will be revisited on your return trip.

Further Information:

Alberta TrailNet: www.albertatrailnet.com

City of Edmonton (Trails): www.edmonton.ca/activities_parks_recreation/parks_
  rivervalley/trail-system.aspx

Explore Edmonton: www.exploreedmonton.com

Fort Edmonton Park: www.fortedmontonpark.ca

Strathcona Science Provincial Park: www.albertaparks.ca/parks/central/
  strathcona-science-pp

Talus Dome

To the southeast of the Quesnell Bridge sits one of Edmonton's most admired — and reviled — pieces of public art. Nearly 1,000 shiny massive silver balls are piled into a tall dome sitting on the grass near the southeast bridge. Its controversial design and $600,000 price tag virtually guaranteed a measure of outrage, and it has been criticized for distracting drivers to looking at "a giant pile of rabbit turds." Its supporters claim that it is an ambitious, visionary project, one that becomes a lightning rod for different points of view and public debate.

The Public Art Archive describes it thus: "*Talus Dome* is both a sculpture in the landscape and a mirror to the landscape. It reflects the sky, the weather and the river of cars that pass by. The hollowed dome is part of a holistic landscape where nature and culture are inextricably linked." What is certain is that you cannot miss it!

Alberta TrailNet Society

Alberta's provincial trail council and charitable organization is tasked with coordinating the development of more than 3,000 km (1,864 mi) of The Great Trail in Alberta. Founded in 1989 and headquartered in Edmonton, TrailNet has worked tirelessly with the national body, the province, municipal governments, and regional and local groups to develop the route and provide funding and other support, and has partnered with government on developing policy and legislation in support of trails.

Extensive as The Great Trail is, it is one of several national initiatives incorporated into Alberta's provincial trail structure: the Wild Rose Trail System. TrailNet's mandate is "Promoting a trail network, including the Trans Canada Trail, connecting all Albertans." The Wild Rose Trail System includes portions of The Great Trail, the Sentier National Trail (hiking only), the Great Canadian Snowmobile Trail, the Alexander Mackenzie Voyageur Route (canoe), as well as thousands of regional trail networks and local pathways. This is truly a massive undertaking and an impressive vision shared by Alberta TrailNet, its partners, and its many dedicated volunteers.

Bridges for Canada

To commemorate 100 years of existence, which would be in 2003, the Canadian Military Engineers began a three-year program in 2000 to assist communities in every province to build or restore bridges for the Trans Canada Trail. Their effort was critical to the success of numerous routes, as many volunteer groups often possessed neither the funding nor the expertise to undertake these massive and complicated projects themselves.

In only one day in 2002, the 8th Field Engineer Regiment — now the 41 Combat Engineer Regiment — arrived and installed the 28 m (92 ft) Bailey Bridge over the Tawatinaw River, making The Great Trail connection between Athabasca and Colinton possible.

Canada's Military Engineers completed dozens of bridges by the end of the program and, in the years since, have built many more; particularly in 2016-17 to assist The Great Trail in achieving its goal of coast-to-coast-to-coast completion.

14. Athabasca Landing Trail

Some trails highlight their historical roots, and perhaps none does that with more rigour than the Athabasca Landing Trail. Named after one of the most important pre-railroad land routes into Northern Canada, the Athabasca Landing Trail attempts to follow the path of these earliest settlers into Northern Alberta, connecting Fort Saskatchewan with the present-day community of Athabasca.

Following either isolated range roads or the abandoned track of the railway that replaced the original tote road, the Athabasca Landing Trail links most of the original settlements founded to service the flow of travellers with lodging and resupply. The community trail association highlights that history at every trailhead and each interpretive panel.

The Athabasca Landing Trail is also the start of the only overland route of The Great Trail into Northern British Columbia, the Yukon, and the Northwest Territories. I elected to highlight the final few kilometres/miles, from the village of Colinton to its end in the town of Athabasca. From this point The Great Trail forks, with the overland Peace River Trail continuing north and west, while the 825+ km (513+ mi) water route Athabasca River Trail heads north toward the Alberta/Northwest Territories border near Fort Smith.

Much of this trail passes through private property, and the trail's existence is possible only with permission from landowners. Please respect their generosity by staying on the trail, not interfering with either crops or livestock, and being scrupulous about leaving no trace.

14. Athabasca Landing Trail

TRUE
MAGNETIC

Contour Interval: 10M
2 KILOMETRES

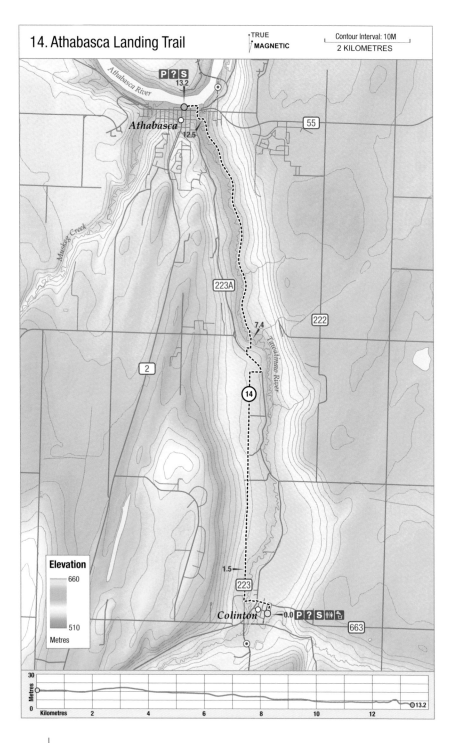

Athabasca River

P ? S
13.2

Athabasca
12.5

55

Muskeg Creek

223A

7.4

222

Tawatinaw River

(14)

Elevation
660

510
Metres

1.5
223

Colinton — 0.0 P ? S 👫 🚻

663

Metres 30 / 0

Kilometres 2 4 6 8 10 12
13.2

14. Athabasca Landing Trail

Distance: 13.2 km (8.2 mi), one way
Ascent: 33 m (108 ft)
Descent: 70 m (230 ft)

Trail conditions: asphalt, crushed
stone, natural surface
Cellphone coverage: no
Hazards: road crossings, wildlife

Permitted Uses								
Walking	Biking	Horseback Riding	Inline Skating	ATV	Snowshoeing	Cross-country Skiing	Snowmobiling	
✔	✔	✔	—	—	✔	✔	—	

Finding the trailhead: From Highway 2, turn onto Highway 663 E and drive 5.6 km (3.5 mi) to the T-intersection with Railway Avenue. Park in the lot directly ahead, near the trailhead kiosk.

Trailhead: 54°37'13.1" N, 113°14'57.5" W (Start: Colinton)
54°43'19.1" N, 113°17'05.6" W (Finish: Athabasca)

Observations: This was a very enjoyable route to bike on a late-summer afternoon and evening. The terrain was gentle, the pastoral landscape peaceful, if undramatic, and the sense of connection with some of the nation's history was particularly strong, especially on some sections of Range Road 223 when the route resembled the original cart track and there were no buildings in sight. In many respects, I think that the Athabasca Landing Trail perfectly captures the essence of The Great Trail.

A great deal of work was done on this trail recently. So much so that the route changed significantly, both in Colinton and Athabasca, between when I travelled it in August 2016 and when I wrote the description in the summer of 2018. My thanks to Linda Strong-Watson of Alberta TrailNet for sending me the GPS coordinates for the revised route.

Route description: This park is a good place to start this route, with its Discovery Panels, trailhead kiosk, and other interpretive panels about the Athabasca Landing Trail on-site. There is also good parking, some covered picnic tables, and other facilities in the large green space. Water, washrooms, and other supplies are available in the Colinton General Store, which is just across Railway Avenue.

Turn left and follow the clearly defined track through the middle of a field. In 175 m/yd it, reaches Highway 663. Turn left, cross the road, and follow 1st Street North to its end in another 300 m/yd. Follow the path out of the village, across the Tawatinaw River on a new bridge, and onto Range Road 223. Turn right, and follow this pleasant dirt road, passing tidy houses surrounded by large, well-tended yards.

1.5 km (0.9 mi) Continue past McNabb Road and on to where vehicle access ends. A broad selection of signage decorates this spot. There are some regulatory signs, including one that states the speed limit is 30 kph (19 mph), but another that says no motorized use is permitted. (There must be some fast cyclists!) There is a trailhead kiosk, but it was bare when I travelled through. Most impressive is a large custom metal sign and artwork for the Athabasca Landing Trail. Above its lettering is a figure wearing a pack and leading a laden

horse. This is a striking introduction to the pathway.

The route heads into the forest, narrowing but still wide enough for wagons. Its surface is quite sandy, which makes cycling somewhat more challenging. The trail is quite straight, and nearly level, which is how it will continue for a considerable distance. Fields will be visible from time to time on both sides of the path, but it will mostly remain shaded by tall aspen.

At 2.8 km (1.7 mi) you encounter the first structure, a small bridge crossing a wet area that is not quite a creek. About 1 km (0.6 mi) further, a road crosses the trail. A gate bars access to the left. Almost immediately afterwards there are a number of houses on the right, and at 4.1 km (2.5 mi), it is clear that automobiles share this track, although only for a short distance before the road departs to the right.

From time to time, there will be barbed-wire fences; remember that the land adjacent is private property, so stay to the trail at all times. At about 4.9 km (3 m), there is another road intersection, with a house on the right and the Great Spirit Lake Campers Village Co-op to the left. An impressively large and intimidating sign cautions against trespassing.

Trail and road again share the route for about 200 m/yd before the motorized track leaves to the right. Continue straight, passing more houses, fences, and fields, until you reach the end of the straight trail at 6.2 km (3.9 mi).

Turn right onto a dirt road that drops down about 250 m/yd toward Range Road 222A, which is a well-used dirt highway. There are many cultivated fields in this area, and views across the river valley are possible. Just before reaching

the highway, a track turns left, onto the grass-covered edge of the cultivated field. The route moves between two rows of fencing, sandwiching the trail between the road and the crops, for the next 600 m/yd, before turning right and arriving at a gate on the road. On the opposite side of the road is another gate, where there is a TCT marker. There is even a ladder over the barbed wire, in case the gate is locked.

On the opposite side of the road, the trail is again bordered by fence. Instead of cultivated fields, this is pasture, so the fence is mutually protective. This part of the trail, like the section alongside the road, was neither range road nor abandoned rail line, so it is far more uneven and bumpy. The path heads downhill, straight for 100 m/yd, 90° right for 100 m/yd, and then 90° left for a further 200 m/yd – all the while closely hedged by high barbed-wire fence.

7.4 km (4.6 mi) The trail crosses the modest-sized Tawatinaw River on the Allen Yee Bridge, which was built by the Canadian Military Engineers. A special Discovery Panel commemorating their contribution is located on the far side. The land around the bridge does not appear to be used for either agriculture or pasture, perhaps because the river describes several oxbows – large U-bends – and this flat section may be prone to flooding.

A wide mown track leads through the high grass to the trees and a small ridge in 200 m/yd, where the trail intersects the former rail of the brief-lived Edmonton and Slave Lake Railway. There was no directional sign there, but the well-worn path to the left was sufficient clue of the correct direction of travel.

The ride becomes level again, if not as straight as Range Road 223, and is situated on a small rise above the river. Many stands of trees border the path, but these are not tall enough to provide overhead shade, and there are frequent gaps, which allow views of the river valley and the occasional farms on the opposite bank. The land to the right is generally higher.

One challenge through this section is that the treadway is often soft sand, so thick that sometimes I needed to dismount and walk. Either the usual rock ballast on rail lines was completely removed, or this particular short line used a practice more common in the United States than Canada and to save money laid their tracks directly on the natural surface.

This is generally an uneventful cruise on the level track, since Colinton has overall been gently descending, although there is an elaborate new bridge over a small stream at 11.1 km (6.9 mi). Once past this bridge, side trails become much more frequent, though they generally branch to the right. By 12.1 km (7.5 mi), the sounds of vehicles can be heard, and houses come into sight on the left.

12.5 km (7.8 mi) The trail arrives at an impressive new bridge that crosses the Tawatinaw River, which links the MRM Wildlife Habitat to the rail trail. There is a trailhead kiosk here, a high-quality structure featuring impressive historical and pictorial displays and, best of all, a large, clear map. And as you can see, the community is all around us. The MRM Wildlife Habitat is in a 9 ha (22 ac) protected area between the river and the urban area of Athabasca.

Turn left, leaving the rail trail and crossing the bridge. Once across, turn right and follow the path as it follows the river with a ridge on the left. At 12.8 km (8 mi), the trail passes beneath multi-lane Highway 55, and for the first time the broad Athabasca River comes into view. Little more than 100 m/yd later, the trail reaches the river and the asphalt-surfaced Rotary Way, which follows the south bank of the river. Turn left and continue alongside the river.

13.2 km (8.2 mi) Arrive at the Riverfront Boardwalk, on the banks of the Athabasca River. Appropriately enough, as this was once named Athabasca Landing, there is a boat launch. This is an excellent place to end this route; there are many benches and picnic tables nearby, including several covered ones. Or, if you prefer to stretch out on the grass, there is a large tended lawn area. Interpretive panels are scattered throughout the park grounds, and services are nearby in the town. When ready to return, retrace your route back to Colinton.

Further Information:
Athabasca County: www.athabascacounty.com/visitors/trail-systems
Athabasca Landing Trail: www.athabascalandingtrail.com
Visit Athabasca: www.visitathabasca.ca

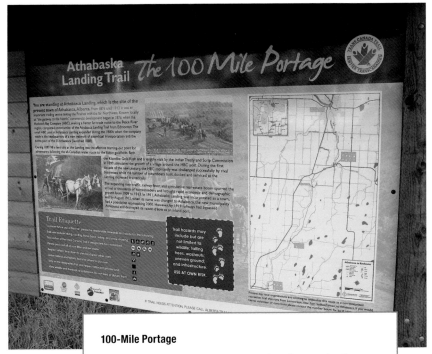

100-Mile Portage

Before the railroads, the fastest and easiest method of travel was by water, so communities tended to be established at key points at lakeheads and along river systems. Land connections between navigable waters were known as portages, from the Latin *portare* (to carry).

Ideally, portages were as short as possible. However, sometimes longer distances were unavoidable, such as the more than 100-mile (160 km) overland trek required between Fort Saskatchewan and Athabasca Landing. The former was near Edmonton and the railroads; the latter provided access to the vast Mackenzie River system.

The first Athabasca Landing "trail," or cart track, was developed by the Hudson's Bay Company to facilitate transportation between Edmonton and the company's northern outposts. Others, such as settlers, prospectors, and independent traders, used the trail as well, and by the late 1800s it had become Canada's busiest access route to the north.

15. Mirror Landing Trail

The Mirror Landing Trail is the name for a water route on the Lesser Slave River and a land path beginning in the community of Slave Lake and continuing along the eastern and northern shores of Lesser Slave Lake. The combined total of these two routes exceeds 150 km (93 mi). The trail contains a varied mix of urban, rural, and wilderness sections.

Situated in boreal forest, this route possesses a distinctly Northern Canada appearance. In fact, more than 50% of Alberta lies within the boreal forest region. Generally the landform is similar to that of the southern grasslands with low rolling hills, but the boreal forest enjoys much higher annual rainfalls and shorter, cooler summers. As a result, it is often thickly forested, although the region near Slave Lake is in a transition zone between forest and grassland.

This area is a birder's paradise, and there is a permanent observatory and a research centre inside Lesser Slave Lake Provincial Park. Because of migratory patterns, hundreds of songbirds and many other passerine species travel through a narrow corridor beside the lake every spring and fall.

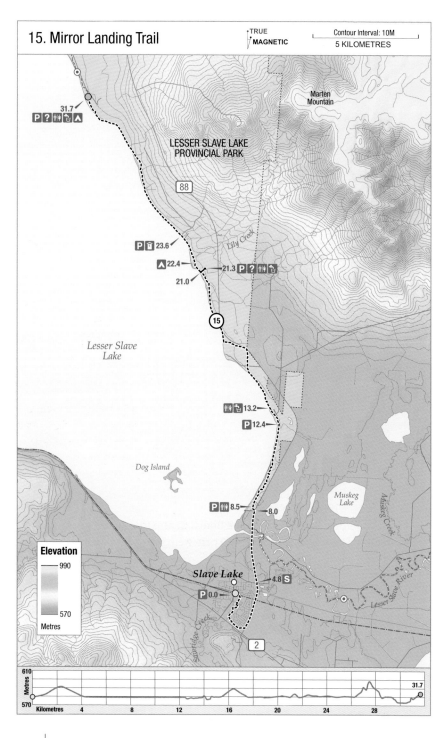

15. Mirror Landing Trail

15. Mirror Landing Trail

Distance: 31.7 km (19.7 mi), one way
Ascent: 88 m (289 ft)
Descent: 93 m (305 ft)

Trail conditions: asphalt, crushed stone, natural surface
Cellphone coverage: partial
Hazards: road crossings, wildlife

					Permitted Uses			
Walking	Biking	Horseback Riding	Inline Skating	ATV	Snowshoeing	Cross-country Skiing	Snowmobiling
✔	✔	—	—	—	✔	✔	—

Finding the trailhead: From the intersection of Highway 2 and Main Street, follow Main Street SE for 1.3 km (0.8 mi). Turn right onto 1A Avenue NE. Park in 100 m/yd, where the street turns left and becomes 2nd Street NE.

Trailhead: 55°16'55.4" N, 114°46'10.7" W (Start: Slave Lake)
55°28'42.8" N, 114°53'53.2" W (Finish: Marten River Campground)

Observations: I found this a particularly challenging experience. From the town to the park boundary the path is a well-defined asphalt-covered pathway, fairly level and suitable for any level of cyclist. Once inside the park, the track switched to compacted earth; it was still easy riding but required more effort. Beyond the Lily Lake Campground, the track was often overgrown with thick grass and featured numerous wet areas. My hybrid bike struggled; a mountain bike would be preferable.

But once the trail reached the Boreal Centre for Bird Conservation, the treadway improved considerably. There were still sections where grass had covered the trail, but the bridges were in good repair, the trail fairly straight, and despite this being the hilliest section of the route, it seemed much easier.

Cyclists should plan for a full day for a return trip. Some hikers can complete this in two days, but I recommend three: Slave Lake to Lily Lake Campground — or, better, to The Nest — to Marten River and back to Lily Lake, then return to Slave Lake.

Route description: The trail begins at the corner of 1A Avenue NE, next to a lovely flowerbed and a bear-proof garbage can. It is paved and in good condition and immediately climbs up a railway embankment and crosses the tracks.

It then spans a narrow steel bridge over Sawridge Creek, turns right at the next junction, and follows the creek upstream, with a large school and an off-leash dog park on the left.

At 600 m/yd, the pathway crosses 6 Avenue SE on a crosswalk, then winds its way through a forested area – passing multiple side trails – until it emerges at 1.9 km (1.2 mi) at Spruce Park, where there is a map kiosk for the Slave Lake Community Trail and a garbage can. Highway 2 is to the right, across a grass-covered field.

For about 450 m/yd the path continues straight, highway to the right, trees and houses on the left, before curving left to avoid another road. However, it soon snuggles up alongside Highway 88, where it remains. At 3.5 km (2.2 mi), the path again crosses 6 Avenue SE, here at its intersection with Highway 88. There is a crosswalk, and a TCT marker, and a sign that requests that cyclists dismount to cross the street.

Once across, the pathway parallels Highway 88, though with a little grass buffer between them. There is a small bridge 400 m/yd from 6 Avenue SE, then the trail crosses the railway 100 m/yd further. From the tracks, the pathway moves a little distance away from the busy road – there is plenty of room – and continues to parallel it. It comes close again on the bridge crossing Sawridge Creek, after which there are several ball fields on the left, and again when it reaches Caribou Trail NW.

4.8 km (3 mi) The crossing of Caribou Trail NW is probably the most dangerous on this route. It occurs at the intersection with Highway 88, there is no crosswalk, and on the opposite side of the road there is a large, busy shopping centre. Caribou Trail is the recommended route to the downtown and hospital and so is usually quite busy.

Once safely across, it is an easy ride until crossing 12 Ave NE about 600 m/yd later. From there to the crossing of Tamarack Road NE at 6.5 km (4 mi), to your left is a continuous strip of commercial/industrial businesses. An ATV trail runs on the right side of the road, which is forested. About 300 m/yd later,

the trail uses the road bridge to cross the Lesser Slave Lake River, which is where the water route connects. Lining the far shore on both sides of the road are large RV parks.

At 7.3 km (4.5 mi), the trail crosses the next (dirt) road. From this point, there are almost no houses in sight, and on the right is a large wetland. Ahead, on the right, the entrance sign for Lesser Slave Lake Provincial Park comes into view.

8 km (5 mi) The asphalt pathway ends at Devonshire Lane. On the far side, the trail enters the park on a boardwalk, which curves left, away from the highway, and crosses a Ducks Unlimited marsh. The asphalt track resumes after 100 m/yd of boardwalk. It is now among trees and continues for about 400 m/yd before ending at a parking lot. This is the access to Devonshire Beach, which is to the left. Picnic tables, garbage cans, and washrooms are scattered throughout the nearby trees. Continue straight; after about 200 m/yd there is a gate, beyond which are more tables and a shelter, as well as a mounted park map.

This is the entrance to the Whispering Pines Trail, which was my favourite section. For the next 2 km (1.2 mi), the path is a winding, sand-surfaced track that rambles through an area of sand ridges. Numerous interpretive panels describe both the interesting landscape and the plants that grow on them. The trail climbs up and down several small hills and navigates around taller ones. As there was a large fire in this area in 2011, the vegetation is somewhat sparse and not very high.

At 10.8 km (6.7 mi), the Whispering Sands Trail ends at a dirt road. Turn right and follow this wide track, which traces the lakeshore. It is a little higher than the lake, so there are some good views available, and several side paths permit access to the sandy shoreline. For 1.6 km (1 mi), remain on this quiet park road, which is also Range Road 55. At 12.4 km (7.7 mi), there is a small parking area, with a garbage can, to the left. At the far end of the small lot, a narrow trail – almost a footpath – heads into the trees.

Follow this bumpy path for the next 800 m/yd until it arrives at the parking are for the North Shore Day-Use Area. There are many facilities available in this area: picnic tables, shelters, washrooms, and drinking water. There are also numerous access points to the lake. Keep left, and watch carefully for the TCT markers that direct you correctly through the next two trail junctions.

At 13.9 km (8.6 mi), you should pass a park sign with a large hiker, stating that you are heading toward the Boreal Centre for Bird Conservation. The trail is in thick forest, a cleared path between the trees. And this it remains for some distance, except for intervals when it follows a power line. It also begins to curve away from Lesser Slave Lake.

Around 15 km (9.3 mi), you might notice the grounds of the Gilwood Golf Course and Country Club through the trees on the right. The trail skirts its boundaries, crossing Township Road 740 at 15.6 km (9.7 mi). The most challenging section of trail follows: uneven, with large wet patches and grass so long that it was difficult to cycle through, so I frequently had to dismount.

About 750 m/yd after crossing the township road, the trail reaches Highway 88 and actually runs on its grassy shoulder for a short distance. It makes this detour because there is private property to the left, the North Shore Homestead

Boreal Centre for Bird Conservation

Lesser Slave Lake and nearby Marten Mountain act as barriers for migrating birds, which prefer to fly around rather than over them. As a result, the eastern shore of the lake is a natural funnel through which disproportionately large numbers of birds pass every spring and fall. In addition, several species at risk, such as the tundra swan and western grebe, are found in large numbers in the lake. In 1994, the Lesser Slave Lake Bird Observatory was established to monitor migrating populations, and it is one of the few bird banding stations located in a boreal forest.

In 2006, the Boreal Centre for Bird Conservation (BCBC) opened its doors, the only educational and research facility worldwide studying boreal birds in their breeding grounds. In addition to its research, the centre maintains a large public display area and offers a variety of interpretive and educational programs.

Located next to the centre is the Nest, a facility sleeping up to ten guests, which is available to house visiting researchers but is also open to public reservations between May and October.

development. After only about 100 m/yd, the path turns left and back into the forest, but it is still rough going until it reconnects with the old road, beside the lake, at 17.6 km (10.9 mi), crossing the power line along the way.

The trail turns sharply right and is great for about 400 m/yd. But then it touches Highway 88 again, in a narrow spot where road and lakeshore are very close. For another bumpy, uneven 500 m/yd, road and trail are together, with no tree buffer between them.

Once it moves away from the road, the trail improves, returning to a grass-surfaced track among the trees, which are predominantly birch or aspen. There are more small bridges over tiny brooks, and several footpaths leading down to the water, where there are some lovely small sandy beaches.

About 400 m/yd after leaving the road, the trail connects to the power line corridor and follows that for a short distance. However, at about 18.8 km (11.7 mi), trail and power corridor link for an extended stretch. The adjacent foliage is quite dense, but about 800 m/yd later you should see an oil pumping station to the right. Some 100 m/yd later, the trail dips to cross a small bridge, then climbs again on the other side. This is a tricky spot: I almost spilled hitting the uphill bump on the far side.

Only 150 m/yd further is a junction; keep left and after another 150 m/yd the trail passes through a meadow, then heads back into the forest on a winding pathway. After 300 m/yd, it reaches a wide level track at a well-signed junction. Cross a small bridge 100 m/yd further and reach a park signpost listing distances only 200 m/yd later.

21 km (13 mi) You have reached the side trail connecting to the Boreal Centre for Bird Conservation, one of the highlights of this route. Details about the centre may be found in the sidebar, but even if you are not particularly interested in birds, the 700 m/yd (return) diversion is worthwhile because there is a water source, washrooms, picnic tables, and other facilities on-site.

Return to the junction; the park signpost states that the Lily Creek campsite is 1.4 km (0.9 mi) further. The first 450 m/yd is along the forested pathway, then the trail rejoins the power corridor, which it follows, crossing a bailey bridge over Lily Creek 200 m/yd later. After another 150 m/yd in the power corridor the trail curves left and connects to a dirt road. Lily Creek Group Campsite is to the left, but you will pass a shelter, water pump, and picnic tables.

A park signpost indicates that the Lesser Slave Lake Bird Observatory is to the right: head that way, following the road for another 1.1 km (0.7 mi).

23.6 km (14.7 mi) Arrive at the Lesser Slave Lake Bird Observatory. There is a large parking area, picnic tables, garbage cans, outhouses, and a number of information and regulatory signs. The automobile road turns right here, heading to Highway 88, and there is a gate blocking further vehicle access directly ahead. The lakeshore is only a few metres/yards distant on the left, and paths cut through the vegetation to reach the beach.

One of the signs here mentions the Freighter Lake Trail, which explains that much of the route you have been using follows a path that was cut by hand in the early 20th century. This path followed the north shore of Lesser Slave Lake and was used by Klondike gold prospectors to reach the Yukon.

There is also a park signpost stating that the Marten River Campground is 8 km (5 mi) further. Several red picnic tables are conveniently placed for bird observation, and some branching footpaths are signed Staff Only. About 200 m/yd from the parking lot is a small cabin, on the right, with solar panels on its roof. This belongs to the observatory and is not open for public use.

The next 500 m/yd features numerous picnic tables, always on the water side of the trail. The pathway itself is excellent, being wide and level, and offering smooth walking/riding. This section provides the best views of Lesser Slave Lake of the entire route.

Until about 26.3 km (16.3 mi), the good surface continues. Then the trail turns 90° right, then 90° left, and then crosses a bridge over a small gorge. On the far side, the path is more uneven, with the trees crowding the edges of the path.

For the remaining distance, the path passes through a mostly forested stretch, mostly hardwoods, although it does have 200 m/yd following the power corridor. This is also the hilliest section and crosses at least five small bridges. I found this enjoyable and tranquil.

About 800 m/yd from the finish, keep left at a junction. The trail soon narrows to a footpath, drops into a little ravine, crosses a bridge, and climbs up to another junction. Keep straight.

31.7 km (19.7 mi) The trail arrives at Marten River Campground, at a road. There is a trailhead kiosk, with a map. A water source is right there, and washrooms are nearby, but there are no benches or picnic tables, unless one of the nearby campsites is empty.

If you are not camping, refill your water bottle and retrace your route back to Slave Lake.

Further Information:
Boreal Centre for Bird Conservation: www.borealbirdcentre.ca
Lesser Slave Lake Bird Observatory: www.lslbo.org
Lesser Slave Lake Provincial Park: www.albertaparks.ca/parks/northwest/
    lesser-slave-lake-pp
Slave Lake Region: www.slavelakeregion.ca
Town of Slave Lake: www.slavelake.ca

Lesser Slave Lake

One of Alberta's largest bodies of water, Lesser Slave Lake covers an area of more than 1,160 km² (448 mi²) about 300 km (186.4 mi) northwest of Edmonton. Important to the fur trade, the Dene First Nations inhabitants were displaced by Cree who were searching for new sources of fur. Today, five First Nations bands — all Cree — have reserves bordering the lake.

Europeans first arrived in 1799 and soon established an outpost near the mouth of the Lesser Slave River, which ultimately became the community of Slave Lake. In the early years of the 20th century, steamships plied the lake, providing access for settlers and supplies to the Peace Country, until the railroad arrived in 1915.

A commercial fishery for whitefish and caviar existed until 2014, but today this large and relatively shallow lake is managed only for sport fishing: walleye and northern pike. Lesser Slave Lake is also one of the top destinations for ice fishing in Alberta.

16. Iron Horse Trail

At slightly more than 300 km (186.4 mi), the Iron Horse Trail became Alberta's longest section of the Trans Canada Trail when it opened in 2001. Of course, the abandoned rail-line corridor had only been obtained from Canadian National (CN) in 1999, so it was a little rough initially. However, every year since then, improvements have been made and the Iron Horse has become very popular, especially with horseback riders and ATVers. Snowmobilers make up the bulk of its winter use.

Unlike most other sections of The Great Trail, the Iron Horse is also popular among aficionados of horse-drawn wagons, and every year there is a large ride between Lindbergh and St. Paul through the remote Moose Hills Creek Valley. Many of the rest areas on the route of the Iron Horse are situated where once there were small communities, with the rest area being all that now remains.

With its many rest and staging areas, most of which permit camping, the Iron Horse is designed to accommodate multi-day excursions, particularly for hikers and cyclists. The section profiled could easily be cycled in two days: St. Paul to Heinsburg, camping at the latter and returning the following day. At 125 km (77.8 mi) return, hikers will require considerably more time: five to six days.

The Iron Horse is open to all uses, including ATVs and horse-drawn wagons. As a walker or cyclist, be prepared to yield to wagons and people on horseback. You may also encounter cattle on the trail over much of the route.

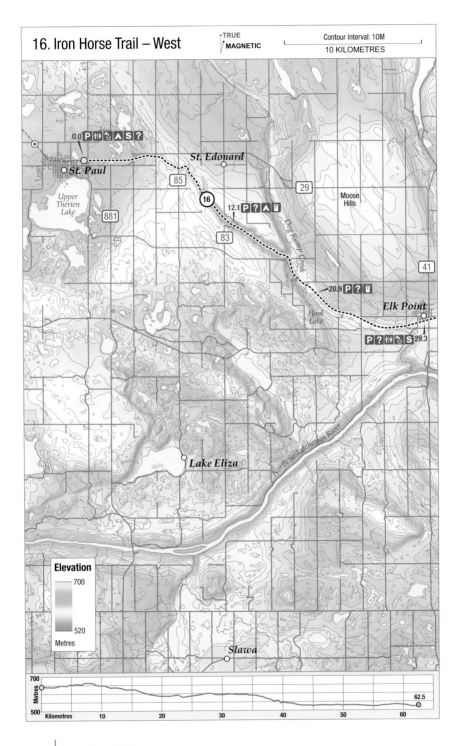

16. Iron Horse Trail – West

TRUE
MAGNETIC

Contour Interval: 10M

10 KILOMETRES

0.0 [P][††][⟲][▲][S][?]

St. Edouard

St. Paul

85

16

Upper Therien Lake

881

29

Moose Hills

12.1 [P][?][▲][†]

83

Dog Rump Creek

41

20.9 [P][?][†]

Elk Point

Hook Lake

[P][?][††][⟲][S] 29.3

Lake Eliza

North Saskatchewan River

Elevation

700

520

Metres

Slawa

700

Metres

500 Kilometres   10   20   30   40   50   60

62.5

16. Iron Horse Trail

Distance: 62.5 km (38.8 mi), one way
Ascent: 265 m (869 ft)
Descent: 383 m/ (1,257 ft)

Trail conditions: crushed stone, natural surface
Cellphone coverage: partial
Hazards: road crossings, ticks, wildlife

Permitted Uses							
Walking	Biking	Horseback Riding	Inline Skating	ATV	Snowshoeing	Cross-country Skiing	Snowmobiling
✔	✔	✔	—	✔	✔	✔	✔

Finding the trailhead: From 50th Avenue (Highway 29) of the community of St. Paul, turn north onto 42nd Street. At its end, in 350 m/yd, turn right onto 53rd Avenue. The trailhead is on the left in 200 m/yd.

Trailhead: 53°59'40.9" N, 111°16'12.5" W (Start: St. Paul)
53°46'01.3" N, 110°31'18.0" W (Finish: Heinsburg)

Observations: Very few cyclists or walkers appear to use this part of the Iron Horse Trail, although I did encounter quite a few ATVs. All the ATVers I encountered behaved well, and a number stopped to ensure that I was not in trouble. I was very much left with the impression of a rural community trail, where the majority of the adjacent population enjoyed an evening or weekend drive on their ATVs.

This route does not pass through very dramatic landscape, but because it follows the bottom of slender valleys it often feels quite isolated, even though farms and ranches are found throughout this area. Birders will appreciate the numerous opportunities to observe waterfowl. My most intimate encounter with wildlife anywhere on The Great Trail occurred on the Iron Horse, when a black bear munching on Saskatoon berries blocked my path for about an hour. I could not get around him, and it refused to be frightened away.

Route description: Begin at the large, elaborately decorated metal gate at the entrance to the Iron Horse Campground. A trailhead kiosk beside it names this point as the St. Paul Staging Area. On the other side of the gate sits what appears to be only the front wall of the former CN station. Water and washrooms can be found in the campsite, and other services are available in the community.

The trail is wide and straight; head left (east). The multi-use path is paralleled by a paved walkway for the first 200 m/yd, until it crosses 40th Street/Highway 881. On the other side, a large sign states that the next services will be found in Elk Point, 31 km (19.3 mi) distant.

The pathway shows signs of heavy ATV use, including deep ruts in the treadway, and most of the signage appears to be for ATVers and snowmobilers. The adjacent terrain is gently rolling but relatively flat, and it alternates between thickets of trees and grassland. Occasionally farm buildings can be seen nearby.

Raptors seem abundant; I saw several in the first 2 km (1.2 mi), and shortly after the 2 km (1.2 mi) mark the trail moves alongside a small pond and wetland, the first of many. At about 3.1 km (1.9 mi), a bright yellow sign indicates that a designated rest area is 10 km (6.2 mi) further. About 300 m/yd beyond that, Highway 29 is crossed.

Caution should be exercised here: the speed limit on the road is 80 kph (50 mph), and there is no notice for drivers that this is a trail crossing. Obey the stop sign posted on the pathway.

A Texas gate

On the far side of Highway 29 the treadway became rougher, with more sand and loose gravel making up the trail surface. At 4.3 km (2.7 mi), there is a Texas gate (a lattice of metal bars across a road spaced to prevent wildlife from walking across it) over the trail. The next gate is at 4.9 km (3.1 mi), after which the trail climbs a small hill to cross Range Road 90, then continues down the other side. From here, the trail descends into a low gully, the land slightly higher on both sides. This defile is mostly wooded, which blocks views of the nearby agricultural land, so it feels somewhat remote. Several small ponds border the path, and these usually are busy with waterfowl.

The next road crossing, Range Road 85 at 6.9 km (4.3 mi), is also raised, and there is another Texas gate on the trail below. From here the hills rise even higher above the trail, with larger ponds on both sides. This is an excellent section for birdwatchers – and duck hunters. Perhaps because of beaver activity, the water in some of these ponds is almost as high as the trail. I quite liked this area, with all its birdlife.

At about 9.4 km (5.8 mi), another Texas gate must be crossed; I found it easier to walk than to cycle over. Cell reception disappears as you continue down this ravine, which keeps sinking lower than the bordering plateau. After the pond's end is a long straightaway.

📍**12.1 km (7.5 mi)** The trail reaches the Édouardville Rest Area, where there are picnic tables, an outhouse, a Discovery Panel, and a large trailhead kiosk featuring a map and considerable historical background information. Camping is permitted, and TCT markers are posted on the trail facing both directions.

About 100 m/yd later, the trail crosses Range Road 83, after which a long, remote section follows, with the only human structures being the occasional Texas gate. Thick forest, mostly hardwoods, borders the trail, with grassy knolls only infrequently intruding. The sandy trail surface makes cycling more difficult, rather like an exercise bike with the tension very high.

At about 17.1 km (10.6 mi), the hills to the left recede, providing views of pasture. The trail curves right, and at the next Texas gate, about 300 m/yd later, is a Discovery Panel on porcupines. About 250 m/yd beyond that, the trail crosses Township Road 573. From here, cell reception should be regained. After the next road crossing, at about 18.5 km (11.5), you can begin to see farms and cultivated land. The ground to the right remains high.

At 20.1 km (12.5 mi), the trail crosses its first bridge, a narrow structure over the tiny Atimoswe Creek, where there is wetland all around and a large pipe for water diversion. A paved road now runs quite close to the left, with houses and farms beyond that.

📍**20.9 km (13 mi)** The trail reaches the Armistice Rest Area, with its outhouse, picnic tables, and trailhead kiosk. There is a large area for parking as well, although it does not appear as if camping is permitted. Hook Lake is nearby, but vegetation kept it mostly hidden.

For the next 3.2 km (2 mi), paved road and trail stay within a few metres/yards of each other. Several dirt roads cross the trail, and for a short distance, there is even a dirt road paralleling on the right. But at 24.2 km (15 mi), the paved road begins to separate from the pathway.

For another 3.6 km (2.2 mi), the trail curves along a gentle slope. Atimoswe Creek, though nearby to your right, is rarely visible through the trees. At 27.8 km (17.3 mi), the Elk Point grain elevator is in view, and an Iron Horse Trail directional sign indicates that a golf course and campground are to the right.

Continue straight; the community of Elk Point is in sight, to the left but still some distance away.

📍**29.3 km (18.2 mi)** The trail arrives at the former train station, which is now the Visitor Centre, and beside which stands a large solar panel. There are also numerous facilities: washrooms, tables, benches, and garbage cans. Community businesses are in sight, across the grass-covered park. Elk Point is a good place to rest and restock.

16. Iron Horse Trail – East

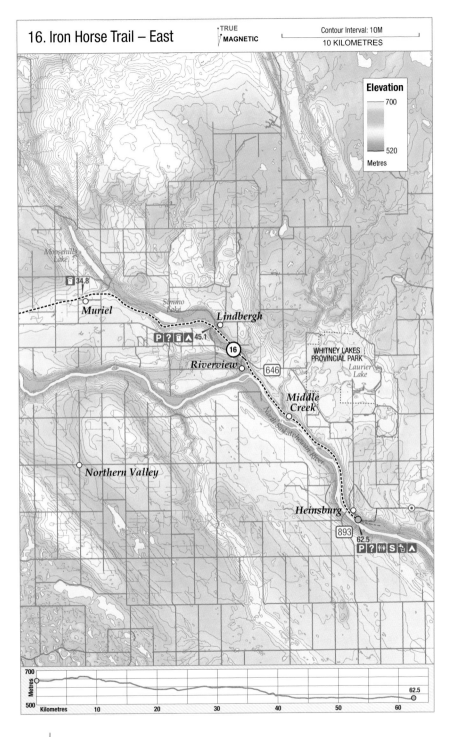

Elevation
700

520
Metres

Contour Interval: 10M

10 KILOMETRES

TRUE
MAGNETIC

Mooshills Lake

34.8

Muriel

Sammo Lake

Lindbergh

P ? i ▲ 45.1

16

Riverview

646

WHITNEY LAKES
PROVINCIAL PARK

Laurier
Lake

Middle
Creek

North Saskatchewan River

Northern Valley

Heinsburg

893

62.5

P ? ⁖ S ⬧ ▲

The trail continues, crossing Highway 41 about 200 m/yd from the Visitor Centre. It is straight for 900 m/yd, until it reaches the next road, where the route has been adjusted to permit it to cross at a 90° angle. Cultivated fields follow as well as several road crossings, and you might sight several oil pumping stations nearby until 34.2 km (21.3 mi), when the trail actually shares the paved road for a short distance. After crossing Range Road 63, there is another Texas gate 300 m/yd later: expect cattle

34.8 km (21.7 mi) An outhouse labelled "Muriel" was the only indication I saw of another rest area. There is considerable tree cover along this section, tall poplars and aspen providing shade, with fields just beyond them. At 36.4 km (22.6 mi), just after the next Texas gate, the ground appears dry and sandy, the trees first shrink and then disappear, and there are soon signs of digging on both sides of the trail and large piles of gravel. Signs warn of ongoing excavation work and to remain on the trail.

These excavations extend for some length. But then the trail curves right and a deep valley appears on the left, with Moose Hills Creek at its bottom. The pathway appears to hug the west slope of this valley, and once again trees line it. Cell reception disappears soon afterwards.

At 42.6 km (26.5 mi), at another Texas gate, there is a Discovery Panel on magpies. Beyond this the hillside slope, both above and below, grows steeper, and the softwoods beside the path are taller. Winding down the valley, the trail is usually bounded by steep hillsides, but it sometimes crosses ravines on high embankments. Another Discovery Panel, on berries, sits all alone at 47.4 km (29.5 mi).

As the trail descends, softwoods give way to tall hardwoods, and through gaps houses and cultivated fields become visible. Rather abruptly, the pathway emerges from its shroud to cross Moose Hills Creek. Directly ahead, the houses of a community are visible. About 300 m/yd later, the trail crosses paved Range Road 53a.

45.1 km (28 mi) A large sign announces your arrival at the Lindbergh Staging Area, which covers a large space. There are the usual picnic tables, outhouses, and trailhead kiosk, as well as some sheltered tables and firepits. Camping is permitted on the large grass-covered lot. But Lindbergh is quite small, and soon the trail moves away from houses.

At 47.5 km (29.6 mi), the Iron Horse crosses busy Highway 646. Trail signage indicates that a store is to the left just up the road. From the road the trail descends a ravine to cross a small creek 400 m/yd later then climbs the other side. When it reaches Range Road 51c, 300 m/yd later, there is a large oil and gas facility on the right. Just beyond that, the path is squeezed between another road and a sizeable Canadian Salt Company plant.

However, after crossing the plant's entrance road at 48.8 km (30.3 mi), the trail passes through another Texas gate and leaves this busy stretch behind. The high ground is now to our left, and within 500 m/yd the North Saskatchewan River comes into view on the right. A dirt road joins the trail from the left and does not separate from it for a couple of hundred metres/yards, but this is only to connect a small pipeline pumping facility next to the river. Just after that, a Discovery Panel about the mule deer commands a panoramic view of the river valley.

The remaining distance is quite pleasant, and relatively isolated from other human structures. For most of it, the river is rarely visible, unfortunately. There is another rest area, Middle Creek, about 5 km (3.1 mi) from the salt plant, and a side trail to the Middle Creek Staging Area 500 m/yd later. Another Discovery Panel, Rivers of Life, sits in an open area at 60.3 km (37.5 mi). The trail is in mostly good shape, though there are a few rough patches when it descends to near river level.

You know you are approaching Heinsburg when you pass beneath the Highway 893 bridge that spans the North Saskatchewan. About 600 m/yd later, at 62.1 km (38.6 mi), the trail reaches a gate and crosses Range Road 43b. A large sign announces that you have reached Heinsburg, and the pathway blends into the large lawn.

62.5 km (38.8 mi) After passing the rebuilt railway station, a CN caboose still mounted on rails, a playground, and a washroom, the trail reaches the Heinsburg Staging Area trailhead kiosk and the historic water tower. There are many facilities located in Heinsburg. Camping is permitted on-site, and drinking water is available. A grocery store and diner may be found in the small community.

The Iron Horse continues a little further but ends shortly in the middle of a cultivated field. End your trip here, and retrace your route – now mostly uphill – back to St. Paul.

Further Information:
Iron Horse Trail: www.ironhorsetrail.ca
Travel Lakeland Alberta: www.travellakeland.ca

Heinsburg Water Tower

The original railway engines that revolutionized land-based travel in Canada were steam powered. Water was an essential element in engine operation and was used in far larger volumes than the necessary solid fuel, which was usually coal. Water towers were placed every 30-50 km (19-31 mi) to ensure that a plentiful supply was always available.

When the Canadian National Railway extended its line to Heinsburg in 1928, it was logical that it should build a water tower there as well. Heinsburg was the end of the line, and it became an entrepot for non-connected settlements north, east, and south.

Diesel engines replaced steam in the 1960s, and the rail line was abandoned in 1983. However, the water tower was maintained by the community, where it was originally placed by CN. It also still contains its original water tank and piping, and its excellent condition makes it unique for Alberta.

Birds of Prey

The grasslands of Alberta are home to a wide range of raptors. Hawks, harriers, falcons, and other species can be spotted perched on almost every line of fence posts. Sometimes there are several posted watching the same field. Owls are also raptors, but they hunt at night.

All raptors are carnivores and can be recognized by their hooked beaks — for tearing flesh — and strong feet and talons — for gripping prey. Unlike owls, which depend upon their hearing, most raptors that hunt during the day possess excellent eyesight and can detect small movements at great distances.

Rodents, squirrels, and small birds are their usual meal, but large raptors can even take rabbits and ducks. Most species are migratory, moving south when ground squirrels migrate and snow covers the movements of mice.

Mountain Lion

Second only to the bear in size — but probably first in inspiring respect and fear from humans — the mountain lion is Canada's largest cat and one of the country's top predators. Although originally found from New Brunswick to British Columbia, the cougar remains common only in Western Canada. Attacks on humans are rare, as are sightings, as cougars are ambush predators. However, as a 90 kg (200 lb) mountain lion can take down six times its weight in prey, and as these big cats are opportunistic hunters, humans are wise to be wary when in cougar country.

17. Cypress Hills

The only place in Saskatchewan that everyone insisted that I include in this book — and frequently their very first suggestion — was the Cypress Hills. Once I had hiked there, it was easy to see why. Its rolling hills, deep valleys, and lush vegetation all make for an exquisitely beautiful hike. Métis hunters, mistaking the species of conifer they saw, named the area "les montagnes des Cyprès," hence the current name.

The Cypress Hills constitute the highest land in Western Canada east of the Rocky Mountains, more than 200 m (650 ft) above the nearby prairie, and they were never covered during the last Ice Age. With so much farmland available to the north, railways bypassed the hills, which have remained sparsely settled and used mainly for livestock grazing.

In 1989, Alberta and Saskatchewan amalgamated several protected areas in the Cypress Hills into Canada's first interprovincial park. This comprises a 345 km^2 (133 mi^2) Western Block that spans the provincial border and a separate 54 km^2 (21 mi^2) Centre Block. The Saskatchewan Western Block is preserved as a wilderness area and contains limited facilities. In 2004, the Cypress Hills were declared a dark-sky preserve, an area that maintains the night sky in as unspoiled a manner as possible. This makes the area a fantastic place to camp and stargaze.

Hikers should note that the opportunities to refresh drinking water are few, and the need is high; carry more than usual. Along with other wildlife, cougars —mountain lions (see p. 191) — are present in the hills. Dogs must be on-leash inside Fort Walsh National Historic Site; they are permitted off-leash in the Interprovincial Park.

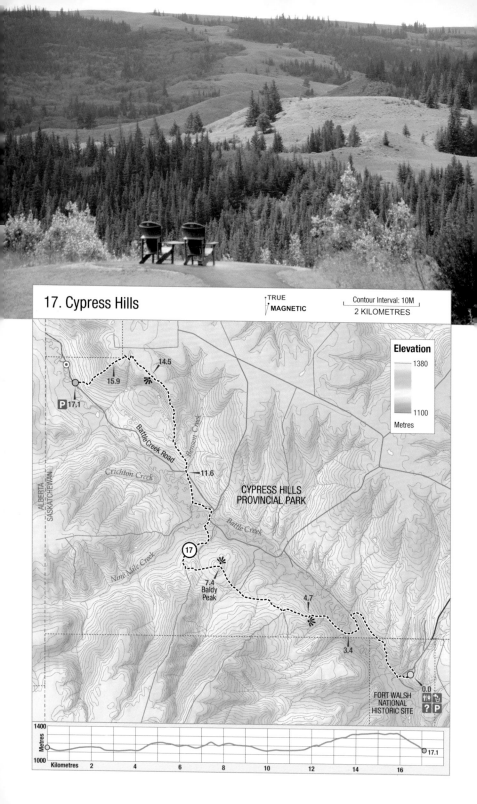

17. Cypress Hills

TRUE
MAGNETIC

Contour Interval: 10M
2 KILOMETRES

Elevation
1380
1100
Metres

14.5
15.9
P 17.1
Battle Creek Road
Crichton Creek
Benson Creek
11.6
CYPRESS HILLS
PROVINCIAL PARK
Battle Creek
17
Nine Mile Creek
7.4
Baldy Peak
4.7
3.4
ALBERTA
SASKATCHEWAN
FORT WALSH
NATIONAL
HISTORIC SITE
0.0

1400
Metres
1000
Kilometres 2   4   6   8   10   12   14   16
17.1

17. Cypress Hills

Distance: 17.1 km (10.6 mi), one way
Ascent: 525 m (1,722 ft)
Descent: 497 m (1,630 ft)

Trail conditions: compacted earth, crushed stone, natural surface
Cellphone coverage: no
Hazards: hunting, ticks, wildlife

Permitted Uses							
Walking	Biking	Horseback Riding	Inline Skating	ATV	Snowshoeing	Cross-country Skiing	Snowmobiling
✔	✔*	✔	—	—	✔	✔	—

Finding the trailhead: From the community of Maple Creek, drive south 54.7 km (34 mi) on Highway 271 south to Fort Walsh National Historic Site. Begin your hike from its parking area/Visitor Centre.

Trailhead: 49°34'26.4" N, 109°52'32.6" W (Start: Fort Walsh National Historic Site) 49°38'21.2" N, 109°59'40.2" W (Finish: Battle Creek Road)

Observations: The Cypress Hills route was one of the most challenging, yet enjoyable, that I hiked in Western Canada. I found the area to be just as exceptionally scenic as everyone had told me it would be. Battle Creek Valley is brilliant, with the alternation between prairie slopes and pine forests providing welcome variety. I was completely surprised and delighted with the profusion of wildflowers in the prairie grasses, particularly the wild roses.

However, the trail was more challenging than it needed to be because the signage was extremely poor, including very poor maps. I managed to wander off the route several times, detours that, while attention grabbing, ultimately meant that this hike required two full days instead of one. Hikers should be comfortable with a high degree of navigational uncertainty, especially between Fort Walsh and the La Barge Trail.

Route description: From the parking lot head into the Visitor Centre to pay the entrance fee and examine the displays. There are washrooms and drinking water in this new facility. Outside, the views are already quite striking. A paved path runs toward a lookout sporting two bright red chairs. Before reaching this, it passes a bronze sculpture of a North-West Mounted Police officer facing a First Nations warrior.

The view from the chairs is impressive, with Fort Walsh at the bottom of the broad valley. Rucked, forested terrain stretches from the stockade toward the far horizon. A crushed-stone path, marked by green signposts, drops down the hillside. At 200 m/yd, the path reaches the entrance road; turn left and follow it toward the fort entrance.

There are washrooms and drinking water inside Fort Walsh. However, shortly before reaching the walls an old road branches to the right. There are no signs, but these are the remains of the former road that connected to the Interprovincial Park. Follow this, keeping to the right at the next few junctions – if you even notice them, as they are fairly indistinct. You will also need to cross unbridged Spring Creek, which is usually just a trickle.

This former road is now used primarily by horseback riders and horse-drawn wagons, so it is little more than furrows worn into the prairie grass. To the left, hidden by trees, runs Battle Creek. Follow this rough track as it gradually ascends the uneven hillside. Expect it to be in rough condition, with significant muddy sections after any rain. Horses tend to churn up soft ground.

At 1.1 km (0.7 mi), you reach the boundary of the Interprovincial Park. A gate blocks the road, which is clearly used by vehicles on the park side. A TCT marker is affixed to the gate, as is another sign stating that the trail is 1 km (0.6 mi) ahead. Follow this wide, dry road. There is no other signage, although there are wonderful views of the valley for the next 1.5 km (0.9 mi).

You arrive at a junction. Directly ahead, the impression made by horses is pronounced and heavy, as it is to your left. When I was there, a wooden post with a Road Closed sign on it was to the left. Turn almost 180° left and follow the horse trail down this closed road, back in the direction of Fort Walsh.

The next section is difficult, because horses have created a number of routes, making it uncertain if you are actually on the correct trail. After 400 m/yd, you should encounter a signpost, bearing a TCT symbol and an arrow. Turn right and follow a much more distinct footpath toward Battle Creek. You should be able to see other signposts ahead and on lower ground.

3.4 km (2.1 mi) Arrive at Battle Creek, a slow-moving, shallow stream that you must ford. Expect to get very muddy feet, ankles, and probably shins, because the ford is also used by horses. (See my YouTube video, "BestofTCT-Cypress Hills SK.") At least the path is distinct on the opposite bank, although it does often have more than one parallel track. It turns right and follows snaking Battle Creek upstream. There are several signposts, and the route is clear for about 650 m/yd. However, the trail forks near a line of trees and there is no signpost. Turn left, even though the most distinct paths – heading toward the equestrian campground, as it turns out – continue straight.

Your far less defined track crosses a tiny stream and begins to climb the hillside, rising nearly 100 m/yd in the next kilometre. Fortunately, over the next small rise – but hidden from the last junction – is a signpost. As you ascend the verdant grass-covered hillside, topping several small hillocks en route, more posts will be found. The trail is also somewhat easier to follow as there appears to be less horse traffic here.

4.7 km (2.9 mi) At the top of the bluff, the trail reaches a wonderful viewing area with a stone bench and large cairn dedicated to Charles Blakley, a deceased volunteer. This is a lovely spot, boasting a panoramic view, and it offers the first cell reception on this route.

A gentle climb continues over the broad grasslands. After a relaxing 600 m/yd, the path connects to a dirt road, where there is a signpost with a rather unhelpful map. Another sign beside it states that this is a designated hunting trail.

Turn right, and follow this wide and quiet road downhill for 1.2 km (0.7 mi) to the next map post, which indicates that this is a junction of the La Barge and Baldy Trails. Turn left off the road and into a stand of thick spruce. Unfortunately, there is a very messy wet area that needs to be crossed about 250 m/yd later, after which you enter another area of open grassland.

7.4 km (4.6 mi) A steep climb follows to the peak of Baldy – so it is signed – the highest point you reach on this side of Battle Creek. It possesses an impressive view of almost 360°. You might even be able to see the Fort Walsh Visitor Centre in the distance. In the pastures below are cattle pens, with their occasional residents grazing nearby – including on your route.

The path curves left and for about 150 m/yd continues along the open ridge, clearly marked with numerous signposts. The trail descends the far side of this hill and crosses a small creek. Once across, it traverses a small band of forested area, climbing again, before emerging onto another driveable dirt road, the South Benson Trail, at 8.3 km (5.2 mi).

Turn right and enjoy the view, both of the scenery and the flora, as you descend all the way to Battle Creek. After 1.1 km (0.7 mi), a footpath separates from the road to the left and heads into pasture. It makes its way cross-country toward another small stream, Nine Mile Creek, before turning right and continuing until it reaches Battle Creek Road, at 10.1 km (6.3 mi). (If there are too many cattle in this field, continue on Benson Road until it intersects Battle Creek Road, then turn left. This only adds about 250 m/yd.)

A modern-looking concrete bridge crosses Battle Creek. On the far side, either continue along the road or turn left onto a track through the sagebrush. For the next 250 m/yd, road and trail run beside each other, until the path reaches another dirt road. Turn left and follow this for about 500 m/yd, then turn right and cross a large field. Battle Creek Road, which also makes a turn to the left, should be in sight the entire time.

This was another spot where I ran into difficulty, partly because of a lack of signposts, partly because a very large herd of cattle obscured the one signpost positioned in the field. If at all uncertain, return to Battle Creek Road and follow it.

11.6 km (7.2 mi) If you are more successful than me, you will uneventfully cross this large field, skirting the forested section to your left, and reach Battle Creek Road near where it crosses Benson Creek. On the opposite side is a signpost featuring the park's poor map (there is no "you are here" indicator). This is the start of the High Vista Trail, the final leg of this route.

The trail immediately begins to climb, at times quite steeply, rising more than 200 m (650 ft) over the next 2 km (1.2 mi). In this first section there are few signposts and multiple paths; keep to the most distinct track at 200 m/yd, to the right. Much of this section is covered by forest, but the narrow footpath frequently works along the edge of the hillside, providing grander views of the valley as you ascend.

After about 900 m/yd, you will see a small pool of water to the left and below. You should also regain cell reception. Within another 200 m/yd, the trail appears to follow a spur, ascending less steeply. The pathway is narrow but worn into the hillside. Not long afterwards, the forest becomes primarily pine, open and attractive.

At 13.8 km (8.6 mi), after a final steep push, the trail emerges onto a large savannah. The treadway is less distinct now, clear but not worn through the grass. Your route continues along the nearly level plateau, keeping close to the bluff's edge. The view keeps getting better, particularly on a small promontory about 600 m/yd later. Little more than 100 m/yd further, you reach a bench that offers broad views across the valley.

The trail leaves the cliff edge here, cutting through the field, where there are wildflowers everywhere. After about 700 m/yd, it heads into a ravine and a complex section. At first the trail looks as if it will avoid this gully, but it turns sharply left then quickly left again to follow the lowest ground. It appears to be heading into the forest, then turns 90° right and climbs back out of the gorge. Several signposts are missing, so exercise caution; you should return to the higher ground on the far side of the ravine.

Fort Walsh National Historic Site

The Cypress Hills of the early 1870s were a lawless frontier, where Canadian sovereignty was very much in question. At least four American trading posts were established there, and with news of the June 1, 1873, Cypress Hills Massacre, when more than 20 Nakoda (Assiniboine) were murdered, the Canadian government decided to act quickly.

Inspector Walsh and "B" Troop of the North-West Mounted Police built the fort a few miles from the site of the massacre, tasked to bring Canadian law to the area. They met with mixed success initially, but with the migration of the Lakota Sioux from the United States in 1877, Fort Walsh was expanded and became headquarters for the NWMP from 1878 to 1882, with a garrison of more than 150.

Once the Lakota returned to the US and the railroad was established further north, Fort Walsh lost its importance. When it was abandoned in 1883, the region had been transformed and its future as part of Canada was secure.

In 1924, the fort was designated as a National Historic Site, and the palisade and buildings were reconstructed in the 1940s.

15.9 km (9.9 mi) This is the highest point of this route, reached just before the path begins its descent toward the finish. Many signposts in this area were lying on the ground, so you might need to follow the wear pattern in the grass. In the first part of the downhill, there are small rocky areas to scramble over, but the route soon heads into the forest, where the thick vegetation growing into the path suggests that fewer people hike this portion of the trail. The drop is also quite steep: 185 m (605+ ft) in the next 1.2 km (0.7 mi).

About 800 m/yd from the crest of the hill, the trail curves right, and about 150 m/yd later the path emerges from the trees and you can see the remains of a cabin in the valley below.

17.1 km (10.6 mi) The path reaches Battle Creek Road, opposite an interpretive panel about Albert and Sylvia Noble, the residents of the old cabin. There is also a signpost mounting map, TCT marker, and directional arrow.

This is the end of the High Vista Trail. Either retrace the path system back to Fort Walsh or trek back along Battle Creek Road, turning right when you reach the Ranger Station.

Further Information:
Cypress Hills Interprovincial Park: www.cypresshills.com
Fort Walsh National Historic Site: www.pc.gc.ca/en/lhn-nhs/sk/walsh
Visit Cypress Hills: www.visitcypresshills.ca

Lodgepole Pine

Lodgepole pine (*pinus contorta*) is a uniquely Western Canadian tree, the most common in the Rocky Mountains and Alberta's foothills region. It also grows abundantly in the Cypress Hills, a tall, slender conifer, with little taper and a straight trunk up to 30 m (98 ft) tall. Lodgepole will grow on a wide variety of sites but prefers well-drained, sandy soils. Fire is one of its principal means of regeneration, and stands of lodgepole pine are often all the same age.

It gained its name because First Nations Peoples valued its straight even-width trunk as the frame for their tipis, or lodges. Railways valued the lodgepole for use as ties, and it is commercially important in the present day.

The lodgepole pine was designated as the province's official tree by Alberta's Legislative Assembly in 1984. (Saskatchewan's tree is the white birch.)

18. Meewasin Trail

Originally an amalgamation of two communities facing each other on opposite banks of the South Saskatchewan River, Saskatoon has expanded fairly evenly to the east and west, and numerous bridges connect its two sides. It has also grown to become the largest urban area in Saskatchewan, with more than 250,000 residents. This section of the South Saskatchewan River is known as the Meewasin Valley, Meewasin being the Cree word for "beautiful."

Saskatoon also boasts one of the most extensive trail networks of any similar-sized city in Canada, with its connected Meewasin Trail extending more than 60 km (37.3 mi) on both sides of the river, linking numerous parks, historic sites, and neighbourhoods. The Great Trail shares part of this network, where it resumes (or ends) on land in Saskatoon; south of the city is a 125 km (78 mi) water route to the Gardiner Dam on Lake Diefenbaker.

The route of The Great Trail is quite specific. However, for most of its length the Meewasin Trail runs on both sides of the river. On your return trip, maybe choose to explore and see both sides of the city. As long as you keep close to the river and recognize Gordie Howe Bridge and Diefenbaker Park, you should have no problems.

18. Meewasin Trail

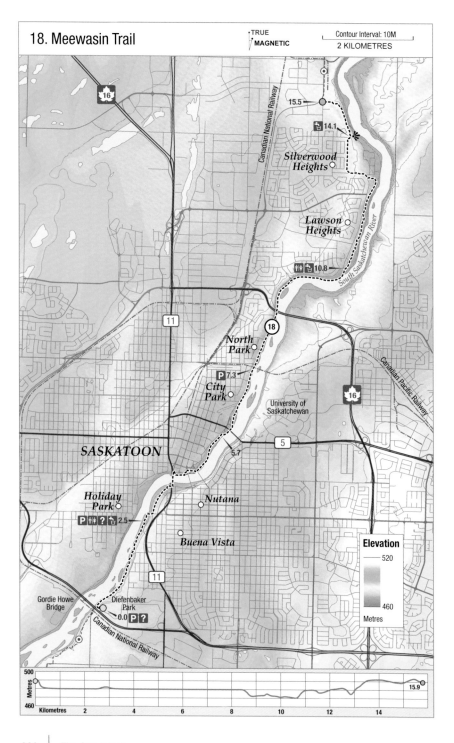

TRUE
MAGNETIC

Contour Interval: 10M
2 KILOMETRES

16

15.5

14.1

Silverwood
Heights

Canadian National Railway

Lawson
Heights

10.8

South Saskatchewan River

18

North
Park

P 7.3

City
Park

University of
Saskatchewan

Canadian Pacific Railway

16

5

SASKATOON

5.7

Holiday
Park

Nutana

P 2.5

Buena Vista

Elevation
520

460
Metres

11

Gordie Howe
Bridge

Diefenbaker
Park

0.0 P ?

Canadian National Railway

500
Metres
460
Kilometres   2   4   6   8   10   12   14

15.9

18. Meewasin Trail

Distance: 15.5 km (9.6 mi) — one way
Ascent: 71 m (233 ft)
Descent: 65 m (213 ft)

Trail conditions: asphalt, crushed stone
Cellphone coverage: yes
Hazards: high usage, road crossings

Permitted Uses							
Walking	Biking	Horseback Riding	Inline Skating	ATV	Snowshoeing	Cross-country Skiing	Snowmobiling
✔	✔	—	✔*	—	✔	✔	—

Finding the trailhead: From the Highway 16 (Trans-Canada Highway)/Highway 11 junction south of the city, turn onto Highway 11 (Circle Drive W). Continue on Highway 11 to Exit 219 S (Ruth Street). Turn left onto Ruth Street E. In 900 m/yd, this ends at St. Henry Avenue. Turn left, and in 450 m/yd turn right into Diefenbaker Park. Turn left and follow the park road until you reach a parking lot overlooking the river, which sits next to Circle Drive.

Trailhead: 52°05'48.4" N, 106°41'29.6" W (Start: Diefenbaker Park)
52°11'38.5" N, 106°37'21.5" W (Finish: Kinnear Avenue)

Observations: I first hiked the Meewasin Trail in the early 2000s and was quite impressed then with its route options and good signage. But this was before the Gordie Howe Bridge, with its pedestrian underpass, was built, and so I tentatively – and irresponsibly, I might add – crossed the river on the undecked and un-railed CN train bridge to reach Diefenbaker Park from the western shore.

Today the pathway system is much better. Its trails are all surfaced with crushed stone or asphalt, signage is even better than in the previous decade, and best of all, there are multiple river crossings available for walker/bikers on excellent, dedicated bridges. Other than the occasional detours for construction projects that plague trails in every major city, the Meewasin Trail is a pleasant, easy trip through attractive urban and natural settings, and I enjoyed this particular route very much, particularly in its downtown sections.

Route description: A large metal signpost, labelled Meewasin and also with a Great Trail sign affixed, sits in the middle of a brick-surfaced circle beside the parking lot. Donor plaques and benches line its edge. A wide staircase

descends to the river below, connecting to the trail, which can be seen running parallel to the water. There is also a separate bicycle path that switchbacks down the hillside.

To the left, the busy Gordie Howe Bridge crosses the South Saskatchewan River, and largely blocks the view south. The dedicated pedestrian/walking bridge beneath it is quite visible and very busy. To the north, both banks of the river appear to be parkland, while the downtown is visible in the distance.

Signs on the trail at river level indicate that Gabriel Dumont Park is the first destination, 2.1 km (1.3 mi) distant. At first asphalt-surfaced, at about 350 m/ yd it switches to crushed stone. Side trails are frequent, as are small bridges, benches, and thickets of trees. The path stays close to the grass-lined river's edge, with lovely views of kayakers casually cruising.

The wide path gently curves left and right, over slightly undulating ground, before reaching a major fork at 1.9 km (1.2 mi): keep left. You might even notice a sign — facing in the other direction — that welcomes you to Memorial Forest. A few hundred metres/yards beyond this, you reach a large signpost for Gabriel Dumont Park.

This is a busy area: there is a large playground to the left, so expect children crossing the trail. Benches line the path, and there are picnic tables on the lawn. There is also a public washroom and a water fountain. Several paths connect from the right, where there is a large parking lot; keep left, heading back toward the river.

2.5 km (1.6 mi) On the right sits Saskatoon's Trans Canada Trail/Great Trail pavilion, in a pleasant lawn with nearby benches and an attractive view of the river. It is connected by a short side trail. Just past this spot, the pathway curves sharply right and heads into an urban neighbourhood, crossing a wooden bridge and snaking through a brick-sided channel up the embankment to arrive at Saskatchewan Crescent W in 200 m/yd.

The off-road trail ends on this quiet residential street, where we turn left, and pedestrians follow the sidewalk while cyclists drive on the street. The trail is quite pleasant, lined with charming older homes and huge elms that provide overhead shade.

At 3.3 km (2.1 mi), you arrive at Idylwyld Crescent, where signs direct you left, onto an asphalt track adjacent to the road. The trail curves right, passing beneath Highway 11 less than 150 m/yd further. This is Rotary Park, but your route is left following the path that leads you onto the bridge and across the South Saskatchewan River.

The trail curves right, then doubles back to deliver you on the north bank of the river at 4 km (2.5 mi). This is another busy location where cyclists will at least need to slow down, and it might be better to dismount. To the left is the River Landing Spray Park, which on a hot summer day will be crammed with screaming, playful children.

The trail continues to follow the river, passing underneath the Victoria Avenue Bridge. Instead climb up from the spray park to the next street up: Spadina Crescent E. Head right, to a roundabout centred with an interesting sculpture called *The Founders*. Cross Victoria Avenue, and take the trail on the far side back down the hill to the river pathway.

At 4.7 km (2.9 mi), the trail crosses beneath the Broadway Bridge and enters the Kiwanis Memorial Park. This is a truly lovely area, right in Saskatoon's downtown. It is an older park, with attractive architecture and many interpretive panels and memorials. You will also pass within sight of the city's iconic landmark, the Delta Bessborough Hotel (locals call it the Bez).

Benches line the pathway, and expect them to be occupied, so this will probably be another area of slow cycling. To the left, the ground is meticulously groomed, but along the river the vegetation is decidedly unkempt. Frequent wide side paths connect the city with the Meewasin Trail; to the right, informal footpaths track through the longer grasses.

5.7 km (3.5 mi) The path narrows significantly as it moves into an area where there are large flower beds. Dismount, and walk to the intersection of Spadina Crescent E and 24 Street E. To the left is Knox United Church, and left of that is St. John's Anglican Cathedral. Just across 24 Street E is the Ukrainian Museum of Canada.

Turn right, and follow the pathway as it passes beneath University Bridge, then moves away from the roadside 400 m/yd from the intersection. This is a pleasant wooded area, where the trail passes the Shakespeare on the

Saskatchewan Festival grounds and the Saskatoon Civic Conservatory. There is some interesting artwork through here.

The trail returns to following the road at 6.6 km (4.1 mi), where Spadina Crescent E intersects Queen Street. It continues close to the road, reaching the Weir – a Depression-era make-work project ostensibly designed to control water levels on the South Saskatchewan River but now a popular birding location – 600 m/yd later. There is a viewing platform here, with several interpretive panels.

⚲7.3 km (4.5 mi) A short distance later the trail arrives at a large parking lot, where a massive metal staircase connects road level to a trail on a rail bridge that crosses the river. If you have time, climb up and have a look; it is a very good view, and the University of Saskatchewan is on the opposite bank. This is one of the very few "rails with trails" bridges in Canada.

Beyond this bridge, traffic on the trails reduces substantially. The Meewasin Trail continues to occupy the space between the road and the river, but it is wider now, and with far fewer users. However, there are many houses across the street, so cyclists should expect plenty of dog walkers, and the hazard that creates. Having a bell on your bike is an excellent idea.

Otherwise, it should be a pleasant, but uneventful, 1.3 km (0.8 mi) to the imposing bridge that transports the multi-lane Highway 16 across the river. In between the two vehicle bridges is the suspended Stew Uzelman Pedway, which connects to the Meewasin Pathway on the eastern shore.

The next 2.1 km (1.3 mi) is either alongside the road or meanders over wide lawns. It is very easy to access the water, but numerous signs forbidding swimming are posted. The path follows the curve of the river, and although there are many houses nearby, the far bank is undeveloped.

⚲10.8 km (6.7 mi) The trail turns away from the river and connects with a side trail that has a crosswalk over Spadina Crescent. It then heads into Meewasin Park, where there is a public washroom and a water fountain. The park also features benches, picnic tables, barbeque pits, playgrounds – if you are feeling perky – and quite a few sculptures. The lawns are wide and well maintained;

this park has the widest grounds of any thus far. Individual trees are sprinkled about, while an interconnected network of paths curves around them. The only dense clusters of vegetation line the riverbank.

This is also the hilliest portion of this route, and the trail manoeuvres over the gently rolling ground. It is a relaxing, pleasant ride until at 12.8 km (8 mi), when the route turns sharply left and begins a noticeable ascent. It quickly reaches Whiteswan Drive then crosses the entrance road to the city's wastewater treatment plant. Paralleling the road, the trail climbs to a fork at 13.6 km (8.4 mi), where there is a bench and some TCT markers; keep right. You also turn right at the next junction, 100 m/yd later, where there is another large steel trail sign.

The path levels, following a wide green space, with houses on the left and a chain-link fence on the right. In 700 m/yd, it reaches another junction. Directly ahead is Adilman Drive, where there is another tall steel Meewasin/TCT marker. Turn right, and in less than 100 m/yd reaches a rest area with three benches and a water fountain, and a lookout over the river valley.

For another 200 m/yd houses are to the left, but these are then replaced by the Silverwood Golf Course. To the right, is quite an extensive view, in part because the land on this side of the river is higher – possibly the highest elevation in the city. Just after reaching the golf course, a sign informs you that you are entering an off-leash dog park.

The trail winds along the crest of the forested hillside for another 500 m/yd, passing some more benches with superb views. At 15.2 km (9.4 mi), there is another junction, with the left path heading between some industrial-looking buildings. Continue to the right, and again at the next junction, which is in sight ahead. After this, the trail turns away from the river.

15.5 km (9.6 mi) The pathway arrives at Kinnear Avenue, where the off-road section ends. Only a garbage can marks the spot, and both the Meewasin Trail and The Great Trail head right, on the road. However, I recommend that you turn back here, and retrace your route back to Diefenbaker Park.

Further Information:
City of Saskatoon: www.saskatoon.ca
Meewasin Valley Authority: www.meewasin.com/visitors/trails
Tourism Saskatoon: www.tourismsaskatoon.com

Magpie

One of the most noticeable birds in Western Canada, the black-billed magpie is almost equally admired and reviled. Champions praise its intelligence and friendliness; opponents rail against its raucous cries and bold thievery. Whatever your opinion, you will not fail to notice the magpie's swaggering walk, long colourful tail, and habit of noisily calling from the tops of trees and fence posts. Magpies are rarely found in the deep forest, preferring open grasslands and meadows. They also are fairly comfortable around humans, so you will find them in cities and parklands, especially near rivers. When a magpie is near, be careful of your food!

Meewasin Valley Authority

The Meewasin Valley Authority (MVA) is a provincially mandated agency dedicated to conserving the cultural and natural resources of the South Saskatchewan River Valley. Jointly run by the Province of Saskatchewan, the City of Saskatoon, and the University of Saskatchewan, the authority strives "to coordinate or control the use of development, conservation, maintenance, and improvement of land within the conservation zone."

Guided by its ambitious Meewasin Valley Project: 100 Year Conceptual Plan, the MVA has become a leader in conservation and education, greening the river lands and restoring damaged areas of the valley. More than just building trails, the MVA offers interpretive programming and encourages volunteer stewardship to improve public awareness of the value of conserving the South Saskatchewan River Valley.

I cannot speak to the success of their other initiatives, but I can attest that the MVA has done an excellent job in developing a first-rate trail network.

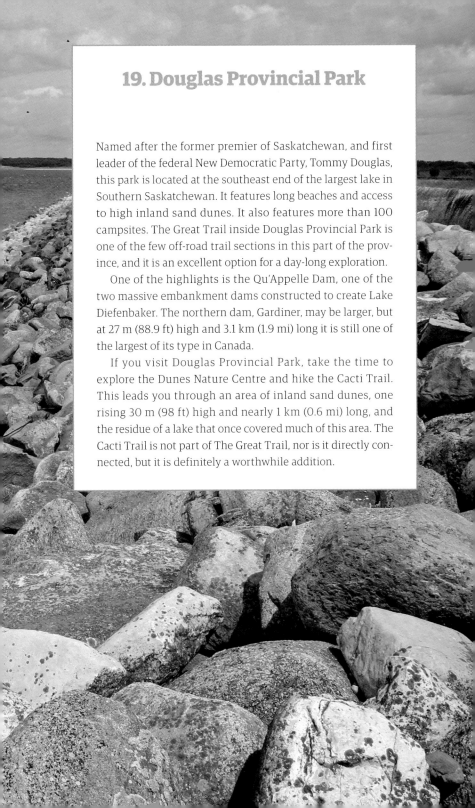

19. Douglas Provincial Park

Named after the former premier of Saskatchewan, and first leader of the federal New Democratic Party, Tommy Douglas, this park is located at the southeast end of the largest lake in Southern Saskatchewan. It features long beaches and access to high inland sand dunes. It also features more than 100 campsites. The Great Trail inside Douglas Provincial Park is one of the few off-road trail sections in this part of the province, and it is an excellent option for a day-long exploration.

One of the highlights is the Qu'Appelle Dam, one of the two massive embankment dams constructed to create Lake Diefenbaker. The northern dam, Gardiner, may be larger, but at 27 m (88.9 ft) high and 3.1 km (1.9 mi) long it is still one of the largest of its type in Canada.

If you visit Douglas Provincial Park, take the time to explore the Dunes Nature Centre and hike the Cacti Trail. This leads you through an area of inland sand dunes, one rising 30 m (98 ft) high and nearly 1 km (0.6 mi) long, and the residue of a lake that once covered much of this area. The Cacti Trail is not part of The Great Trail, nor is it directly connected, but it is definitely a worthwhile addition.

19. Douglas Provincial Park

TRUE
MAGNETIC

Contour Interval: 10M
1 KILOMETRE

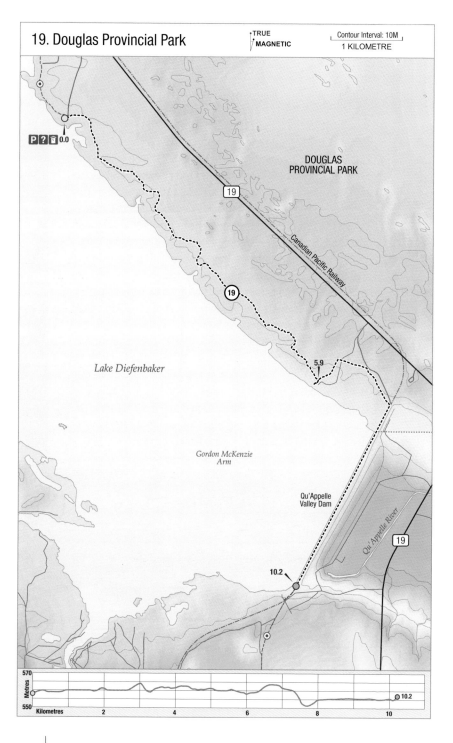

DOUGLAS
PROVINCIAL PARK

P ? ℹ 0.0

19

19

Canadian Pacific Railway

Lake Diefenbaker

5.9

Gordon McKenzie
Arm

Qu'Appelle
Valley Dam

Qu'Appelle River

19

10.2

570

Metres

550

10.2

Kilometres   2   4   6   8   10

19. Douglas Provincial Park

Distance: 10.2 km (6.3 mi) — one way
Ascent: 31 m (102 ft)
Descent: 32 m (105 ft)

Trail conditions: compacted earth, natural surface
Cellphone coverage: yes
Hazards: poison ivy, ticks, wildlife

Permitted Uses							
Walking	Biking	Horseback Riding	Inline Skating	ATV	Snowshoeing	Cross-country Skiing	Snowmobiling
✔	✔	—	—	—	✔	✔	—

Finding the trailhead: From the park entrance on Highway 19, drive 350 m/yd to the park entry office. Once past that, turn left and continue 950 m/yd to the parking lot at the end of the road.

Trailhead: 51°01'42" N, 106°29'14.8" W (Start: Boat ramp parking area)
50°58'24.8" N, 106°26'24.4" W (Finish: End of dam)

Observations: The sandy soil of Douglas Park reminded me of Prince Edward Island beach dunes. Both the size of Lake Diefenbaker and its long, broad beaches surprised me. In fact, if one wished, one could simply walk along the lakeshore from the boat launch to the dam without ever using the official trails. This was a quite pleasant day hike, even the section on top of the dam, and it was considerably enhanced by the large number of Discovery Panels along the route. Signage is excellent, and there are trail maps at all major junctions.

On the other hand, the mosquitoes were ferocious, and when I finished my trek, even though I was cycling and rarely set foot on the ground, I picked an even dozen ticks off myself. I have rarely been so distracted by insect issues. Users should be prepared – or visit in the winter.

Route description: The trail begins on the opposite side of the road from the parking lot. You should be able to see the trailhead, where there is a map, a Discovery Panel, and a tall wooden post on which regulatory signs are mounted all positioned side by side.

The area is all waist-high grasses, with the trail a wide – and obvious – strip mown through them. To the right, a wide sandy beach extends far beyond the

end of the boat launch to the water. There are few trees visible at the start: either white birch or aspen, clustered in low clumps in the distance. A considerable number of scrubs are scattered throughout the grass, which is tall and tough. The ground is dry and sandy.

This area is nearly completely flat, so it is only vegetation that blocks your view. Just 250 m/yd from the start, the trail forks, but there is another map at this junction. The Trans Canada Trail (or Great Trail) is clearly labelled, and you will see that the park's system is a series of three stacked loops. Keep right, on the route that stays closer to the lakeshore.

The path continues through the tall grass, passing a Discovery Panel on the great horned owl, before reaching the first clump of trees at about 550 m/yd. Another Discovery Panel, on the trembling aspen, faces the trail about 100 m/yd further. Occasional metal posts mounting directional arrows and hiker symbols mark the way.

Surprisingly, there is even some wet ground that cannot be avoided in this first kilometre, just before the next Discovery Panel, on the white-tailed jackrabbit. This spot offers a view of some small ponds. At 1.1 km (0.7 mi), at Point B, there is a map and another Discovery Panel, this one on coyote howls. Keep straight on the wide grass-surfaced pathway. It is another 600 m/yd to the next junction, at Point C.

It is here that the Short Loop branches left, and there is another map to ensure you continue on the correct route: straight (right). There are excellent views of Lake Diefenbaker along this section, which is quite open. The trail continues its meandering path around clumps of trees, passing yet another Discovery Panel, on the porcupine, at 2.7 km (1.7 mi).

Just after this, the path enters a forested thicket, and offers some possibly needed shade. A metal bench is located just inside the tree cover. The ground is slightly more uneven through this section, though never climbing more than 2-3 m (6-10 ft). The path works around any small knolls and remains mostly among the trees, reaching the next junction at 3.5 km (2.2 mi).

There is a bench here, a map, and another Discovery Panel, on mule deer. This is where those hiking the Qu'Appelle Loop would head left and onto the Wolf Willow Trail. The Great Trail continues straight, into another copse of mixed birch and aspen, which crowd toward the centre of the path. A fairly long stretch of winding pathway follows, with much of it inside forest. There are only very occasional glimpses of the water.

5.9 km (3.7 mi) The trail arrives at another junction, at what appears to have been an old road. A sign says that the lake is to the right; head in that direction. There is a small rise, after which you are in what appears to be an old parking lot. Beyond that is a wonderful beach, only 100 m/ yd from the junction. The opposite shoreline appears quite close, and the Qu'Appelle Dam is visible to the left, a low rock wall edging the lake.

This is a wonderful location to have a picnic, although there are no tables to use. When ready, retrace your steps to the junction, but keep straight. After little more than 400 m/ yd, the trail connects to the Wolf Willow Trail, where there is a trail map and a plethora of directional signage.

Turn right 90°; the trail soon crosses a narrow dirt road then meanders through the woods, sometimes in sight of a much wider roadway. This is also the largest elevation change on the entire route, dropping 10 m (33 ft) over the next kilometre – and it is still barely noticeable.

The park trail reaches a final junction at 7.5 km (4.7 mi). There is a trail map here, and the road is in sight, connected to the trail by a footpath. Walk onto the dirt road, and turn right. The dam stretches out for a considerable distance. Connecting alongside the road and also running over the dam is an operational Canadian Pacific rail line.

The far end of the dam is visible, but an additional 2.7 km (1.7 mi) of hiking/ biking is required to reach it. I think it is worthwhile, because this section offers the most unobstructed views possible. To the right, Lake Diefenbaker

Lake Diefenbaker (see image pp. 214-15)

Created by the construction of the Gardiner and Qu'Appelle River dams in 1967, Lake Diefenbaker is now the largest body of water in the southern part of the province. Narrow but 225 km (140 mi) long, Lake Diefenbaker supplies drinking water for Regina and Medicine Hat and, with controlled releases, keeps the Qu'Appelle River flowing year round. It is a valuable source of irrigation for neighbouring farmland. With water levels that fluctuate 3-9 m (10-30 ft) each year, and erosion-prone soils, Lake Diefenbaker's shorelines are often broad sandy beaches, making a perfect nesting habitat for piping plovers.

I was impressed by the large numbers of pelicans floating in the deep water near the dam, and the many vultures riding the winds above them.

The lake is named after Canada's 13th prime minister, John G. Diefenbaker, who was the only chief of the federal government to hail from Saskatchewan.

stretches far away to the north, with more revealed the further along the dam you travel. To the left, the Qu'Appelle River Valley, lower than the level of the dam, also opens up for viewing.

The road is easy walking, although you should expect it to be quite windy. When I walked it, dozens of white pelicans bobbed in the shelter of the dam while several vultures soared above me. If you want more of a challenge, the lake side of the dam is lined by boulders – ideal for hopping. As you near the end, there is a small control building, and you can see that the road crosses the railway tracks at the far end of the embankment.

10.2 km (6.3 mi) At the far end of the dam lies one of the largest, sandiest, most deserted beaches you will have seen thus far. It is the perfect spot to stop and relax for a few minutes before beginning your return trek. You may either retrace your route or follow the inland Wolf Willow Trail for a slightly shorter trip.

Further Information:

Douglas Provincial Park: http://www.tourismsaskatchewan.com/
provincialpark/308/douglas-provincial-park#sort=relevancy
Qu'Appelle River Dam: https://www.wsask.ca/Lakes-and-Rivers/Dams-and-Reservoirs/Major-Dams-and-Reservoirs/QuAppelle-Dam/
Ticks: www.usask.ca/vmc/news/2014/ticks-101.php

John Tann, CC BY 2.0

Tick

Ticks are small, eight-legged animals related to spiders — they are not insects — that attach themselves to mammals, birds, and other animals and gorge on their blood. Unfed ticks are small, not much larger than a sesame seed, and they move around on the ground, grass, and bushes, waiting to attach themselves to any animal that brushes past.

Most tick bites cause only skin irritation and swelling, but a small percentage of ticks carry diseases, the most deadly of which is Lyme disease. DEET and Permethrin insecticides sprayed on clothing are effective at repelling ticks, but nothing has proven 100% effective, and other preventative measures are prudent.

Ticks have only recently become established in much of Canada. However, their range is spreading. Currently, there are virtually no ticks carrying Lyme disease in Saskatchewan, but you should check every year for updates.

Qu'Appelle River Valley

The Qu'Appelle Valley extends approximately 400 km (250 mi) across the central portion of Southern Saskatchewan and is one of the most scenic places in the province. Certainly this beautiful valley, lower than the surrounding landscape, is quite different from the flat Saskatchewan prairie found elsewhere. Twenty-three rural municipalities and eight First Nations reserves border this important river.

Canadian poet E. Pauline Johnson, in *The Legend of the Qu'Appelle Valley*, wrote that it received its name from an Indigenous warrior canoeing home one night, who thought he heard his name called out. "Who is there?" he called. "Qu'appelle?" Returning home, he was told that his fiancé had passed away the previous evening and with her last breath called out his name. Less romantically, the river's name may have come from Métis traders, who heard the local Cree inhabitants call "*Kâ-têpwêt*?" which sounds similar to the French "Qu'appelle."

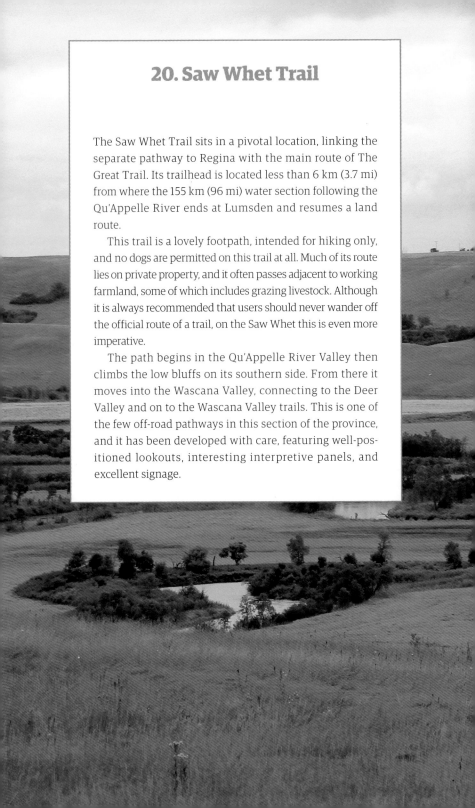

20. Saw Whet Trail

The Saw Whet Trail sits in a pivotal location, linking the separate pathway to Regina with the main route of The Great Trail. Its trailhead is located less than 6 km (3.7 mi) from where the 155 km (96 mi) water section following the Qu'Appelle River ends at Lumsden and resumes a land route.

This trail is a lovely footpath, intended for hiking only, and no dogs are permitted on this trail at all. Much of its route lies on private property, and it often passes adjacent to working farmland, some of which includes grazing livestock. Although it is always recommended that users should never wander off the official route of a trail, on the Saw Whet this is even more imperative.

The path begins in the Qu'Appelle River Valley then climbs the low bluffs on its southern side. From there it moves into the Wascana Valley, connecting to the Deer Valley and on to the Wascana Valley trails. This is one of the few off-road pathways in this section of the province, and it has been developed with care, featuring well-positioned lookouts, interesting interpretive panels, and excellent signage.

20. Saw Whet Trail

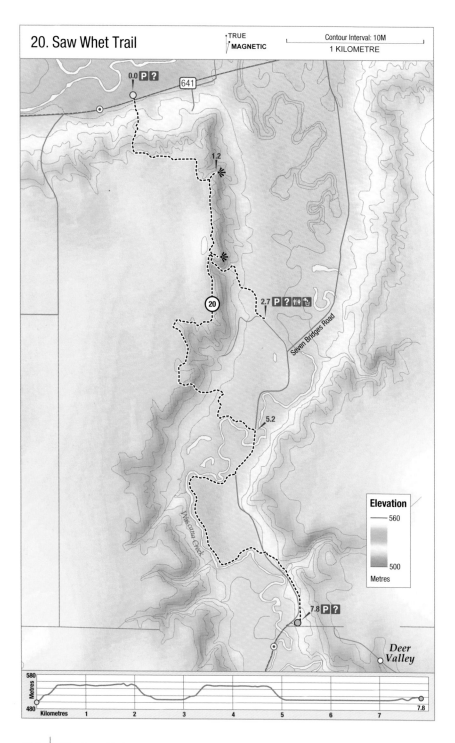

TRUE
MAGNETIC

Contour Interval: 10M
1 KILOMETRE

641

0.0 P ?

1.2

20

2.7 P ? ⚇ ♨

Seven Bridges Road

5.2

Phecara Creek

Elevation
560

500
Metres

7.8 P ?

Deer Valley

580
Metres
480
Kilometres 1   2   3   4   5   6   7   7.8

20. Saw Whet Trail

Distance: 7.8 km (4.8 mi), one way
Ascent: 137 m (449 ft)
Descent: 123 m (404 ft)

Trail conditions: compacted earth, natural surface
Cellphone coverage: yes
Hazards: road crossings, ticks, wildlife

Permitted Uses							
Walking	Biking	Horseback Riding	Inline Skating	ATV	Snowshoeing	Cross-country Skiing	Snowmobiling
✔	—	—	—	—	✔	✔	—

Finding the trailhead: From Highway 11, turn onto Highway 20/641, heading south toward Lumsden. Continue through the town, crossing the Qu'Appelle River and the railway tracks. Immediately after the tracks, turn right on Grid Road 641. Continue 4 km (2.5 mi); the trailhead is on the right.

Trailhead: 50°38'1.4" N, 104°55'13.1" W (Start: Grid Road 641 Trailhead)
50°36'4.5" N, 104°54'13.9" W (Finish: Deer Valley Trailhead)

Observations: With low hills, expansive views, and a winding river to follow, the Saw Whet Trail is a perfect day hike for a family. Despite the fact that the route is mostly only a mown path through the tall prairie grass, it is well signed and very difficult to miss. I would very much like to try this trail on a crisp, clear winter day.

Birdwatchers should enjoy this path. I saw several species of raptors in the trees both along the ridgeline and in the Wascana Creek Valley, and the forests on the slopes appeared to be full of small, colourful passerines. Unfortunately, I did not see any of its eponymous owls.

By way of warning, I should mention that it had rained for two days before I hiked this path. I had no idea that grasslands were home to so many – so very many – tiny, ravenous mosquitoes. If there is any hazard to be aware of here, it is them.

Route description: The red-roofed kiosk sits beside the road, the only structure for a considerable distance in any direction on the grassland. It offers an excellent large map, and there is a little parking lot beside it with a garbage can. There is even a signed crossing over the dirt road, for the path heads up the nearby hill, a distinct track visible in the tall grass.

Within sight of the road, is a barbed-wire fence with a small wooden gate, on which is a TCT/Great Trail marker, to provide passage. The track is natural surface, which means grass, and there is a slender path worn through it. It climbs immediately, and soon moves into low, thick vegetation, winding its way through the uneven ground. The trees are so thick that branches on both sides brush against you. Signage is provided by white-painted wooden posts, often with a trail marker and an arrow affixed.

In little more than 400 m/yd you reach the top of the hill, 50 m (164 ft) higher than your start. The sight at the top is interesting. Directly ahead is a huge cultivated field, just the other side of another barbed-wire fence. Turn left and follow the fence line; another gate provides crossing about 100 m/yd later. There are quite expansive views over the Qu'Appelle Valley below.

The trail traces the edge of the crop – wheat, when I was there – and crosses an access road at about 600 m/yd. The route is easy to follow, keeping cultivated fields on the right with a fence on the left and looking ahead for the tell-tale white signposts.

At 850 m/yd, the path turns 90° right, which is also where the first views of Wascana Creek are available. After another 150 m/yd the route turns left again, and in another 100m/yd it reaches a junction with a side trail to a lookout.

1.2 km (0.7 mi) A short 100 m/yd grassy walk delivers you to a bench overlooking the lower Wascana Valley. This is the Carrsdale Lookout, named for the post office, which was in the house of some of the original settlers to the area: Ed and Linnie Carss. The view is placidly pastoral, with cultivated fields visible in both valleys and on the ground above them.

Return to the main trail, which continues along the crest of the hill, with a few minor undulations to navigate. The next lookout, the McNally, is reached about 600 m/yd later and is also named for a pioneering family with descendants still farming in the valley.

Shortly after returning to the main trail at 1.9 km (1.2 mi), there is a junction. Turn left and follow this downhill, into a shallow ravine. The path soon enters thick forest, but quickly emerges onto a grassy knoll. Directly ahead are some farm buildings, and the sharp-eyed might notice the red roof of a trail kiosk as well. The path leads across the fields to the farm's driveway; turn left.

2.7 km (1.7 mi) The route ends at a trailhead kiosk, similar to the one at which you began the hike. The nearby buildings belong to Griffith's Petting Farm and Campground. Washrooms and drinking water are available there. However, this is just a scenic diversion and some additional exercise; retrace your route the 750 m/yd back uphill to the main trail.

At the junction, turn left. The route continues to follow the ridgeline, marked by the white posts. To the left, the land slopes away into the Wascana Valley, while on the right are either cultivated or grass-covered fields. All the trees are left and below, and there is a fence on the left for part of this section.

For nearly 500 m/yd the route is straight, but then it turns right to work around a wide gulch. It crosses a farm road at 4.1 km (2.6 mi) at the lowest point, but there is only an infinitesimal change in elevation. The trail continues to trace a route around the gulley, always keeping close to the crest of the hill.

At 4.6 km (2.9 mi), the trail makes a sharp turn left at a gap in the fence and begins to descend the hillside. After 350 m/yd, the route heads right to avoid another cultivated field. It meanders between field and trees for another 200 m/yd before reaching the edge of Wascana Creek. Interestingly, the bank on this side is not high but steep sided, almost vertical.

This last few hundred metres/yards contains a limited amount of signage, and there was nothing at this location. Turn left, and saunter alongside the creek toward the road and bridge that were visible as you came down the hillside. There might be no markers, but there is a well-defined treadway through the vegetation.

5.2 km (3.2 mi) The trail arrives at the dirt-covered Seven Bridges Road, beside one of its bridges. There is even a TCT/Great Trail sign hanging on the side, along with others at the roadside, one with a warning that this is a busy road. (Not so when I was there.)

For the next 350 m/yd, you walk along the road. Fences line both sides, and there are cattle among the trees. There is also considerable lively bird life, particularly in the thickets alongside the river. At another gap in the fence, the trail turns right, leaving the road and following the river.

For the next 1.4 km (0.9 mi), the trail follows the winding route of the river. To the left is mostly one large cultivated field, and there is considerable old machinery scattered about near the path, including irrigation equipment. This is excellent birdwatching territory, with warblers darting through the dense wooded thickets that occasionally enfold the path, waxwings feasting on the late-summer berries, and bank swallows whose tunnels dot the vertical clay riverbank, swooping over the water devouring mosquitoes.

Sandwiched between field and river, it is impossible to get lost, so enjoy the ornithology and continue until you arrive once again at Seven Bridges Road at 7.2 km (4.5 mi). This time, however, it merely crosses the lane and heads through a fence, after which it turns right.

Almost immediately you are confronted by a gate with a notice. If the gate is closed so is the trail, and hikers must return to and follow the road. As this relates to the presence of cattle, do not ignore this warning: hikers are killed by cows every year. Fortunately for me, it was clear for passage, so I followed the far less well-worn footpath as it worked along the base of a hill. In fact, because it had not been mowed, it was nearly waist high and at times was challenging to force through.

In addition, there were several cattle paths and no trail markers, so I kept to the track that stayed in sight of the road. This moves into a forested area, where there were even some downed trees across the path. However, it soon returned to following the barbed-wire fence, which is itself adjacent to the road.

7.8 km (4.8 mi) The trail arrives at the trailhead kiosk and parking lot, marking the end of the Saw Whet Trail and the start of the Deer Valley section. There is a garbage can but no picnic table. Retrace your route back to the trailhead on Grid Road 641. It will be only a 6.3 km (3.9 mi) walk if you do not include the side trail back to Griffith's Farm.

Further Information:

Lumsden/Deer Valley Trail Brochure: http://lumsden.ca/wp-content/uploads/2017/06/2017-Trail-Brochure.pdf
Saskatchewan Trails Association: www.sasktrails.ca
Town of Lumsden: www.lumsden.ca

Northern Saw-whet Owl

A tiny nocturnal owl with a large head and bright yellow eyes, the northern saw-whet is more often heard than seen. Its rasping call, a screech likened to a saw being dragged over a whetstone, is supposedly what gives this feisty little predator its name. Nesting in hardwood forests but ranging in all types of woodland, the saw-whet preys primarily on mice, shrews, and voles — one of which makes several meals for this robin-sized hunter — but it will also take small birds such as chickadees and sparrows. Though some remain resident year round, most saw-whets migrate south for winter, stealthily conducting their journey at night.

24. South Whiteshell Trail

MANITOBA

21. Rossburn Subdivision

The Rossburn Subdivision is a 170+ km (106+ mi) [I found three different measurements listed online] route that follows an abandoned rail line between the communities of Russell and Neepawa. The Rossburn Subdivision – a railroad term indicating a branch route off the main line but with its own dedicated crew – was opened in 1905 to speed up delivering grain to market. It also reduced the travel time for passengers to Winnipeg to as little as twelve hours, much faster than by horse and buggy.

But like railroads all over North America, the rise of the automobile and trucking led to the loss of business, declining revenues, and the abandonment of unprofitable lines. Rossburn station closed in 1975; the last freight train rolled through in 1996. Soon afterwards the entire subdivision was abandoned, but it was quickly purchased by the provincial government for use in the Trans Canada Trail.

For much of its length, the Rossburn Subdivision is relatively close to the southern boundary of Riding Mountain National Park. The official Great Trail connector to the park is located near the community of Erickson, but Deep Lake Campground can be reached by road from Rossburn, only 27.5 km (17.1 mi) due north along quiet Provincial Road 264.

ATVs are not officially permitted on this trail but are frequent users nonetheless. Do not be surprised if you encounter one.

21. Rossburn Subdivision

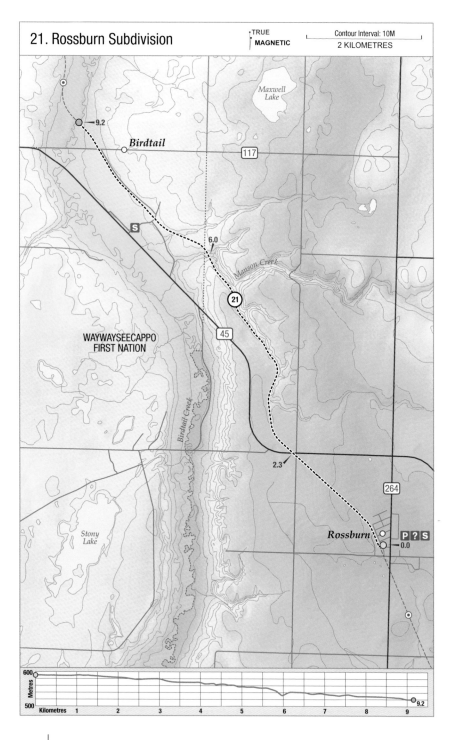

TRUE
MAGNETIC

Contour Interval: 10M
2 KILOMETRES

Maxwell Lake

9.2

Birdtail

117

S

6.0

Manson Creek

21

45

WAYWAYSEECAPPO
FIRST NATION

Birdtail Creek

2.3

264

Stony Lake

Rossburn

P ? S

0.0

600
Metres
500

Kilometres 1 2 3 4 5 6 7 8 9

9.2

21. Rossburn Subdivision

Distance: 9.2 km (5.7 mi), one way
Ascent: 22 m (72 ft)
Descent: 94 m (308 ft)

Trail conditions: crushed stone, natural surface
Cellphone coverage: yes
Hazards: motorized use, rattlesnakes, road crossings, ticks

Permitted Uses							
Walking	Biking	Horseback Riding	Inline Skating	ATV	Snowshoeing	Cross-country Skiing	Snowmobiling
✔	✔	✔	—	—	✔	✔	✔

Finding the trailhead: Turn left from Highway 45 onto Victoria Avenue. After 950 m/yd, turn right onto Centennial Road. Trailhead parking is on the left in 200 m/yd.

Trailhead: 50°40'11.4" N, 100°48'46.7" W (Start: Rossburn)
50°43'51.6" N, 100°53'18.4" W (Finish: Birdtail Creek)

Observations: I elected to profile a fairly small portion of this long trail, beginning in its namesake community and extending to the Waywayseecappo First Nation community and the Birdtail Bridge, constructed by the First Combat Engineer Regiment of the Canadian Army. This was sufficient, I believed, to provide the opportunity to view excellent examples of the type of terrain found in this part of the province and capture the spirit of the route.

This trail contains long straight stretches, with no obstacles, and although there is a reasonable amount of elevation change, it is so gradual as to be barely noticeable. The rolling topography, cut by the steeply sloped drainages bordering the small streams, provided more opportunities for wildlife viewing than I expected. The number and variety of raptors, for example, surprised me, as did the diversity of flowering plants.

This is a very easy bike ride but an even better hike.

Route description: From the parking area, where a row of trees has been planted between it and the trail, you pass beneath a steel gateway into the Queen Elizabeth II Diamond Jubilee Park. In the open area beyond sits a

trailhead kiosk, a number of Trails Manitoba interpretive panels, garbage cans, and picnic tables.

A small steel bridge is directly ahead. It crosses a shallow ditch and connects you to the rail trail. In addition to The Great Trail signage, there are local route markers for the Centennial and the Activity Trails. In the wide expanse of carefully tended lawn, several pieces of exercise equipment are visible – should you feel the urge to "pump up" before your hike/bike.

Turn right, toward the grain elevator, which towers above the rest of the community. The main trail is distinct, a strip of crushed stone partly grown over with grass. It crosses the first road just 250 m/yd from the trailhead; a large stop sign warns trail users that vehicles have precedence.

Straight for the first 400 m/yd, the path begins a gentle curve left before settling into another long straight section about 250 m/yd later. Once it leaves Rossburn, flourishing and flowering vegetation crowds the edges of the pathway. Thick grass even grows in the centre of the trail, reducing the crushed stone to two thin strips, like separate lanes for traffic travelling in opposite directions. The effect is striking, and charming.

For the first 1 km (0.6 mi), the ground is essentially level before beginning an almost imperceptible descent. A fair number of low trees provide a visual barrier on both sides of the trail, though frequent breaks reveal large areas of cultivated land. At 2.1 km (1.3 mi), the path crosses a gravel road, and 100 m/yd later, it crosses Highway 45.

2.3 km (1.4 mi) Be especially cautious crossing the highway; this is a high-speed road and there is no crosswalk or indicator that this is a trail crossing. On the opposite side sits a distance marker: Waywayseecappo 7 km (4.3 mi), Russell 42 km (26.1 mi).

Fields line both sides now, with broad views in every direction: Big Sky. The horizon seems limitless over the treeless ground. The trail begins another gentle turn, this time to the right. By 3 km (1.9 mi), the descent becomes more noticeable, with the land to the left high enough to block the view. As it moves into this ravine, no human habitation is visible, and the trail feels more remote than previously.

To the right, the ground is lower, and the route begins to parallel Manson Creek, although this cannot at first be seen. However, at 4 km (2.5 mi) a beaver dam has created a pond, which is quite evident. As it follows the river gully,

Rail Trail Trivia

Did you ever notice that most trails developed from abandoned railroads are about the same width? That is because they are generally made from railways that used standard gauge — the distance between rails — of 1.435 m (56.5 in). North American standard gauge is the same as Great Britain's, because our first railway engineers came from there.

But how did Great Britain choose such an odd number? Quite simply, they made the first railway cars the same width as their horse-drawn wagons, which was the size required to use their roads. England's first roads, however, had been built by the Romans, who constructed them for their war chariot, and 1.435 m just happened to be the distance apart that a chariot's wheels had to be to not get tangled up with their horse's legs.

So when next you hike/bike on a rail trail, you can imagine you are walking on a direct descendant of the Roman roads of Europe, first built more than 2,000 years ago.

---

there are a few more minor curves in the route, and a fair number of trees grow on the left hillside. About 100 m/yd later, on the right, is a Discovery Panel on the broad-winged hawk.

Most of the embankment on the far side of Manson Creek is grassy, and occasionally some cattle might be spotted grazing there. At 4.5 km (2.8 mi) is another Discovery Panel, titled A Skulk of Foxes, and there is a third a few hundred metres/yards later on the North American elk. As you continue descending the ravine, it becomes clear that there are multiple beaver dams in Manson Creek, creating several large pools and – judging by the vigorous quacking – outstanding waterfowl habitat.

At 5.6 km (3.5 mi) comes the most pronounced decline on this route, as the trail drops to cross Manson Creek.

6 km (3.7 mi) A long earthen embankment crosses Manson Creek, which turns sharply left at this point. When I travelled this section in 2016, the embankment was so severely eroded that I had to carry my bicycle over the thin strip that remained. I was assured by the local association that the embankment has since been completely rebuilt.

The embankment is higher than all the surrounding terrain, so once again extended views are possible, including Highway 45 and (possibly) the Waywayseecappo business complex. Also, for the first time since leaving Rossburn, houses can be sighted, directly ahead.

The trail is now inside the Waywayseecappo First Nation, and there are houses and roads all throughout the surrounding area, on both sides of the trail. The terrain is mostly treeless, with the land sloping gently down to the left, where Highway 45 and a large cluster of buildings – the business complex – are visible, and quite close.

At 6.6 km (4.1 mi), the path crosses Disappearing Stream. (There was no water when I passed there, suggesting the topographical feature is aptly named.) Then a number of dirt roads and driveways are crossed, with houses often only a few metres/yards away from the trail. When I passed though, this section was entirely covered in grass, with the vegetation thick enough to significantly slow my bike's progress. But it was also quite lovely, with a riot of small wildflowers scattered in the thick, tall grasses on either side of the track.

The much wider road at Birdtail is crossed at 8.6 km (5.3 mi). On the far side, a sign states that Angusville is 15 km (9.3 mi); Russell is 35 km (21.7 mi). Leaving the houses behind, the trail continues to gradually descend, although higher ground is visible ahead. Rich-looking farmlands are in sight in the distance, but close at hand it is pastureland, with cattle grazing or watching as you pass by.

Before you sight the bridge you encounter a small bronze plaque, mounted atop a piece of pole-drilling machinery. (As it is entirely brown in colour, it blends into the vegetation and is easy to miss.) This tells you that the upcoming bridge, crossing Birdtail Creek, was refurbished by the First Combat Engineer Regiment in 2003.

9.2 km (5.7 mi) Just a few steps later, and you reach Birdtail Creek, where a single-file footbridge, rigid-framed, not suspended, crosses the deceptively tranquil river. If the mosquitoes (and cows) will permit, this is a pleasant place to take a break and have a snack before retracing your route back to Rossburn.

Further Information:

Asessippi Parkland Tourism: www.asessippiparklandtourism.com

Riding Mountain National Park: www.pc.gc.ca/en/pn-np/mb/riding

Trails Manitoba: www.trailsmanitoba.ca

Waywayseecappo First Nation: https://www.youtube.com/watch?v=DbUU-zqJKn4

Mixed-Grass Prairie

Richer in ecological diversity than the short-grass prairie to the west and the long-grass prairie to the east, mixed-grass prairie occurs in a semi-arid climactic zone, with average annual rainfalls in the 50 cm (20 in) range. Prairie grasslands once made up the largest vegetation zone in North America, with the mixed-grass prairie comprising about 22% of the total area. Today, it has been reduced to less than 30% of its former range by conversion into cropland and pasture.

As a result, most of this region's large mammal populations — of bison, elk, pronghorn antelope, and Great Plains wolf — have disappeared from the wild. Many resident bird species, such as the greater prairie chicken, burrowing owl, and loggerhead shrike, are endangered.

As its name suggests, the vegetation within the mixed-grass prairie will be a constantly changing blend of short and long grasses. Drought and frequency of grazing will generally determine which species dominate, with fire another major factor.

22. Winnipeg Forks

If there is a geographic central city in Canada, it must be Winnipeg, which sits astride the vast Canadian Shield barrier of Northern Ontario and the prairie grasslands. Although to eastern Canadians Winnipeg is part of the west, ask Albertans and they will probably say it is not. In the second half of the 19th century, Winnipeg was known as the Gateway to the West, the railway nexus from which large numbers of immigrants spread to populate the prairies. At that time, Winnipeg was also known as the Chicago of the North, a boom town of infinite potential, its population doubling – or more – every decade.

The Forks is the heart of Winnipeg, its cultural and social centre, originally the site of First Nations encampments, fur trapping trading posts, home of the Métis, and location for the first European settlements. Today it is bounded by shops and museums, a large public space crisscrossed by pathways, and a natural location to experience the city on The Great Trail. There is so much to be found in this small area, so many interpretive panels, so many displays, that it is impossible to list them all. Allow yourself plenty of time to explore.

Things can happen quickly in boom towns, and in Winnipeg trail development over the past decade has exploded. With one of the most ambitious active transportation plans of any Canadian city, Winnipeg has built a large network of shared-use pathways, and plans to build far more. For The Great Trail, this means that current road connections may be able to be transferred onto off-road paths in the future.

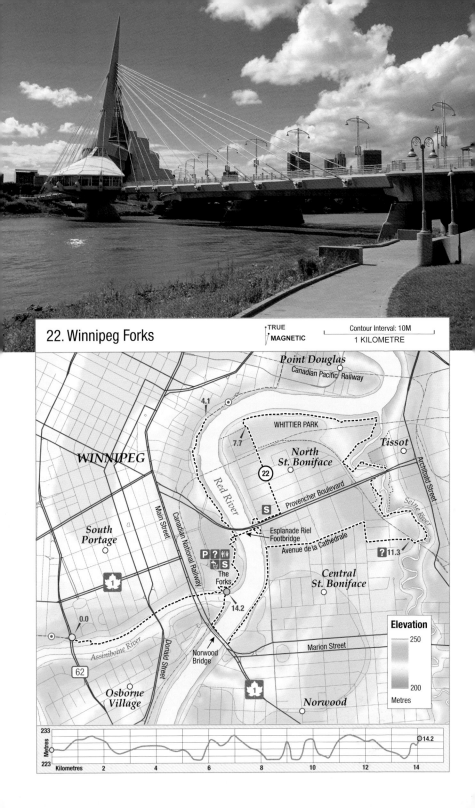

22. Winnipeg Forks

TRUE
MAGNETIC

Contour Interval: 10M
1 KILOMETRE

Point Douglas
Canadian Pacific Railway

WHITTIER PARK

4.1

7.7

WINNIPEG

*North
St. Boniface*

Tissot

22

S

Provencher Boulevard

Red River

*South
Portage*

S

Esplanade Riel
Footbridge

Avenue de la Cathédrale

1

P **?** **†**
S

*The
Forks*

? 11.3

*Central
St. Boniface*

14.2

0.0

Assiniboine River

Marion Street

62

Donald Street

Norwood
Bridge

Canadian National Railway

Main Street

Elevation

250

200

Metres

1

*Osborne
Village*

Norwood

Seine River

Archibald Street

233

Metres

14.2

223 Kilometres   2   4   6   8   10   12   14

22. Winnipeg Forks

Distance: 15.8 km (9.8 mi) — return
Ascent: 129 m (423 ft)
Descent: 133 m (436 ft)

Trail conditions: asphalt, crushed stone
Cellphone coverage: yes
Hazards: road crossings, road sections

Permitted Uses							
Walking	Biking	Horseback Riding	Inline Skating	ATV	Snowshoeing	Cross-country Skiing	Snowmobiling
✔	✔	—	✔*	—	✔	✔*	—

Finding the trailhead: Begin at the intersection of Assiniboine Avenue and Osbourne Street. There is on-road parking on a nearby side street.

Trailhead: 49°52'57.7" N, 97°08'53.5" W (Start/Finish: Assiniboine Avenue)

Observations: Winnipeg is one of the few places that I actually cycled off several kilometres/miles – ok, quite a few – in the wrong direction. It was definitely my mistake, but better signage with posted maps would have helped. I didn't mind, of course, because, Winnipeg is a tremendously attractive urban setting for walking and/or cycling. This is particularly so near The Forks, where architectural masterpieces such as the Canadian Museum of Human Rights and the Esplanade Riel provide arresting visual stimuli.

Originally I had intended only to profile the loop around St. Boniface and The Forks, but the scenery, both natural and human made, along the Assiniboine and Red Rivers induced me to include this short section as well. (One of the benefits of riding in the wrong direction? Maybe.)

Route description: Begin at the intersection of the two streets, where a bike path comes up to the intersection. This is an attractive area, with the Manitoba Legislature on the opposite side of Assiniboine Avenue, and the Great-West Life Company head office across Osbourne. The actual route of The Great Trail is along Assiniboine Avenue, and there is a bidirectional bike track that extends as far as Main Street. If, however, the River Walk is open – it is often closed because of severe spring floods – I recommend following that.

From the intersection, follow the asphalt path downhill. This quickly connects to the Cornish Path, which leads to a statue of Louis Riel, and a set of stairs down to the Assiniboine River Walk, where there is a water taxi dock. Turn left and follow this wide path, which runs alongside the broad waterway. Dozens of benches line the path, and there is lighting for nighttime uses. A dense buffer of trees largely blocks your view of the city above, although frequent staircases provide access back to Assiniboine Avenue, which this path parallels.

A remarkably peaceful interlude follows while the trail passes beneath the massive bridges for Donald and Main Streets. Except for the background drone of the urban environment, this is a somewhat isolated, almost deserted, stretch of pathway.

At 1.4 km (0.9 mi), just after passing beneath a railroad bridge, the trail arrives at a very busy spot. Directly ahead are a small artificial cove, which the trail curves around, and a boat tour dock. To the left, there is a semicircular area with several rising levels, each broad enough to accommodate picnic tables. Above this area is a large building that contains a wide variety of restaurants. On sunny days, this amphitheatre swarms with people, most of them enjoying a meal in sight of the river.

At the far side of the cove, before passing beneath the next bridge, turn left and follow a broad curving path to higher ground. At the next junction turn right, and at 1.6 km (1 mi), at another junction, you should find yourself next to a shallow amphitheatre bordered by steel sculptures, on the left, known as the Oodena Celebration Circle. To the right is a pedestrian bridge crossing the Assiniboine River, at the near end of which is The Forks Trailhead kiosk.

This is a busy area, with many attractions and a confusing network of paths. Take the route that keeps the Oodena to your left, then straight at the next intersection, keeping the Children's Museum on the left. Continue until you reach a circular junction. The Adventure Park should be on the right, the 1999 Canada Games Flame on the left. Turn right, heading past The Forks National Historic Site entrance – where there are public washrooms – until you reach another circular junction next to the Peace Park and the Esplanade Riel.

There are uncounted benches and picnic tables to stop and reorient if you get misdirected. There are so many plaques and interpretive panels that you will need to decide whether to use your time to read or to hike/bike. If these directions sound too complex, just follow the river until you reach the funky suspended bridge.

Take the trail underneath the Esplanade Riel. This wide track follows the Red River and also crosses beneath the Provencher Bridge. Keep right at the next major junction; you head onto a pathway with fences on either side. This eventually heads up to run alongside Waterfront Drive, linking with it at 2.6 km (1.6 mi).

The pathway is now running next to the street like a sidewalk, but it is clearly a shared-use trail. Little more than 100 m/yd later, you will pass an interesting artistic display: what appear to be five aircraft wings. This piece, called the *High Five*, is in fact supposed to be an abstracted human hand.

In another 100 m/yd the trail crosses beneath a railroad bridge and enters Stephen Juba Park, where it veers away from the road and passes through a lovely area of overhead trees with many flowerbeds and benches. There are even additional examples of public art, visible when the trail briefly touches Waterfront Drive again, at the roundabout with Bannatyne Avenue.

Follow the path until it passes the colourful and creative-looking Mere Hotel, at 3.3 km (2.1 mi), and returns to alongside the road. The trail passes a parking lot, crosses Alexander Avenue, then moves into Fort Douglas Park. This is mostly lawn, so there are excellent views of the Red River – and maybe even Fort Gibraltar on the opposite bank. You might also notice The Scots Monument, on the road side of this park.

At 3.8 km (2.4 mi), trail and road diverge, with the path heading into a forested area and surfaced in crushed stone. Several side trails permit access onto adjacent streets.

4.1 km (2.5 mi) The off-road pathway finishes, connecting to the end of Annabelle Street, where The Great Trail begins an on-road section. Instead of continuing, retrace your route back to The Forks until it passes underneath the Esplanade Riel, in about 1.9 km (1.2 mi).

Once back at Esplanade Riel, climb up and cross over the Red River to St. Boniface – the predominantly Franco-Manitoban district of Winnipeg. As you

cross the sleek and stylish Esplanade Riel, you might notice something distinctive: this is the only bridge in Canada with a restaurant on it.

Once across the bridge, turn right and follow the winding path down to water level. It curves right, back underneath the bridge. It then climbs back up to Taché Avenue; there is a parking area to the left. At Taché, turn right and return to Provencher Boulevard. (This almost complete circle is designed to avoid the heavy automobile traffic on Provencher.)

Turn left on Provencher Boulevard, where there is a bike track incorporated into the broad sidewalk. Even so, because this has so much pedestrian traffic, cyclists may wish to dismount for the 200 m/yd until the intersection with Rue Saint Joseph. Here, turn left, and continue – cyclists on the road, walkers on the sidewalk – to the end of the street 800 m/yd later.

7.7 km (4.8 mi) Arrive at the intersection of Rue Saint Joseph and Rue Messager. On the right is Fort Gibraltar, a 1978 reconstruction of a fur-trade era fort built in 1809 by the North West Company at the confluence of the Red River and the Assiniboine River.

The trail continues straight on a crushed-stone path, the Promenade Saint Boniface, toward a large wooden platform. When it reaches the river's edge, less than 200 m/yd later, turn right and follow the trail right beside the reconstructed fort.

Once past the fort, the nearly straight track continues for more than 1 km (0.6 mi), with river and trees lining the left and large lawns containing sports fields on the right: Whittier Park. At 9 km (5.6 mi), you reach a bronze plaque recognizing Jean-Baptiste Lagimodière and Marie-Anne Gaboury, two early European settlers and grandparents of Louis Riel. A short walk down a side trail leads to where the Seine River joins the Red.

The trail turns sharply right, following the Seine upstream, and enters Lagimodière-Gaboury Park. It passes beneath railway tracks then meanders through dense forest. Side trails abound, so be careful to stay on the main track. About 500 m/yd from the plaque, you arrive in the parking area for the park. Turn left; this follows a railway track for about 1 m/yd, then turns sharply left and crosses the Seine River on a very nice bridge.

In another area of lawns, the trail turns right again, arriving at Provencher Boulevard at 10 km (6.2 mi), at the end of a road bridge over the Seine River. There is no crosswalk over this four-lane road, but you must cross to the opposite side. Once safely over, turn left and continue 150 m/yd to where there is a trail sign and map, just before reaching a store parking area.

Turn left, onto the narrow Gabrielle Roy Trail. This is a lot of fun, a slender, twisting path hugging the riverbank and set among the trees. It only lasts for 1.1 km (0.7 mi) before crossing beneath a rail bridge and reaching a junction. Turn right, and climb the stairs.

11.3 km (7 mi) Reach the end of Rue Deschambault, where there is a trailhead kiosk with a map. An extended road section follows: 350 m/yd on Rue Deschambault, right onto Des Meurons Street for 175 m/yd, then left onto Avenue de la Cathedrale. There is good local trail signage; there are also small TCT/Great Trail stickers on power poles.

At 12.7 km (7.9 mi), the route reaches and crosses Taché Avenue to resume on an asphalt-surfaced trail: the Promenade Taché. To the left is the stately Saint Boniface Cathedral. The trail has also returned to the Red River and within sight of the Esplanade Riel. Turn left and follow this route for the next 900 m/yd, as it passes the St. Boniface Museum and the St. Boniface General Hospital. There are many benches and pleasant areas to stop and rest in this narrow strip of green space between road and river.

Just before it reaches a massive road bridge, the trail splits. Turn left, and climb up to road level and the Sentier La Liberté Trail. Turn right, and cross this busy bridge. Fortunately, there is both a wide pedestrian walkway and a separate cycling track. As soon as you are across the Red River, turn right onto a crushed-stone pathway, toward The Forks. In 200 m/yd it arrives at a wide pedestrian bridge that crosses the Assiniboine River.

14.2 km (8.8 mi) Cross the river: On the far side of this bridge, you reach The Forks, and reconnect with the trail on which you began your hike/bike. Turn left to retrace your route back to your start point at Assiniboine Avenue and Osbourne Street. Only 1.6 km (1 mi) remains.

Further Information:
Canadian Museum for Human Rights: www.humanrights.ca
The Forks National Historic Site: www.pc.gc.ca/en/lhn-nhs/mb/forks
Tourism Winnipeg: www.tourismwinnipeg.com
Trails Manitoba: www.trailsmanitoba.ca
Winnipeg Trails Association: www.winnipegtrails.ca

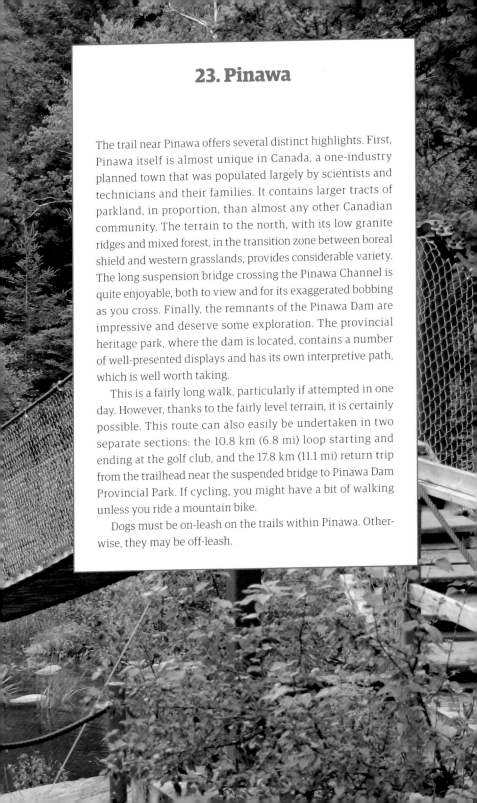

23. Pinawa

The trail near Pinawa offers several distinct highlights. First, Pinawa itself is almost unique in Canada, a one-industry planned town that was populated largely by scientists and technicians and their families. It contains larger tracts of parkland, in proportion, than almost any other Canadian community. The terrain to the north, with its low granite ridges and mixed forest, in the transition zone between boreal shield and western grasslands, provides considerable variety. The long suspension bridge crossing the Pinawa Channel is quite enjoyable, both to view and for its exaggerated bobbing as you cross. Finally, the remnants of the Pinawa Dam are impressive and deserve some exploration. The provincial heritage park, where the dam is located, contains a number of well-presented displays and has its own interpretive path, which is well worth taking.

This is a fairly long walk, particularly if attempted in one day. However, thanks to the fairly level terrain, it is certainly possible. This route can also easily be undertaken in two separate sections: the 10.8 km (6.8 mi) loop starting and ending at the golf club, and the 17.8 km (11.1 mi) return trip from the trailhead near the suspended bridge to Pinawa Dam Provincial Park. If cycling, you might have a bit of walking unless you ride a mountain bike.

Dogs must be on-leash on the trails within Pinawa. Otherwise, they may be off-leash.

23. Pinawa

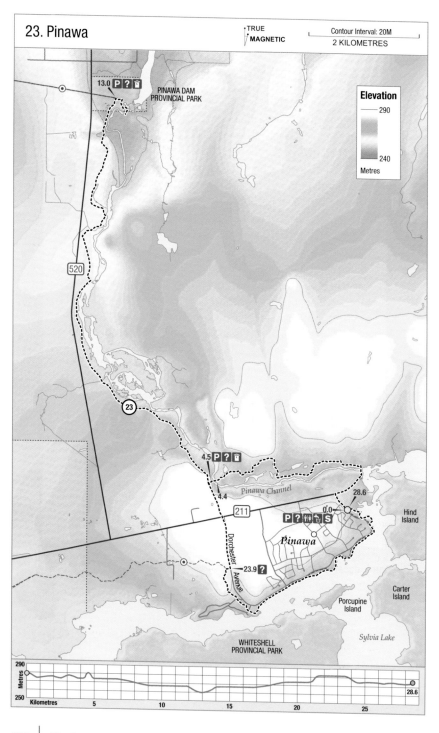

TRUE
MAGNETIC

Contour Interval: 20M
2 KILOMETRES

Elevation
— 290
240
Metres

13.0 **P** **?** 🚻

PINAWA DAM
PROVINCIAL PARK

520

(23)

4.5 **P** **?** 🚻

4.4

Pinawa Channel

211

28.6

0.0 **P** **?** 🚻🚻🚲 **S**

Pinawa

Hind
Island

Dorchester Avenue

23.9 **?**

Carter
Island

Porcupine
Island

Sylvia Lake

WHITESHELL
PROVINCIAL PARK

290
Metres
250

Kilometres   5   10   15   20   25

28.6

23. Pinawa

Distance: 28.6 km (17.8 mi), loop
Ascent: 56 m (184 ft)
Descent: 58 m (190 ft)

Trail conditions: compacted earth, crushed stone, natural surface
Cellphone coverage: yes
Hazards: poison ivy, road crossings, ticks, wildlife

Permitted Uses							
Walking	Biking	Horseback Riding	Inline Skating	ATV	Snowshoeing	Cross-country Skiing	Snowmobiling
✔	✔	✔	✔	✔*	✔	✔	✔*

Finding the trailhead: Begin your walk in the Pinawa Golf and Country Club parking lot.

Trailhead: 50°09'14.3" N, 95°52'17.9" W (Start/Finish: Pinawa)

Observations: This is a remarkably easy hike, with little elevation change throughout the entire route. I was surprised how little fatigue I felt after nearly 30 km (18.6 mi) of walking. The signage is excellent, and it was almost possible to follow the path without paying much attention to directional indicators — though I do not recommend ever doing that!

The community of Pinawa is lovely, and its lakefront trail has an astonishing array of amenities for such a small community. But I most enjoyed the Pinawa Dam site, with its impressive ruins and well-developed interpretive program. This route provides interesting historical, as well as natural, qualities to recommend it.

Route description: A clear path is visible on the north side of the parking lot, with blue diamond-shaped signs and white arrows indicating the direction. There is also a TCT/Great Trail marker. The golf course remains to the right as the path reaches and crosses Highway 211 about 350 m/yd from the start. Turn right, and walk alongside this road to its end, at a parking area next to Sylvia Lake, at 900 m/yd.

There is a trailhead kiosk at the far end of the parking lot, where an off-road pathway continues. There are also garbage cans and a picnic table or two nearby. There is even a Discovery Panel on the bald eagle. A wide

Spillway Viewpoint

The First Dam

To meet the growing demand for electricity in Winnipeg in the early 1900s, an ambitious — some said foolhardy — experiment was attempted on the Winnipeg River near present-day Pinawa: the construction of the first year-round producer of electrical power between Sault Ste. Marie and the Rocky Mountains. Between 1903 and 1906, the Pinawa Dam was built in this rough, unsettled territory. Lacking railroads or roads, heavy equipment had to be ferried by scow or hauled by horses over the ice of Lac du Bonnet.

Initially the dam produced more than 18,000 kW of power — more than critics said that Winnipeg would ever use. But by 1916, the population of the city had quadrupled, and the Pinawa Dam was already inadequate. Despite constant upgrades, by the 1920s it was clear that larger, more efficient power generators were required.

A thriving community had risen to build and service the new dam, but when construction began on the Seven Sisters project, workers and their families began to drift away. After the Pinawa Dam closed, in 1951, the final few families moved, and the town was abandoned and became known as Old Pinawa.

crushed-stone-surfaced pathway crosses the diversion dam, a low, wide rock structure, which spans the Pinawa Channel. Sylvia Lake is to the right; the channel on the left.

At the end of the dam, where there is another Discovery Panel, the trail turns left, narrowing to become a footpath. The terrain around here is interesting; the rock scooped out when the Pinawa Channel was created is littered about in huge mounds. In some places, this rock was used to create embankments; the path uses some of these as its route. There are other spots where the trail crosses bare rock, and trail signage in these areas are posts set in rock cairns.

A system of mountain bike trails shares the Pinawa Channel Trail; they use separate signage, and for a short distance this is part of their Red Trail. Most cyclists we encountered were mindful that there were pedestrians – but not all, so be cautious.

The route soon becomes a single-track footpath, with frequent intrusions of bare rock, and there are numerous turns and junctions in these first few kilometres/miles. However, signage is quite good, so it is simply a case of paying attention to stay on the correct route. An example of this is at 1.9 km (1.2 mi), when the Red Trail turns left, while the Pinawa Channel Trail curves right: signs clearly indicate the divergence.

There are occasional views of the channel, to the left, but the trail is mostly within the forest. By 2 km (1.2 mi), the path has widened so that two may walk comfortably side by side. Another Discovery Panel, ominously on the black bear, is at 2.7 km (1.7 mi).

Trail junctions are too numerous to mention – or remember. Fortunately, each has the blue diamond marker with a white arrow pointing in the correct direction. As the trail meanders through the thick forest, there is scarcely any climb required. Indeed, except for trail junctions and interpretive panels, there are few views.

At 4.2 km (2.6 mi), the trail emerges briefly from the vegetation to pass alongside a small pond, and then onto the first natural vertical rock face on this route.

4.4 km (2.7 mi) The trail arrives at one of its highlights: the suspension bridge spanning the Pinawa Channel. This remarkable 54 m/yd long, 1 m/yd wide structure bows deeply down from its two supporting beams, and bounces enough to satisfy the most playful hiker. Since it was completed in 1998, this suspension bridge has been attracting walkers from all over the province.

On the far side of the bridge is a large pavilion recognizing community supporters of the trail. Sometimes a picnic table is found here as well. A short footpath leads to a parking area, where there is a trailhead kiosk and a map. There is also an outhouse for trail users.

Turn right, onto the Alice Chambers Trail, which appears to be an extension of the road that led to the parking area. A gate limits car access, but trail signage near the gate shows that ATVs and snowmobiles are permitted. What follows is a pleasant, wide, and mostly downhill trek through a mixed forest of spruce and aspen. In fact, the trembling aspen is the subject of a Discovery Panel about 650 m/yd along this track.

There is clear signage at regular intervals, and occasionally – depending on how thick the adjacent foliage is – views of the Pinawa Channel to the right. There is at least one bench and a few more interpretive panels before the trail reaches an important junction at 7.2 km (4.5 mi), where there is another bench. The motorized track curves left; the hiking/biking path continues straight but onto a grass-covered surface.

Within sight of the junction, a narrow wooden bridge crosses a small brook. To the right, Sylvia Lake is visible. Once over this bridge, the trail resembles an old road, but it is completely grass covered and clearly not open to vehicle use. Once again the trail heads into forest, with tall trees lining both sides.

The area seems quite secluded, but occasional car sounds remind you that a road, Highway 520, parallels the trail and is actually quite close. Breaks in the vegetation to the right reveal Sylvia Lake and the Pinawa Channel, which also roughly parallels the trail. Occasional signs and a bench are found in this stretch, but the lush ground growth suggests low usage of this part of the trail.

At 9.3 km (5.8), you arrive at an area known as The Rapids. Two interpretive panels mark the spot, and a distinct side trail leads out less than 100 m/yd to where you can view the constricted and rapidly flowing river. The main pathway is much rougher now, looking more like a footpath and less like a former woods road. Watch for poison ivy near here.

After leaving the rapids, there is a minuscule hill – worth mentioning only because it's so rare – after which the trail resumes as an old, grass-covered road. About 700 m/yd later, road and trail almost touch, then the road turns right and away from the highway. Barely 200 m/yd further, another narrow bridge spans a tiny rivulet. On the far side are a bench and a Discovery Panel on the beaver.

There is another rough patch, where the trail goes onto an area of bare rock. Off to the right, a granite bench sits on the rock at the edge of the water, an enticing swimming spot. But the main pathway soon veers away from the water and back into the forest. It soon narrows into a single track, with a grass-covered treadway.

The forest cover begins to change, with spruce giving way to aspen and poplar. Soon, even these open stands or hardwoods begin to have gaps of grasslands between them. By 11.9 km (7.4 mi), there are wide views in nearly every direction, particularly ahead and toward the river on the right. At 12.8 km (8 mi), another tiny, railed bridge is crossed.

13 km (8.1 mi) Barely 100 m/yd later is a junction where you should turn left. Almost immediately, the path reaches a well-maintained field, with a trail-head kiosk, picnic tables, and other amenities; you have reached Pinawa Dam Provincial Heritage Park and the site of Old Pinawa.

This is a fascinating site. The concrete ruins of the Pinawa Dam are massive, and there are various displays, including the remains of power-generating equipment, scattered throughout the grounds. The park has its own interpretive trail, with panels outlining both the story of the dam's construction and of the community that lived, and died, around it.

At a minimum, I recommend that you head toward the dam and cross over the sturdy metal bridge that crosses the narrowest section of the channel. Turn right, and continue as far as the bare rock beside the rapids, about 500 m/yd from the trailhead kiosk. This is a favourite swimming location and certain to be busy on hot summer days. There should be an empty picnic table or bench nearby for you to rest and have a snack.

Once you have finished your explorations of Old Pinawa, retrace your route back to the parking area close to the suspension bridge. Your total distance covered to this point will be at least 22.4 km (14 mi). Instead of returning via the suspension bridge, continue straight along the gravel road. In 600 m/yd, when it reaches Highway 211, cross and continue straight on Dorchester Avenue. There are no houses along this gravel road, at least for the 850 m/yd you travel before you reach a trail junction, on the right.

A Special Community

In 1963, Atomic Energy of Canada Limited (AECL) constructed the Whiteshell Laboratories nuclear research facility in what is now Pinawa, Manitoba. The facility was initially the site of a nuclear reactor, as well as an underground research centre to study the disposal of nuclear waste. This area was selected because it was relatively unpopulated and far enough from Winnipeg in case of accidents.

The new community of Pinawa was biult to house the scientists and their familites. Designed as a Garden City, Pinawa features expansive lots, extensive public recreation spaces, and cultural amenities far beyond what might be expected in a remote, modest-sized community.

AECL began decommissioning the facility in 1998, and Pinawa has had to adjust to a changed, less-secure economic future. Even today this small town of barely 1,300 retains a vibrancy rarely equalled in much larger communities, and its outsized lawns have proven so attractive to wildlife that Pinawa is known as the Deer Capital of Manitoba.

23.9 km (14.9 mi) Turn off Dorchester Avenue and onto a pathway. Immediately there is a trailhead kiosk, followed by a junction; turn left. The trail is wide, level, and dry. It is lined by tall hardwoods, and over the next kilometre it winds its way to the lakeshore, crossing several gravel roads en route. Once it reaches the water, it curves left and begins to trace the shoreline.

An additional 3.6 km (2.2 mi) remains. However, for the remaining distance the trail hugs the water's edge as it passes through the community of Pinawa. And there is so much to see that it is impossible to do it justice: playgrounds, benches, covered picnic tables, dozens of interpretive panels, the yacht club, canoe launches, interesting houses, islands in Sylvia Lake – a widening of the Winnipeg River – and much more. The entire shoreline of Pinawa is public land, and it has been developed as a superb recreational property.

28.6 km (17.8 mi) The path leads back to the parking area of the golf club, where you began. There is a restaurant inside the club, which is accessible to the public and open year round.

Further Information:

History of the Pinawa Dam: http://www.granite.mb.ca/oldpinawa/opbh1beg.html

Pinawa Dam Provincial Heritage Park: https://www.gov.mb.ca/sd/parks/popular_parks/eastern/pinawa.html

Town of Pinawa: www.pinawa.com

Manitoba's Boreal Forest

When thinking of Manitoba, most envision vast prairie farmlands, but in fact much of the province is covered by boreal forest, including a great deal of the area east of Winnipeg. Characterized by its rugged Precambrian volcanic rock base, thinly covered by soil and often exposed on hilltops, the boreal forest is a mixture of white spruce and balsam fir, with pockets of trembling aspen and poplar. Its poorly drained bogs are rich in peat and usually edged by tamarack and black spruce.

The boreal forest sustains a wide range of wildlife. Vast numbers of migratory waterfowl nest in the many ponds and lakes, while animals such as the endangered woodland caribou require this habitat to survive. Canada's, and Manitoba's, boreal forest is one of the few remaining landscapes in the world still shaped primarily by natural processes, such as fire, insects, and wind.

24. South Whiteshell Trail

Large Whiteshell Provincial Park, 2,729 km² (1,054 mi²), sits along the Manitoba-Ontario border like a screen. It covers a significant tract of Canadian Shield terrain and the same boreal forest found throughout Northern Ontario. Being close to Winnipeg, Whiteshell Park has become a major recreation area, containing thousands of cottages and offering sailing on its many large lakes, extensive canoe routes, and several long-distance hiking/biking trails, such as the well-known 63 km (39.1 mi) Mantario Trail.

Whiteshell Park is also where an uninterrupted land route of The Great Trail ends, if you are coming from the west, or resumes, if you are heading west. From Vancouver to Whiteshell it is possible to walk or cycle the entire Great Trail, with only a few short exceptions. From this park begins a more than 2,000 km (1,243 mi) water route that continues until near Sault Ste. Marie, Ontario.

Within Whiteshell Park are nearly 180 km (112 mi) of walking/cycling pathway, extending from the Seven Sisters Dam in the north, to High Lake in the south. When I was exploring the area for this book, the Seven Sisters area was closed because of work on the dam, and forest fires had closed much of the North Whiteshell Trail. Ironically, short portions of the South Whiteshell Trail near Falcon Lake were flooded. This is a beautiful area, and if you enjoy the portion profiled, it is well worth exploring the sections I had to bypass, should conditions permit.

24. South Whiteshell Trail

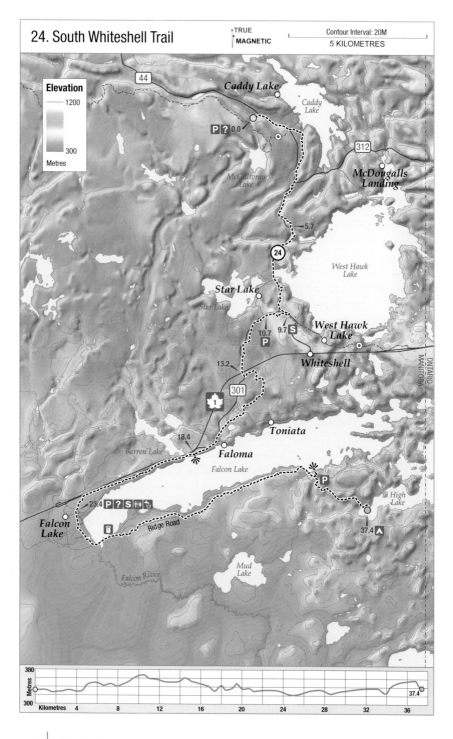

TRUE
MAGNETIC

Contour Interval: 20M
5 KILOMETRES

Elevation

— 1200

300

Metres

44

Caddy Lake

Caddy Lake

P ? 0.0

312

McDougalls Landing

5.7

24

West Hawk Lake

Star Lake

Star Lake

9.7 S

West Hawk Lake

10.7 P

13.2

Whiteshell

301

1

18.4

Toniata

Barren Lake

Faloma

Falcon Lake

P

High Lake

23.4 P ? S 👫 🚻

37.4 ⛺

Falcon Lake

Ridge Road

Falcon River

Mud Lake

ONTARIO | MANITOBA

380

Metres

300

37.4

Kilometres   4   8   12   16   20   24   28   32   36

24. South Whiteshell Trail

Distance: 37.4 km (23.2 mi), one way
Ascent: 318 m (1,043 ft)
Descent: 312 m (1,024 ft)

Trail conditions: asphalt, crushed stone, natural surface
Cellphone coverage: partial
Hazards: poison ivy, ticks, wildlife

Permitted Uses							
Walking	Biking	Horseback Riding	Inline Skating	ATV	Snowshoeing	Cross-country Skiing	Snowmobiling
✔	✔	✔	—	—	✔	✔	—

Finding the trailhead: From Highway 1, take the West Hawk Lake exit (Highway 44) and drive north for approximately 10.5 km (6.5 mi). Turn left into the McGillivray Falls picnic area; the parking lot is in about 200 m/yd.

Trailhead: 49°48'34.5" N, 95°14'16.0" W (Start: McGillivray Falls)
49°41'23.1" N, 95°10'55.8" W (Finish: High Lake)

Observations: I was entirely unfamiliar with this part of Canada and did not know what to expect. North of Falcon Lake it was typical Canadian Shield terrain: lots of hills with small bodies of water filling every low spot between them. I rather enjoyed that the trail had to wind its way around the frequent wet spots, and that it went up and down the many (thankfully) low hills.

Between the community of Falcon Lake and High Lake, the terrain was often somewhat different, with longer straight sections and fewer wetlands. The tree cover changed as well, with more aspens. That is, however, until the final 2.5 km (1.6 mi), which featured the most demanding climbs of the entire trek. This is a very enjoyable bike ride and a marvellous cross-country ski route.

Dogs must be on-leash inside the urban area of Falcon Lake but are permitted off-leash elsewhere.

Route description: Start at the McGillivray Falls parking area, where there are picnic tables and garbage cans but no cell reception. The small waterfall is a short walk from the parking area, but our route follows the access road back to Highway 44, turning right and continuing along the paved roadway to the entrance of the Caddy Lake camping and picnic area, at 1.3 km (0.8 mi). Cross the road; behind the large Caddy Lake sign is a forest pathway, marked as the Trans Canada Trail. Follow this into a thickly wooded and soggy area, emerging 500 m/yd later onto a rather solid bridge with a view, on the left, of Caddy Lake and a canoe launch area. Once across the bridge, the treadway improves, becoming wide with a gravelled, rather than a grass-covered, surface.

The trail follows a tiny brook through the forest, with occasional glimpses of Highway 44. At 3.8 km (2.4 mi), the path crosses Highway 312, at its junction with route 44. A large stop sign warns cyclists not to use the short steep downhill section to dash across the road.

The trail parallels Highway 44 and is often in sight of the road, but it is much more challenging, climbing a number of steep little hills. At about 4.9 km (3 mi), there are several large, rusting pieces of equipment beside the path, and just afterwards, large boulders line and define the track. Several access roads cut across the route, and these are usually unsigned.

5.7 km (3.5 mi) Arrive at the junction with the Lost Lake Trail, a 3 km (1.9 mi) dead-end side path, and the first major junction along this route. Continue straight, through a series of very steep hills and sharp curves, with wetlands and open water on both sides of the trail. After crossing another dirt road, the trail moves to the other side of Highway 44, at 6.6 km (4.1 mi), just at the intersection with the Moonlight Bay Road. (There is no crosswalk, and the speed limit on Highway 44 is 80 kph [50 mph], so please be cautious.)

The off-road trail continues for another 750 m/yd but ends at a business parking lot opposite Fire Road W7. For the next 600 m/yd, walk/cycle on the road, along the edge of Permiac Bay. At 8 km (5 mi), an off-road pathway resumes on the left side of the highway.

The longest and most extended climb of this route begins, as the trail works its way toward the community of West Hawk Lake. The lake is to the left, and several side roads connect to the many cottages along its shoreline. You might notice one or more granite benches alongside the trail in this section; these are in memoriam to various local nature enthusiasts.

9.7 km (6 mi) The trail crosses Highway 44 one final time. To the left, barely 200 m/yd away, is the Nite Hawk Café – a popular restaurant. However, at the junction on the opposite side of the road, turn right, and head away from the village. The climb continues for another 800 m/yd before reaching the very highest point on this route, where a welcome and extended downhill section begins.

About 200 m/yd later, the trail comes out to Highway 301, where there is a large parking area, then returns into the forest where it must negotiate its way around a large wetland and open ponds. Several times the path returns close to Highway 301, only to veer away briefly into the forest.

13.2 km (8.2 mi) Road and trail converge, crossing beneath the Trans-Canada Highway together. Signs advise particular caution by cyclists and pedestrians using this narrow passage. The route parallels the road for a further 150 m/yd, then turns left and into the forest, this time for a considerable distance.

The next 3.8 km (2.4 mi) were among my most enjoyable of this route. It is mostly forested – with ranks of tall pine – and almost entirely downhill. And except for crossing the asphalt Toniata Road, at 16 km (9.9 mi), there are almost no human structures visible. (Well, there is one: a TCT Discovery Panel.) The sylvan sojourn ends at 17.2 km (10.7 mi), when the trail reconnects with Highway 301. Just 350 m/yd later, Falcon Lake comes into view when the path crosses the entrance to the Faloma Beach Marina.

The trail experience changes radically from this point. Falcon Lake is lined with cottages, and innumerable access roads and driveways must be crossed. The pathway is often squeezed into a very slender space between the road and Falcon Lake. Even the Trans-Canada Highway curves toward the water, and sometimes lakeshore, cottages, Highway 301, and Highway 1 are all in sight from the path. The terrain also resumes climbing multiple small hills, where the sandy trail surface sometimes defeated my hybrid bike's attempt to ascend.

18.4 km (11.4 mi) The path reaches a peaceful lookout with an excellent view of Falcon Lake. There is a granite bench and a picnic table as well as three Discovery Panels on the bald eagle, lady's slipper, and white pine. This is a welcome respite from the challenging terrain.

The trail continues alongside the road, traversing hummocky ground and navigating over multiple driveways, and you will rarely be out of sight of the road. Finally, at 22.8 km (14.2 mi), the trail curves left, away from the road, and arrives at a large grass-covered playing field. About 500 m/yd further, passing picnic tables and other amenities, the path reaches a large parking area, where there is a water fountain and a trailhead pavilion.

23.4 km (14.5 mi) You arrive at the intersection of Falcon Boulevard and Park Road, where you continue straight, on the road surface; it is very well signed. For the next 600 m/yd, the route follows the road, passing restaurants, grocery stores, and all manner of services. TCT signs and blue diamond arrows mark the way. The community of Falcon Lake is busy but small: a resort centre.

Park Street ends at a tiny boat launch area. The path veers right, then crosses the extensive wetland aided – not entirely successfully – by a couple of bridges, to arrive at the Falcon Lake Marina after a soggy 500 m/yd. After steering through the parking lot, the trail heads through the tall grass to reach Ridge Road at 25 km (15.5 mi). Stay on the road for the next 900 m/yd, crossing Falcon Lake Dam and passing another picnic area, with outhouses, before re-entering the forest to the right.

The next section is wonderful. The track is wide and in excellent condition, and it winds sinuously through the trees. The forest is mostly aspen and permits good views. Although slightly hilly, the knolls only require a little effort to surmount and are fun to descend. There are multiple junctions and side trails to lakeside cottages, but the signage is clear. I found that this area flew past.

A small granite bench at 31.3 km (19.4 mi) overlooks a small wetland that is extremely busy with several species of waterfowl. Birdwatchers will appreciate this spot. The pleasant forest ramble continues for a further 2.1 km (1.3 mi), at which point the trail crosses Ridge Road and quickly descends to the edge of Falcon Lake. Following the lakeshore for a short distance, at 34 km (21.1 mi) a sturdy metal bridge spans a tiny brook, and the path moves away from the water.

What might be the most difficult hill on this route immediately begins, although it is only a 25 m (82 ft) climb over 350 m/yd. At the crest is a short footpath to a lookout of Falcon Lake: a granite bench topping a granite knoll. Eventually, this will be extended to connect to the Falcon Trails Resort, but when I travelled it, the path ended at the bench.

Return to the main trail and continue. It crosses Ridge Road one final time, less than 200 m/yd from the junction with the lookout footpath. Here is a trailhead parking area. After this, the route traces a twisting path over the rocky ridges. As it does, coniferous trees soon dominate, with the area more closely resembling a boreal-shield forest than did the aspen groves closer to the lake.

Western Painted Turtle

One of the most widespread freshwater turtles in Canada is the painted turtle, which can be found in every province except Newfoundland and Labrador. There are three distinct subspecies in Canada, the largest and most brightly coloured of which is the western (*Chrysemys picta bellii*), which ranges from Northern Ontario to British Columbia. Western painted turtles have olive-coloured shells on top, but the bottom is cream and red with bold patterns. Bold yellow stripes on the head and legs make this an easy species to identify.

D. Sharon Pruitt from Hill Air Force Base, Utah, USA

Although they spend most of their time in or close to bodies of water, during breeding season in May/June, females search for sandy or gravel soil to lay their eggs, and they often wander quite far from ponds and streams to find a location that suits them. They also will search for other ponds to colonize. During these months, it is not unusual for them to cross roads, so if you see a turtle-crossing sign while driving, slow down and keep an eye out turtles on the road. And if you want to move a turtle off a roadway, take it to the side it was already heading toward.

37.4 km (23.2 mi) The wide path ends abruptly, on the shore of High Lake, in a secluded bay called Manitoba Cove. Camping is permitted in this area. High Lake lies in both Ontario and Manitoba, and though not on the Path of the Paddle, it can be accessed by canoe from Kenora. Retrace your route to McGillivray Falls.

Further Information:
South Whiteshell Trail Association: www.swtatrails.com
Whiteshell Provincial Park: www.gov.mb.ca/sd/parks/popular_parks/eastern/
    whiteshell_info.html#05a

28. Pukaskwa National Park

25. Pigeon River Provincial Park

Sitting on the border between Minnesota and Ontario, Pigeon River Provincial Park is a natural historical museum. For more than 100 years, the canoe was the principal means of travel on the lakes and rivers of Canada, and the transport vehicle of the fur trade. Positioned at the head of Lake Superior, and providing the easiest route into the interior of Northwestern Ontario and Minnesota, Pigeon River became a major terminus until it became the political boundary for the new United States.

Today, most people visit to view the impressive 28 m (92 ft) waterfall that, like its grander cousin on the Niagara River, separates the two countries. No evidence remains of the earlier history except for the many interpretive plaques that attempt to provide visitors with an understanding of the heritage and importance of this place.

Pigeon River and the parks on both sides of the border make up an important location for the water route that connects The Great Trail between Thunder Bay and White Lake in Whiteshell Park in Manitoba. It is the longest, and most physically demanding, portage on that entire 1,200 km (745 mi) route.

25. Pigeon River Provincial Park

MAGNETIC TRUE

Contour Interval: 10M
1 KILOMETRE

PIGEON RIVER
PROVINCIAL PARK

593

61

Finger Point

14.0

Animikii Water Trail

6.4

Elevation

330

3.9

Pigeon River

25

190

Lake
Superior

CANADA
USA

Metres

2.3

0.0, 16.5

P ? 🚻 ♿

MINNESOTA

350
Metres
150

16.5

Kilometres   2   4   6   8   10   12   14   16

25. Pigeon River Provincial Park

Distance: 16.5 km (10.3 mi) — return
Ascent: 486 m (1,594 ft)
Descent: 486 m (1,594 ft)

Trail conditions: natural surface
Cellphone coverage: no
Hazards: cliffs, ticks, wildlife

Permitted Uses							
Walking	Biking	Horseback Riding	Inline Skating	ATV	Snowshoeing	Cross-country Skiing	Snowmobiling
✔	—	—	—	—	✔	—	—

Finding the trailhead: From the Highway 17/Highway 61 junction in Thunder Bay, drive south on Highway 61 for approximately 60 km (37.3 mi). The trail begins from the parking lot of the Ontario Travel Information Centre.

Trailhead: 48°00'17.6" N, 89°34'55.4" W (Start/Finish: Tourist Information Centre)

Observations: This route was a pleasant surprise. I was completely unaware of this park, or of its tall waterfall, before I visited. I also very much enjoyed the second section of the walk, onto Finger Point, with its views of Lake Superior and the many tiny Boundary Islands that dot the outflow of Pigeon River. With its large number of interpretive panels, I found this a pleasant change to the more remote and demanding treks elsewhere in Northern Ontario.

When I hiked this in 2016, park maps showed the Old Logging Road Trail in the park's interior, and I originally intended to make this route a loop by returning along it. However, that section was not maintained, resulting in a challenging time spent thrashing about on overgrown paths. Accordingly, I suggest walkers retrace their route from the Middle Falls parking area back to the start of the Finger Point Trail. However, if the Old Logging Road is cleared, it will be a much quicker and easier return option.

Route description: The footpath begins from the parking lot for the tourist information centre, which, when open, provides both washrooms and potable water. Excellent trailhead signage, including a trail system map, is located near the steps and ramp that descend from the parking lot to river level. At the base of these steps is a panel describing the Path of the Paddle, the water route that connects Thunder Bay to Manitoba.

The walk begins on the Boardwalk Trail, a short wheelchair-accessible path to Pigeon Bay. Although this leads to an observation deck overlooking the lake, which contains several interesting interpretive panels, turn left at the next junction, after only 75 m/yd on a slender, natural-surfaced footpath. There is a map at this junction.

The surrounding forest was quite lush when I was there in late summer. Although the route is quite close to Pigeon Bay, the water was almost never visible. And except for several short bridges spanning nearly dry brooks, there is little to see until the next junction 450 m/yd later, where there is another map.

Turn left, onto the High Falls Trail, which a bright blue sign states is 1.5 km (0.9 mi) long. The path initially looks about the same, a well-defined footpath snugly shrouded by trees, though the ground to the right is higher, while the land on the left is wet (and there are lots of mosquitoes!). After another 500 m/yd, the path emerges from its tree cover – briefly – to pass underneath Highway 61. Just before it does, another long boardwalk traverses a large soggy area.

On the far side of the road the trail veers right for a short distance, until it reaches another large map board. Turn left and follow what was clearly a forest road. This wide track has been surfaced with crushed stone, and it makes for an easy stroll through another thickly forested area.

A junction is reached after about 300 m/yd; both lead to the High Falls, but keep left. Soon after, some wet areas require boardwalks to cross, after which the trail returns to a footpath. At 1.7 km (1.1 mi), the path arrives at The Chimney Site, where an interpretive panel explains that the stone chimney rising nearby is all that remains of a hunting/fishing resort that was popular in the 1930s and '40s. A short side trail, to the left, in 50 m/yd leads to the banks of the Pigeon River and a Canadian Heritage Rivers plaque, which outlines this river's historical importance to the fur trade. By this point, cell reception will have disappeared.

Return to the main trail, which now parallels the shallow river upstream. The United States shore appears to be only a short wade away. However, even though the land at this spot is quite low, rocky cliffs soon appear ahead, and the trail quickly begins to ascend. As the grade steepens, a series of staircases provides assistance, and soon a protective fence lines the left, along the cliff edge. At 2.2 km (1.4 mi), the trail reaches a wooden, railed bridge named the Rock Sluice, which crosses a deep crevasse.

2.3 km (1.4 mi) On the far side of the Rock Sluice bridge, the path arrives at a large viewing area facing the 28 m (92 ft) High Falls. This is an excellent lookout, with superb views of both the cascade and the deep ravine it has created. Benches are available for those fatigued from the short but fairly strenuous climb, and there is one of several interesting examples of stylized metal artwork. Similar viewing platforms on the Minnesota side of the river, in Grand Portage State Park, are also likely occupied. High Falls is the tallest cataract in the state.

Return over the bridge and turn left. In 85 m/yd, this path ends at the river above the waterfall, where it is possible to scramble over the rocks right to the edge where the river plunges. The view upstream looks remarkably calm and ordinary.

The main trail turns inland just before this little viewing site. Almost immediately, forest once again envelops the trail, the thick vegetation rapidly deadening the crash of the cascading waters. The path soon resembles a forest road, fairly wide and making for easy walking.

At 2.7 km (1.7 mi), you reach the junction with the new path to Middle Falls, where a Trans Canada Trail – or possibly a Great Trail – marker indicates that you turn left. This slender footpath almost immediately begins to climb. There are few views during this dark forest ascent. After 700 m/yd, you might notice attractive flecks of pink and red granite occasionally peeking through the thin soil. This is a warning: the steepest climb of the hike is about to begin, more than 50 m (165 ft) in the next 300 m/yd.

As you near the top of this hill, you should take in the views back in the direction of Lake Superior and Pigeon River. The crest is reached at about 3.7 km (2.3 mi), where the path turns left and follows the ridgeline for slightly more than 100 m/yd. There are a few open areas looking east, with decent vistas because you are quite high and the path runs along the top of a cliff. There is cell reception once again, but check carefully as it will probably be from an American service provider.

3.9 km (2.4 mi) There is one final viewpoint, The Lookout, then the trail turns sharply right, back into the forest, and begins an almost equally steep descent. Stones intrude into the treadway, and they are often wet and slippery. For almost 900 m/yd the path works down and up the hillsides, until at 4.8 km (3 mi), it connects once again with the broad and shallow Pigeon River. No human structures are visible anywhere, and once again there is no cell reception.

Sadly, the path follows the water barely 150 m/yd before returning into thick forest, where it remains until it reaches a junction with the former Old Logging

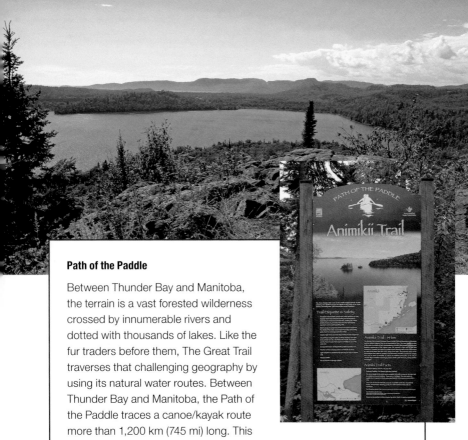

Path of the Paddle

Between Thunder Bay and Manitoba, the terrain is a vast forested wilderness crossed by innumerable rivers and dotted with thousands of lakes. Like the fur traders before them, The Great Trail traverses that challenging geography by using its natural water routes. Between Thunder Bay and Manitoba, the Path of the Paddle traces a canoe/kayak route more than 1,200 km (745 mi) long. This is further divided into six regional trails, most given Ojibwe names, honouring the First Nations Peoples who inhabited the region before the arrival of Europeans.

The trail section in Pigeon River Provincial Park links the Animikii (**Thunderbird**) Trail, which runs the 136 km (85 mi) between Fort William Historical Park on the Kaministiquia River and Grand Portage National Monument on Lake Superior in Minnesota, and the Omimi (Pigeon) Trail, which continues another 100 km (62 mi) to Quetico Provincial Park.

Road Trail 500 m/yd later. There is a sign that says it is 1.6 km (1 mi) back along the route to The Lookout.

Turn left, where there is a parking area, and follow the gravel road. Pigeon River is soon visible to the left, and Highway 593 is directly ahead. Just before reaching the highway, there is a shuttered park building, the former office for the now-closed campground, and a trail map located at a road junction; turn left and follow the former campground road. It is an easy walk on the wide, gravelled track, with the river to the left, the highway on the right, and visible ahead, Middle Falls.

6.4 km (4 mi) Arrive at the end of the trail, on the rocks of the modest – 6 m (20 ft) – Middle Falls. This is a pleasant location to have a snack and far less visited than High Falls. When you have finished exploring the rapids, retrace your route. Do not attempt the Old Logging Road Trail, which is overgrown. Continue as far as the junction of High Falls and Finger Point Trail.

At this junction, it is only 500 m/yd back to the trailhead; to this point you have walked about 12 km (7.5 mi). Should you have the energy, continue onto the Finger Point Trail for the best views of Lake Superior and the islands. There is a map at the junction, and a separate sign states the lookout is only 2 km (1.2 mi).

Almost from the beginning, many roots and rocks intrude into the pathway. This route appears far less well travelled than the High Falls Trail. Within 150 m/yd, there are views to the right into Pigeon Bay. Soon the path is almost touching the water, with wonderful views across the small cove.

However, the surface is rocky, with higher ground to the left. The trail undulates up and down small knolls, particularly at 600 m/yd, when it turns away from the water and makes a short, steep ascent. For the next 500 m/yd, it is mostly downhill, with occasional views of the water. Care is required to pick your way over the rocky ground.

The path descends once again to lake level, beside a tiny sheltered cove. Then it continues into a thickly forested area, and 500 m/yd of easy walking while gently climbing. At 1.6 km (1 mi) from the High Falls Trail junction, the climb steepens, delivering you, in 200 m/yd, to a hilltop with superb views back toward Pigeon River.

14 km (8.7 mi) The trail continues, dropping back downhill about 10 m (33 ft) in only 30 m (99 ft) before making the final 25 m (82 ft) ascent to the Finger Point Lookout, where there is a bench – in the shape of Lake Superior – artwork, and a 360° view. There is even Canadian cell reception here.

To complete this hike, walk the 2 km (1.2 mi) back to the High Falls Trail junction, then turn left and complete the 500 m/yd to the trailhead, for a total trek of approximately 16.5 km (10.3 mi).

Further Information:

Path of the Paddle Association: www.pathofthepaddleassociation.com
Pigeon River Provincial Park: www.ontarioparks.com/park/pigeonriver

26. Sleeping Giant Provincial Park

The Sleeping Giant is one of Lake Superior's geological highlights, a distinctive landform that is both massive in size and instantly recognizable when viewed across the wide waters of Thunder Bay. It sits entirely protected in the large — 24,400 ha (60,292 ac) — provincial park of the same name, which was one of the first created in Ontario, in 1944.

Clearly, the highlights for most at Sleeping Giant Park are the trails that climb the Head, Chest, and Knees of the Giant, delivering hikers to majestic views from the top of the highest cliffs in Ontario. The Great Trail route, however, circles the escarpment, remaining almost entirely at its base. Yet this is not a lesser option, as the views of the fortress-like cliffs from the shoreline of Thunder Bay and Lehtinens Bay are as unforgettable as those from the summit.

The Kabeyun Trail, the name of the route around the Giant, is also a path that is less travelled by hikers, particularly so once past its junctions with the Talus Lake Trail. As a result, it retains a remote feel that is sometimes missing from the trails to the lookouts, and campsites along the Kabeyun Trail are more often available than those in the park's interior.

This is the one of the few of the sixty routes profiled in both volumes of *The Best of The Great Trail* where it was possible to create a loop rather than a linear trek. That is in part because of the landscape, where the trail rings the tip of the Sibley Peninsula, but also because of the extensive trail network inside the provincial park. The final 7.1 km (4.4 mi), mostly along the Sawyer Bay Trail, are not part of The Great Trail, but using it enables a return to the starting trailhead.

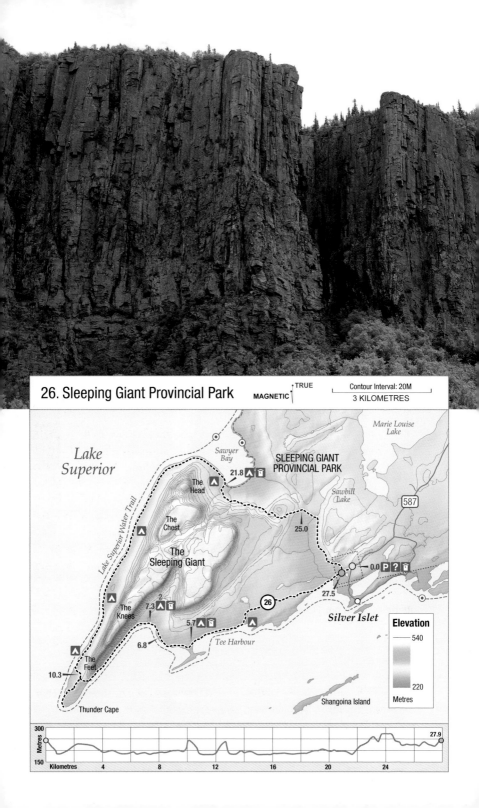

26. Sleeping Giant Provincial Park

MAGNETIC | TRUE

Contour Interval: 20M
3 KILOMETRES

Lake Superior

Marie Louise Lake

Sawyer Bay

SLEEPING GIANT PROVINCIAL PARK

21.8

The Head

Lake Superior Water Trail

The Chest

The Sleeping Giant

Sawbill Lake

587

25.0

0.0 P ?

27.5

The Knees

7.3

2

5.7

6.8

Tee Harbour

26

27.5

Silver Islet

The Feet

10.3

Thunder Cape

Shangoina Island

Elevation

540

220

Metres

300
Metres
150

Kilometres 4 8 12 16 20 24

27.9

26. Sleeping Giant Provincial Park

Distance: 27.9 km (17.3 mi), loop
Ascent: 584 m (1,916 ft)
Descent: 584 m (1,916 ft)

Trail conditions: crushed stone, natural surface
Cellphone coverage: partial
Hazards: isolated, wildlife

Permitted Uses							
Walking	Biking	Horseback Riding	Inline Skating	ATV	Snowshoeing	Cross-country Skiing	Snowmobiling
✔	✔*	—	—	—	✔	✔*	—

Finding the trailhead: Turn off Highway 17 onto Highway 587 (Pass Lake Road) and drive 36.5 km (22.7 mi) to the large provincial park parking lot.

Trailhead: 48°20'24.4" N, 88°49'20.7" W (Start/Finish: Kabeyun South Trailhead)

Observations: This is a fantastic hike, even though much of it is along what once were former logging roads. True, this route does not climb to the top of the Giant, but it works around the base of its towering cliffs and provides exceptional views of both the escarpment and Lake Superior. Most of the trail is fairly easy to hike, but there is one short section where you must hop from one massive boulder to another, and it is as challenging as almost any trail I have encountered.

This is a long hike for one day, and with the many campsites available, it is worthwhile turning it into a two-day trek. Should you have no time constraints, consider undertaking the roughly 40 km (25 mi) trek between the Kabeyun South and North Trailheads, and return. That will require four or five days, but it will be time well spent.

Route description: The Kabeyun South Trailhead parking lot is huge, the start location for all the trails that climb or circle the Sleeping Giant. A large pavilion displays a map of the entire park, along with some regulatory information (including fees). Several picnic tables sit nearby, as well as garbage cans and outhouses.

The path appears to be a continuation of the road, though somewhat rougher as it has not been maintained for vehicle use. ATV tracks are evident, but these are of park service vehicles only. The surrounding forest is quite thick at first, and the path is surprisingly rough with many loose stones. It also descends quite rapidly, losing nearly 61 m (200 ft) of elevation in the first 800 m/yd.

At 400 m/yd, you reach the intersection with the Sawyer Bay Trail, on which you will return. On the post there, you will see for the first time the park's unique signage, contributed by a "Friends of" organization: pink rect-

angles with black or white symbols and text. You continue straight, in the direction of Tee Harbour and the Sea Lion. After another 400 m/yd, the trail reaches the lakeshore at Perry Bay and the junction with the 500 m/yd side trail to the Sea Lion. This picturesque rock formation, a stone arch jutting into Lake Superior, is worth the short diversion – though perhaps not if you are attempting this full walk in one day.

Views of the water and the many nearby islands are fleeting. Within 50 m/yd, the trail bridges a small creek and a ridge rises up on the left. To the right is a fairly large boggy area, and I found that the large number of hungry mosquitoes discouraged loitering. (In fact, I broke into a jog to escape them.)

Until the bridge crossing the outflow from Shuniah Lake, at 3.6 km (2.2 mi), this becomes a peaceful sylvan stroll, with no views except the vegetation and an occasional bird or small mammal. However, I was pleased to spot an indigo bunting here, the only time I have ever seen this species. Just 400 m/yd later, the trail reaches the first campsite on the shore of Tee Harbour, where there is an outhouse. Essentially, the walk from Perry Bay to here was all uphill for the first half, all downhill for the remainder.

5.7 km (3.5 mi) After an extended section that is often in sight of the water, though also through an extremely wet and messy length, the trail arrives at the Tee Harbour camping area. There is another signpost here festooned with pink distance markers. A cursory inspection quickly reveals that most vary from both the information found on the park map and what I recorded. In my books, I note what I observe when I travel the route, even when it is different from other published sources. As a general safety rule, always be prepared for the longest distance.

The Tee Harbour campsites are left, along a short side trail, where there is a lovely beach for those who are tempted by the lake. The main trail continues straight with fewer rocks and wet areas, and, with a break in the vegetation, the Sleeping Giant is visible directly ahead, an imposing wall of rock.

6.8 km (4.2 mi) Arrive at the junction with the Talus Lake Trail, a challenging but much shorter route to Sawyer Bay and one that provides access to the top of the Giant. Taking it is the only opportunity to choose a shorter trek than the entire 27.9 km (17.3 mi) loop.

However, it is not the path of The Great Trail, which continues straight. About 500 m/yd further, after it crosses a lively brook on an unrailed bridge, the trail reaches Lehtinens Bay and its stony beach. Several campsites are situated in this sheltered cove. Directly ahead, the Knees of the Giant appear to be an impenetrable high-cliff barrier.

By 7.8 km (4.8 mi), the trail has curved left and now parallels The Knees, towering above with large talus deposits extending almost into the water. Within another 200 m/yd, the former road has narrowed into a slender footpath congested by tree roots and large rocks. The path becomes increasingly more difficult until by 8.5 km (5.3) it is a wall of massive boulders. For the next 300 m/yd, you do not hike, you rock hop, picking your way across a scree landscape.

Fortunately, by 9 km (5.6 mi) the trail has returned to something more normal: a rocky footpath, but with no scrambling required. A comparatively easy stroll remains, quite close to the water, until 10 km (6.2 mi), when the trail reaches the Feet of the Giant. Here the path turns sharply right and begins to climb.

10.3 km (6.4 mi) After quite a steep – but mercifully short – climb, and equally quick descent, the path arrives at a signed junction. Just before reaching it, once over the crest of the Feet, you will have cellphone reception for the first time in this hike. Turn left, onto the side trail to Thunder Cape.

This is less well used than the main trail, so vegetation might obscure the track somewhat in the summer. It continues to drop gently downhill, until it reaches the water on the western side of the peninsula. After another few hundred metres/yards, it ends among the buildings and birdcages of the Thunder Cape Bird Observatory, perched on the very tip of the Sibley Peninsula. On clear days you can see the city of Thunder Bay to the west and Isle Royale National Park in the United States to the south.

Retrace the 1.2 km (0.7 mi) back to the junction with the main trail, and turn left. You have now travelled 12.6 km (7.8 mi). The path quickly descends to reach lake level in 400 m/yd, where it turns right and parallels the shoreline.

Thunder Cape Bird Observatory

Established in 1992 to monitor migratory bird populations in Northern Ontario, the Thunder Cape station is located where a lighthouse once guided ships safely around the Sibley Peninsula. In spring and fall, groups of students and volunteers observe the annual migrations while capturing and banding a variety of species.

Visitors are welcome. Camping is available on site and all guests are provided with tours of the facility. However, as the only entry is either by boat or the long hike from the Kabeyun South Trailhead, the observatory is fairly inaccessible.

To the left is Thunder Bay, city and body of water; to the right, visible only through gaps in the leaves, the highest cliffs in Ontario form an impressive rampart.

The pathway is mostly level and provides quite easy walking, with surprisingly few rocks. Campsites are common along this shoreline, and because they are moved every few years, they may not be located where they appear on the park map. My only disappointment was that there were so few good views of the cliffs. Perhaps late fall or early spring is the best time to hike this trail.

Fortunately, at about 15 km (9.3 mi), there is one open area near the base of the Chimney, a particularly scenic lookout at the end of The Top of the Giant Trail. The trail also touches upon a nice gravel beach with fantastic views of the cliff wall to the south, an excellent site to enjoy lunch.

From here until the junction with the Head Trail, at 21.3 km (13.2 mi), the walk remains the same. To the left, except for occasional stretches when the path briefly moves slightly inland, are views of Thunder Bay (the body of water). On the right is thick vegetation, with the cliff face of the Chest of the Sleeping Giant visible only occasionally. In the final kilometre, the trail bends right, following the shoreline as it curves into Sawyer Bay, a popular anchorage site for sailors. Just before reaching the junction with the Head Trail, cell reception will disappear.

The Head Trail is only 1 km (0.6 mi) long, but it is rated as extreme, should you consider adding that to your trek. From this junction, the Kabeyun Trail becomes wide enough for two to walk side by side and makes for an easy stroll to the next junction.

♀ 21.8 km (13.5 mi) The trail arrives at the junction with the Talus Lake Trail. Turn right to turn this into a loop walk. You are officially leaving The Great Trail, which continues straight to the Kabeyun North Trailhead, about 17 km (10.6 mi) further – and far from your starting point.

By now, the pathway is unmistakeably a former roadway, so it is fairly easy rambling. Unfortunately, the most challenging climb of the entire hike begins, with 68 m (223 ft) of elevation gain in the next 1.2 km (0.7 mi). At the next junction, after only 200 m/yd on the Talus Lake Trail, turn left onto the Sawyer Bay Trail. Continue your climb.

For the remainder of the hike, this is a walk mostly shrouded by adjacent vegetation. Although a former logging road, the track is quite windy, with many climbs and descents – fun when riding a bike. It works around the side of Thunder Mountain, but the summit can only rarely be seen, to the right. Almost the only view available on this entire section is of tiny Shale Lake, from about 23.8 km (14.8 mi).

♀ 25 km (15.5 mi) The junction with the Sawbill Lake Trail arrives suddenly. Be sure to take the fork to the right, otherwise you will be making a long detour. Your trail drops down to cross Sawbill Creek 500 m/yd later, then follows a roller coaster route over numerous small knolls before its final descent to the junction with the Kabeyun Trail.

♀ 27.5 km (17.1 mi). Turn left. After a final 400 m/yd trek uphill, the trail returns to the Kabeyun South parking area.

Further Information:
Explore Northwest Ontario: http://visitnorthwestontario.com
Sleeping Giant Provincial Park: www.ontarioparks.com/park/sleepinggiant
Thunder Bay Field Naturalists: www.tbfn.net

The Sleeping Giant

This rock formation dominates the eastern horizon in Thunder Bay, a massive, recumbent, apparently human form, head and torso distinct, arms folded over its gigantic chest. No imagination is required to see a giant sleeping in the hills across the bay. A First Nations Oral Tradition claims that it is Nanabijou, the Ojibwe Spirit of the Deep Sea Water, turned to stone.

Geologists assert that it is an igneous rock tableland that erosion has moulded into its present shape, its 240 m (787 ft) cliffs the highest in Ontario. This distinctive profile of the Sleeping Giant, jutting into Lake Superior, is the southernmost tip of the 52 km (32.3 mi) long Sibley Peninsula, which covers an area of 243.9 km^2 (94.2 mi^2). The Sleeping Giant was voted #1 in the Seven Wonders of Canada contest by CBC viewers/listeners in 2007.

27. Mount Gwynne

Between the communities of Rossport and Terrace Bay, the Casque Isles Trail traverses the rugged north shore of Lake Superior for 53 km (32.9 mi). Originally developed in 1975-76, this challenging footpath, maintained by volunteers, picks its way over a truly wilderness landscape characterized by forbidding rock hills, dense boreal forest, and the constant overshadowing presence of one of the world's largest fresh-water lakes. Mount Gwynne is the highest point on the Casque Isles Trail, which is affiliated with the Voyageur Trail, the National Hiking Trail, and The Great Trail, and provides commanding views in every direction from its summit.

The Casque Isles Trail features several difficult sections, and although the route from Schreiber Beach to Worthington Bay is not its most challenging, it is definitely not easy. The first 5 km (3.1 mi) is essentially all uphill to the summit. However, most of this elevation – 230+ m/yd (755+ ft) – is lost in the final 2 km (1.2 mi) to Worthington Bay, some of it on rocky, uneven ground. More than half the effort of this hike is expended just in traversing this demanding section, so unless you want a tough grunt down and up the hillside, limit your hike from Schreiber Beach to Mount Gwynne's summit.

27. Mount Gwynne

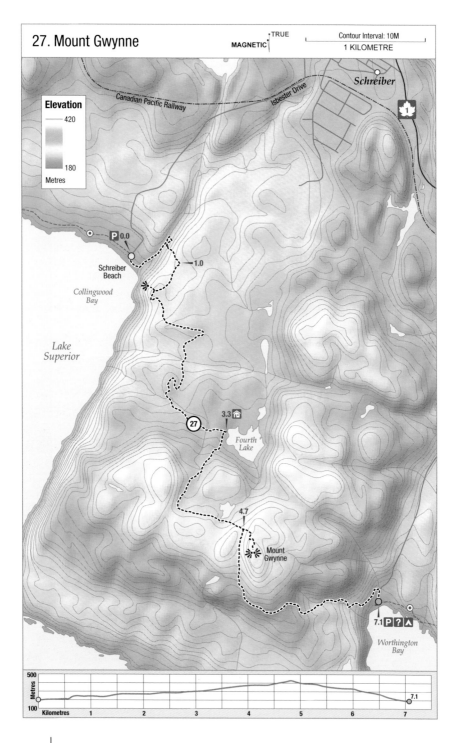

MAGNETIC TRUE

Contour Interval: 10M
1 KILOMETRE

Elevation

420

180

Metres

Schreiber

Canadian Pacific Railway Isbester Drive

P 0.0

1.0

Schreiber
Beach

*Collingwood
Bay*

*Lake
Superior*

27 3.3

*Fourth
Lake*

4.7

Mount
Gwynne

7.1 P ? ▲

*Worthington
Bay*

500
Metres
100 Kilometres 1 2 3 4 5 6 7 7.1

27. Mount Gwynne

Distance: 7.2 km (4.5 mi), one way
Ascent: 288 m (945 ft)
Descent: 282 m (925 ft)

Trail conditions: natural surface
Cellphone coverage: yes
Hazards: cliffs, isolated, rugged terrain, wildlife

Permitted Uses							
Walking	Biking	Horseback Riding	Inline Skating	ATV	Snowshoeing	Cross-country Skiing	Snowmobiling
✔	—	—	—	—	✔	—	—

Finding the trailhead: From Highway 17, take Winnipeg Street and follow the signs to Schreiber Beach, about 3.2 km (2 mi).

Trailhead: 48°47'37.0" N, 87°17'23.2" W (Start: Schreiber Beach)
48°46'09.2" N, 87°15'43.0" W (Finish: Worthington Bay)

Observations: This is a beautiful walk, without a single section that I did not enjoy. Schreiber Beach was lovely, and I took a quick, invigorating dip there. The terrain is rough but exceptional, and the views from the top of Mount Gwynne are vast and picturesque. Evidence of human habitation is minimal in this sparsely populated corner of Ontario, so when there is a panorama, it is of mostly undisturbed forest or the vast expanse of Lake Superior.

In a strange twist of fate, when I hiked toward Worthington Bay, the trail was so overgrown that I worried that I might not be able to use it. Small spruce had grown up thickly and were now head high, making it sometimes difficult to ensure that I was still on the pathway. It seemed as if the trail had been abandoned, or at least rarely used. However, on my return I encountered a crew of workers from the trail association, who were clearing a distinct route and were racing through the vegetation. Ironically, my progress was slowed significantly by the many felled trees they had not yet cleared but that now barricaded the trail for nearly 2 km (1.2 mi).

Route description: The path begins at the beach, a short distance from the parking lot. A large sign prominently marks the trailhead, which is Access Point #5, and 27 km (16.8 km) from the Casque Isles Trail's beginning in Rossport. Sadly, there is no map of the route. Benches are available, shaded beneath some taller white birch, close to the water's edge.

Turn left and shuffle through the sand until it ends at a creek mouth. On the left, a Voyageur Trail marker – yellow diamond with blue text and arrow – directs you onto a narrow footpath cut through the vegetation. Another diamond-shaped maker, the blue with white text of the Casque Isles Hiking Club, indicates that Worthington Bay is 6 km (3.7 mi) distant.

The path roughly parallels Cook Brook and is fairly easy walking, though it begins to climb immediately. On the opposite bank, a vertical rock face soon dominates as the path continues into a narrow gorge. At 500 m/yd, the spindly looking Tom McGrath suspension bridge – capacity one person, warns a notice – crosses Cook Brook, and the hike begins in earnest. For the next 200 m/yd, the trail climbs a slender cleft in the rock face, scrambling over rocks on a thin path hacked into the hillside. All four limbs will be required to scramble up this section.

📍 **1 km (0.6 mi)** Arrive at the junction with a side trail to Access Point #6, at 28 km (17.4 mi), which is 1.5 km (0.9 mi) at the end of Winnipeg Street in Schreiber. One tree is decorated with at least five signs, the most important of which (probably) indicates that 3 km (1.9 mi) remain to the Mount Gwynne junction. Continue straight, to the right of the signs, and within another 150 m/yd the trail climbs out of the trees onto an area of bare rock and pine. To the right is a picnic table, situated to provide a view of Collingwood Bay and where you started at Schreiber Beach.

For a short distance the route continues along this hilltop; watch for directional arrows painted on the bare rock. However, at 1.3 km (0.8 mi), the path makes a sharp cut left and is swallowed up again by the forest. Thick vegetation enfolds the trail, which is a slender footpath. Fortunately, route markers are rarely more than 200 m/yd apart, and each kilometre is indicated with a more sophisticated sign.

Generally the walking is dry, with only occasional small wet areas. At 2.2 km (1.4 mi), a tiny brook must be crossed on a simple log bridge. In summer, it might be barely noticeable. Only about 200 m/yd after this, the trail curves sharply right to climb out onto an area of bare rock where there is a bit of a view of Lake Superior. It does not linger, quickly turning left and back amongst the trees. Not too much later, the km 30 marker is found affixed to a stump, almost at ground level.

📍 **3.3 km (2.1 mi)** After working through some alder thickets, and crossing another tiny watercourse, the trail arrives at Fourth Lake, an excellent picnic and swimming location. The main trail swings right, passing a camping shelter – roofless and in disrepair when I visited – and then resumes climbing, now

more steeply. It was at this point that I met the crew clearing the trail, and the difference in experience was remarkable thanks to their efforts, with the path being wide and unmistakeable.

About 450 m/yd from Fourth Lake is the wettest section of this route, when the path skirts the edge of a soggy meadow for 50 m/yd. The trail continues straight, more or less, for another 350 m/yd until it reaches the junction to the Abyond Lookout. When I hiked this, the signage was illegible and the side trail had not been cleared, so I chickened out and did not explore it. I have heard that I missed a highlight of this hike, so if conditions look favourable when you are here, do it.

I turned 90° left, following the main trail. Soft, wet ground continues for another few hundred metres/yards in a rare level section, then the climb resumes.

♀4.7 km (2.9 mi) You reach the junction with the side trail to the Mount Gwynne summit after a short, sharp descent into a small depression. At this intersection sits a picnic table, and another sign-decorated tree, which also hosts the Mount Gwynne sign-in box.

The final scramble to the summit is 250 m/yd of continuous climb, although the sign says it is 300 m/yd. It is worthwhile, for from it there is a vast 360° view, both far out onto Lake Superior and deep into the forested interior. The town of

Schreiber is visible, and the rugged lakeshore stretches off into the misty distance in both directions.

At the top sits a small weather station, and bolted to one nearby rock is a bronze plaque dedicated to Tom McGrath, founder of the Casque Isles Trail. The view is magnificent, and even on a scorching summer day a refreshing breeze made a rest break here even more appealing.

Anyone who returns from here to Schreiber Beach will have completed a 10 km (6.2 mi) hike, longer than that if they include the side trail to the Abyond Lookout. However, for those who wish to more than double their exercise, I recommend continuing to Worthington Bay. To do so, turn left once back down to the junction and picnic table at 31.5 km (19.6 mi).

Almost immediately the treadway becomes more difficult as the path threads a narrow saddle between adjacent hills. Although nearly level, boulders litter the route; they are slippery in the summer humidity, and care must be taken to work your way among them. Shortly after reaching the km 32 marker, the descent quickly becomes fairly steep.

Fortunately, this challenging section does not last long, as the footpath reaches, then follows, an old road. After this, even though the descent is rapid, walking is quite manageable. The slope on the right, occasionally visible through the vegetation, is often nearly vertical.

Except for the sense of dread inspired by the thought of the return climb, the trail is uneventful until it reaches a fork at 6.5 km (4 mi), or 1.4 km (0.9 mi) from the Mount Gwynne junction. Keep left; it is well marked. This road, now surfaced in gravel and wider, continues to drop. Watch for a large cliff on the left and a deep drop on the right. For the first time in this hike, cell reception disappears, for the final 500 m/yd.

9 7.1 km (4.4 mi) The trail reaches another large trailhead sign, Access #7, marked as 34 km (21.1 mi). This is the official end of the Mount Gwynne segment, with the next 10 km (6.2 mi) named – intriguingly – the Death Valley section. There is a picnic table here, and camping is permitted. However, to access the stony beach, another 100 m/yd of walking is required.

From here, retrace your route back to Schreiber Beach. Subtracting the 500 m/yd side trail to the summit of Mount Gwynne, your return walk will be 6.7 km (4.2 mi).

Further Information:
Township of Schreiber (Maps): www.schreiber.ca/visiting/tourism-maps
Voyageur Trail Association (Casque Isles): www.voyageurtrail.ca/
    trailscasqueisles.html

Voyageur Trail Association

In the 1970s, Ontario experienced its greatest boom of trail building for hikers prior to the inception of the Trans Canada Trail. Many of the province's long-distance walking routes, such as the Oak Ridges, the Ganaraska, the Rideau, the Grand Valley, and the Avon, were largely developed during that decade.

So too was the Voyageur Trail, planning for which began in 1973. Originally, it was hoped that an unbroken footpath could be constructed along the entire shoreline of Lake Superior, connecting to and extending the Bruce Trail, by water, between Tobermory and Manitoulin Island.

Largely built and maintained by volunteers, the Voyageur Trail has never achieved its goal of a continuous trail. However, significant sections have been built, including the Casque Isles Trail, and many of these have become part of The Great Trail.

28. Pukaskwa National Park

This 1,878 km² (725 mi²) carpet of boreal forest, edged by a bleak, rocky shoreline occasionally punctuated by attractive sandy beaches, sits on the rim of Lake Superior, the largest freshwater body of water in the world. Pukaskwa is Ontario's only wilderness national park and is the largest in the province.

The Coastal Trail of Pukaskwa follows the wild shore of a vast inland sea, with deadly cold water and unpredictable weather. The path begins from the Visitor Centre and ends more than 60 km (37 mi) later at the North Swallow River — a location even more remote than the trailhead. Hikers must either retrace their route on foot or arrange for a water shuttle to collect them.

Designated in 1978, Pukaskwa was established to represent the Central Boreal Uplands natural region of Canada. In a transition zone between the northern boreal forest and the Great Lakes/St. Lawrence Lowlands, the park's exposed bedrock shoreline is also suitable habitat for dozens of arctic-alpine plant species. Pukaskwa National Park protects a portion of the longest stretch of undeveloped shoreline anywhere within the Great Lakes.

Each night's campsites must be reserved before departure. Park staff, at the pre-hike briefing, stated that the Coastal Trail is considered one of the three most challenging in Parks Canada's system. The route I selected varies slightly from that recommended by Parks Canada; the choice, as always, belongs to each hiker.

Those wishing to sample the rugged terrain, but wanting something less aggressive than the entire Coastal Trail, should consider a day trip to the White River Suspension Bridge, about 18 km (11.2 mi) return.

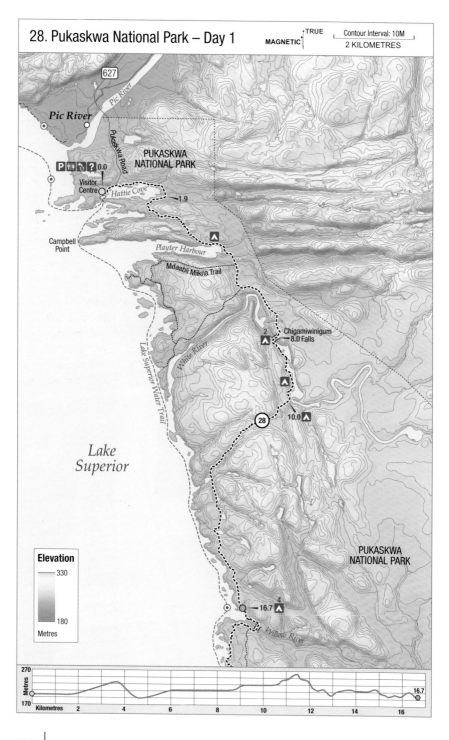

28. Pukaskwa National Park – Day 1

MAGNETIC | TRUE

Contour Interval: 10M
2 KILOMETRES

627

Pic River

Pic River

PUKASKWA
NATIONAL PARK

Pukaskwa Road

P 🚻 🏕 ❓ 0.0

Visitor Centre

Hattie Cove — 1.9

Campbell Point

Playter Harbour

Mdaabii Miikna Trail

White River

Lake Superior Water Trail

Chigamiwinigum
2 — 8.0 Falls

28   10.0

Lake
Superior

PUKASKWA
NATIONAL PARK

Elevation
— 330

180
Metres

4
16.7

Willow River

270
Metres
170
Kilometres   2   4   6   8   10   12   14   16   16.7

28. Pukaskwa National Park

Distance: 63.5 km (39.5 mi), one way
Ascent: 1,449 m (4,754 ft)
Descent: 1,465 m (4,806 ft)

Trail conditions: natural surface
Cellphone coverage: none
Hazards: cliffs, coastal weather, isolated area, rugged terrain, wildlife

				Permitted Uses			
Walking	Biking	Horseback Riding	Inline Skating	ATV	Snowshoeing	Cross-country Skiing	Snowmobiling
✔	—	—	—	—	✔	—	—

Finding the trailhead: Pukaskwa National Park is located on the shores of Lake Superior, roughly halfway between Thunder Bay and Sault Ste. Marie. The nearest community is Marathon, about 26 km (16.2 mi) to the northwest. There is only one access road to the park: from Highway 17, turn onto Highway 627. After 12.2 km (7.6 mi), it becomes the Pukaskwa Road when it crosses the Pic River. Continue for another 2.3 km (1.4 mi), turning left toward the Visitor Centre; the parking lot is 200 m/yd further along.

Trailhead: 48°35'27.1" N, 86°17'24.4" W (Start: Visitor Centre)
48°12'43.5" N, 86°06'37.1" W (Finish: North Swallow River)

Observations: This is a tough multi-day hike, but it is unbelievably rewarding. Somewhere in the middle of day 4 I turned to my hiking companion and said, "I want to meet whoever designed this route. I want to congratulate them on selecting a path that works its way from the water level to the tops of some of the highest granite hills, then back down again, over and over. I want to shake their hand, then I want to kick them in the n**s!"

As much of this route crosses granite ridges, when the weather is dry you should be able to make good progress. However, when wet these rocks are extremely treacherous, and 1 km (0.6 mi) an hour can be a good pace. In addition, if the weather is bad, the boat shuttle cannot make the trip to pick you up. (We had intended to hike this in the reverse direction, but rough weather prevented the boat from sailing for several days – so we started from the Visitor Centre instead.)

Carrying enough food for an extra 1-2 days is strongly advised. If you do this hike, I suspect that you will agree.

Route description

Day 1: Visitor Centre to Willow River
Distance: 16.7 km (10.4 mi), one way
Ascent: 220 m (722 ft)
Descent: 220 m (722 ft)

The path begins near the park's Visitor Centre, in the same parking lot. Washrooms, drinking water, and information kiosks are all available, as well as a replica Anishinaabe camp. The narrow footpath is quickly swallowed by the forest, as it works its way around Hattie Cove. Within 500 m/yd, the first climb up a granite ridge begins, though it's very gentle by later standards. It provides lovely views of the cove.

This is an easy walk, with extensive boardwalks across wet areas. At 1.5 km (0.9 mi), a sturdy bridge spans a small brook, and soon afterwards a long floating boardwalk guides you over the drenched meadow at the end of Hattie Cove. Expect several spots to be submerged.

📍**1.9 km (1.2 mi)** The boardwalk ends at the base of a granite knoll, and immediately the trail becomes a little more challenging. Fortunately, there is only minor climbing required, but there are often large rocks in the path, and their moss and lichen-covered surfaces are slippery. Frequently, the trail passes through a cleft in the granite, requiring careful foot placement on the uneven, broken rock.

The trail works around this first knoll, heading through a ravine before reaching its high point at 3.8 km (2.4 mi). After this, it quickly sheds the slowly gained 40 m (131 ft) as it drops to Playter Harbour 600 m/yd later. At 4.5 km (2.8 mi), the path passes a backcountry campsite with a wonderful view of the slender inlet.

More wet areas follow, spanned by puncheons (narrow plank boardwalks), and when the trail curves right, at 5 km (3.1 mi), a bridge crosses another small creek and the path moves away from Playter Harbour. For the next few hundred metres/yards, there are long stretches of puncheons and several minor bridges. The trail climbs slightly, but what follows is one of the easiest stretches of the Coastal Trail as the path meanders through the thick softwood forest – interrupted only by junctions, on the right, to the Mdaabii Miikna Loop Trail, at 6 km (3.7 mi) and 700 m/yd later.

The ribbon of brown worn into the moss ground cover occasionally crosses tiny bridges traversing mostly dry gullies. By 6.1 km (3.8 mi), the route is nearly level and remains so until 7.5 km (4.7 mi) when it descends and then climbs a deep gully. Sounds of rushing water will soon be heard in the silent woods, and 300 m/yd later the trail turns sharply right.

📍 **8 km (5 mi)** Emerging from the trees, the trail arrives at one of its most dramatic sights: the White River Suspension Bridge. Swaying 23 m (75 ft) above a deep vertical canyon and the raging Chigamiwinigum Falls, this steel footbridge is the only route to the remainder of the park. Beneath it, and visible under your feet, the White River roils through the narrow passage.

Once across, the path turns left and connects to the canoe portage route. Continue straight/left as the path descends to river level. There is a lovely spot for the canoe launch; the river is wide above Chigamiwinigum Falls, almost creating a small lake. The Coastal Trail continues to follow White River upstream for the next 2 km (1.2 mi), working up and down the rugged slope as required. There is even a wooden staircase, at about 8.8 km (5.5 mi).

There are several delightful viewpoints of the river along the way, or detours onto rocky ledges bordering lively cataracts. At 9.7 km (6 mi), there is a wilderness campsite (HF1), with an outhouse, within sight of the largest cascade since the suspension bridge: Hook Falls. There will be two more campsites closer to the waterfall.

📍 **10 km (6.2 mi)** The trail arrives at a junction. To the left is a path to the rocky riverbank above Hook Falls; it is quite scenic and worth the short detour. The main trail turns right and heads away from the river. The next 1 km (0.6 mi) is quite easy, a distinct track through thick forest and almost no rock. After that, the trail climbs the ridge crowding on the right, moving into the open on stretches of bare rock. The hardwoods disappear, replaced by conifers and many jack pines clinging to the thin acidic soil. Small cairns of rock indicate the route as it crosses long rock ridges.

At about 11.5 km (7.1 mi), the trail reaches its highest point of the day, after which it begins to descend into a shallow gully between the granite ridges. Small bogs and ponds are visible to the left, occupying the lowest ground.

Somewhere on this ridge, you will get the first glimpses of Lake Superior since Playter Harbour.

The trail gradually descends to the bottom of the ravine, then follows it toward the lake. At about 12.8 km (8 mi), it crosses the brook and gradually curves left. It reaches its lowest point, 60 m (197 ft) below the ridge, when it crosses another brook feeding into a small pond to the right 200 m/yd later.

The route follows this ravine passing more bogs and ponds, which are to the left. At 14.6 km (9.1 mi), the trail leaves the ponds behind, ascending a low hill for 300 m/yd before descending while curving left. Unless it is an exceptionally calm day, you will begin hearing waves as you go down.

The remaining distance to Willow River might be somewhat frustrating. For most of it, the noise of waves will be quite loud, but the thick vegetation bordering the trail permits only occasional peeks of the water, even at 15.5 km (9.6 mi) when it is barely 50 m/yd away. In addition, the path is also probably its roughest thus far, with the treadway frequently strewn with round, slippery rocks, particularly at about 16.4 km (10.2 mi).

However, you will probably also be buoyed by the knowledge that you are quite close to the end of the day's hike.

16.7 km (10.4 mi) The path arrives at the mouth of Willow River, a sandy beach littered with piles of logs. End your hike here. There are four campsites available — all have their own outhouse and bear-proof food locker, as do all park campsites — three in the trees to the left, and one (my favourite) to the right on a rocky hillock.

Day 2: Willow River to Oiseau Bay
Distance: 18.4 km (11.4 mi), one way
Ascent: 319 m (1,047 ft)
Descent: 337 m (1,106 ft)

From the start of the beach, pick your way carefully over the many felled trees that have washed ashore. Maybe you will find that someone has used this detritus to create some interesting sculpture, as I did when I was there.

After 300 m/yd, at the end of the beach, the path turns left and heads upstream 400 m/yd to the suspension bridge spanning the Willow River. This rather grand 75 m/yd steel structure looks somewhat out of place in this remote setting. However, it is preferable to swimming the broad stream — and it looks strong enough to survive until the next glaciation!

Once across, the path turns right and heads back toward Lake Superior. There is a junction in 200 m/yd; to the left is an inland section. Continue straight, climbing up a steep rocky knoll, to gain a wonderful view of the previous night's campsite. As the trail continues, passing through some forest but

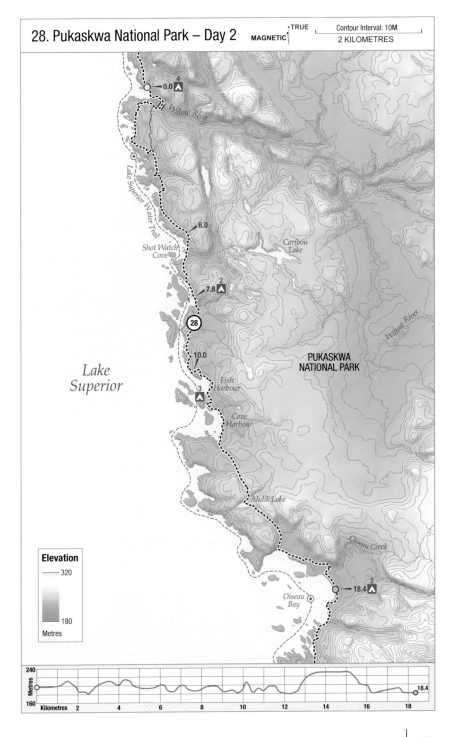

28. Pukaskwa National Park – Day 2

TRUE
MAGNETIC

Contour Interval: 10M
2 KILOMETRES

Willow River

Lake Superior Water Trail

0.0 ▲ 4

6.0

Shot Watch Cove

Caribou Lake

7.8 ▲ 2

(28)

10.0

Lake Superior

Fish Harbour

3 ▲

Cave Harbour

PUKASKWA NATIONAL PARK

Willow River

Ahdik Lake

Oiseau Creek

Elevation
— 320

180
Metres

Oiseau Bay

18.4 ▲ 2

240
Metres
160
Kilometres 2   4   6   8   10   12   14   16   18

18.4

often along rock ridges, navigation quickly becomes an issue. Small cairns of stones are the only route markers, and these are not always well placed or easy to see on the uneven ground.

The path twists and turns over the rough landscape, descending to reach the lakeshore at 2 km (1.2 mi). For the next 600 m/yd, you scamper along the water's edge, hopping from boulder to boulder, picking carefully across cobble beaches or easing over rounded headlands, before the route climbs again. Although it turns away from the water occasionally, or dips into small gullies out of sight of the lake, there are several excellent hilltop views.

At 3.3 km (2.1 mi), the two inland paths reconnect; keep right, crossing a tiny bog about 100 m/yd further on puncheons. Then it is back into thick softwoods, the ground a carpet of bright green sphagnum moss. You reach a large pond, on the left, at about 500 m/yd, and the path curves around it, remaining close for about 250 m/yd before returning among the trees.

Small loose rocks make walking precarious as the path moves down a dry creek bed, at about 4.6 km (2.9 mi). The cobble extends almost until the trail reaches a small cove about 150 m/yd later. Turning back among the trees, the path works up and down the rocky landscape, a continuous staircase. Day 2 is already obviously more challenging than day 1.

6 km (3.7 mi) The route crosses the middle of a huge area covered by small round stones. For 150 m/yd, walkers must negotiate this slippery zone, but it is tremendously interesting, a cobble beach far from the water. About 500 m/yd later, the trail touches the lake above Shot Watch Cove, a pleasant spot to stop for a snack.

The path descends to a small beach, which you cross, but quickly heads back into forest. (Watch for a wildlife camera about 150 m/yd later.) After 500 m/yd among the trees, the trail returns to lakeshore, and you can enjoy a short walk on the sand.

7.8 km (4.8 mi) The first of the two Morrison Harbour campsites is on the right, on the lake but sheltered by a small island. The second site, MH2, is about 25 m/yd further, and the trail crosses a small brook 275 m/yd after that.

For the next 1.7 km (1.1 mi), the route remains mostly inland, although views of the lake from a bare rock hilltop are frequent – as are hills. At about 9.7 km (6 mi), there is another stretch of difficult cobble to negotiate, then the path reaches the lake, where it works along the rugged shoreline for the next 300 m/yd with a cliff rising to your left.

10 km (6.2 mi) You arrive seemingly at a dead end: to your left is an 8 m (26 ft) cliff, while ahead is a 2 m (7 ft) drop to the water. However, the cairns lead to this spot. To proceed, you must lower yourself down the ledge directly ahead, stepping onto some rocks lapped by Lake Superior's waves. Turn left, clamber

over the rocky rubble, and scramble through a narrow crevice in the cliff. This is a challenging spot even in good weather, requiring some dexterity and confidence. In bad weather and high waves, this might be nearly impassable.

Pick your way through the cleft, climbing as you do. Once through, the path turns right and quickly descends to the narrow sandy beach at Fish Harbour. At 11.1 km (7 mi), the route turns inland and climbs a low ridge. Some 300 m/yd later, you reach a junction with a side path to Fish Harbour's two campsites, on the right.

After another 300 m/yd over rocky ground, alongside more vertical rock faces, the path reaches the shoreline at Cave Harbour. For the next kilometre, the path meanders through the low ground near the water, occasionally turning into the forest to cross small brooks but returning soon to the sheltered cove.

At about 12.7 km (7.9 mi), the footpath leaves Cave Harbour and begins its longest climb of the day, working alongside a tiny stream through the forest. For the next 1.3 km (0.8 mi), the ascent is steady, though rarely steep, gaining more than 50 m (164 ft). Then it descends all the way to Oiseau Bay, passing small Ahdik Lake – which may look more like a bog – at 14.5 km (9 mi). There is quite a bit of soggy ground to traverse as well.

At 16.2 km (10.1 mi), the path emerges onto a beach at Oiseau Bay. Enjoy the sand surface for 250 m/yd until you return to a forested section. This is a lovely section, the spruce covered in thick mats of old man's beard and the trail passing beneath moss-covered knolls. It ends by descending a set of stairs and arriving at a long open area covered in sand and sparse vegetation, at about 17 km (10.6 mi).

For the next 700 m/yd, your path is up the middle of this odd clearing, which is actually the former path of Oiseau Creek. Occasional posts mark the route, which continues up the clearing to its end, then curves right and crosses Oiseau Creek at 17.6 km (11 mi) on a "bridge" made up of fallen logs, the remains of a footbridge and whatever other debris has become snagged in the pile. Your footing will be, to say the least, unstable.

From here the path climbs the dunes, turns right, and follows the brook to the main beach of Oiseau Bay – one of the longest sand beaches in the park – 300 m/yd later.

18.4 km (11.4 mi) The campsites are near the middle of the beach, although there is a shallow wet area that must be crossed before reaching them. Nestled among the trees, they are quite nice, with good views of the lake and a background sound of pounding surf.

Day 3: Oiseau Bay to White Gravel River
Distance: 14.5 km (9 mi), one way
Ascent: 467 m (1,532 ft)
Descent: 464 m (1,522 ft)

From the campsite, follow the beach south for its remaining 300 m/yd, where it crosses a small outflow and heads into thick forest. The distinct footpath soon reaches bare rock, close to Lake Superior. Watch for cairns; it is easy to wander off the route. The landscape is rugged, with the path often passing between or alongside the massive granite/gneiss rocks. There is even a small staircase at 900 m/yd in one difficult spot. Although the area is forested, bare rock dominates.

The path works its way through the difficult terrain, making detours inland where required but returning to the lakeshore. It evens crosses small beaches occasionally, in tiny coves, or overlooks small inlets from rock ridges.

2.6 km (1.6 mi) The trail emerges from its forested route to the attractive sand beach at Nichols Cove, which provides a sheltered location for a snack. This small inlet is a popular refuge for kayakers when rough lake chop drives them off the open water.

From Nichols Cove, the route winds its way through the broken ground, though often crossing stretches of bare rock with wonderful views of the lakeshore and several small islands. The uneven terrain demands constant attention, and falls are likely, especially if the slippery rocks are wet. Between km 4-4.5 (2.5-2.8 mi), you will face a particularly challenging stretch, at water level scrambling over large, loose boulders.

From here, the path begins an almost continuous ascent up a high granite ridge. As you climb, better and better views of Fish Harbour are revealed. The

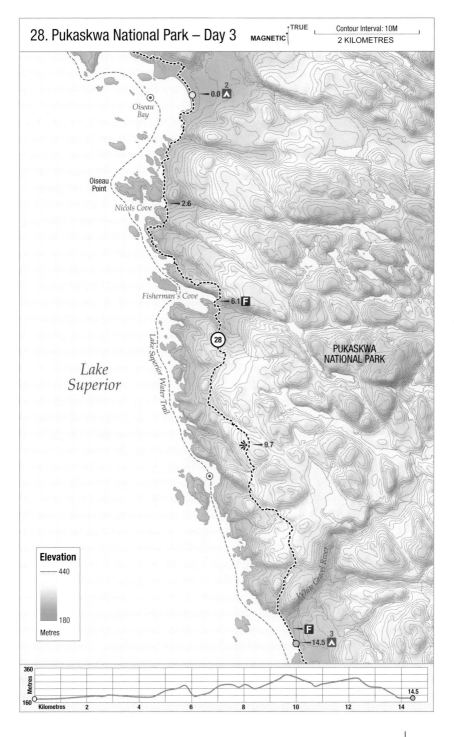

28. Pukaskwa National Park – Day 3

MAGNETIC | TRUE

Contour Interval: 10M
2 KILOMETRES

Oiseau
Bay

2
0.0

Oiseau
Point

Nicols Cove

2.6

Fisherman's Cove

6.1 F

28

PUKASKWA
NATIONAL PARK

Lake
Superior

Lake Superior Water Trail

9.7

White Gravel River

Elevation
440

180
Metres

F
3
14.5

Metres 360 / 160

Kilometres 2 4 6 8 10 12 14.5 14

best viewpoint is at 5.2 km (3.2 mi), after which the trail curves behind still higher ground. By 5.8 km (3.6 mi), the path has risen more than 70 m (230 ft) above the lake. From here it turns sharply right and loses all that elevation over the next 300 m/yd descending in a steep, jagged, narrow gully.

⚐ 6.1 km (3.8 mi) The trail reaches a beach at Fisherman's Cove; after the previous 2 km (1.2 mi), this is another tempting rest stop. At its far end is the first wide brook that must be forded. (The water level when we crossed was waist high, but there was a large log that we were able to cross using trekking poles for support.)

Once across, the trail turns inland and climbs again, reaching the junction to the Fisherman's Cove campsites 300 m/yd later, just before crossing another small brook, which it then follows for a short distance. This area is thickly wooded, and there are few views. Another climb, even higher than the one before Fisherman's Cove, begins.

What follows is a rough slog through some of the most challenging terrain you have yet faced. The trail has moved away from the lakeshore and follows an extended route several hundred metres/yards inland, often with higher ground on the lake side. These rock hillocks, supporting a spare covering of scraggly jack pines, feature long stretches of bare rock. Views of Lake Superior are few; most lookouts reveal an endless vista of similar craggy hills receding into the park's interior.

The route crosses several tiny creeks, and sometimes uses the low gullies they follow. It is an almost steady climb to 7.3 km (4.5 mi), after which it descends – with one notable exception – for the next 1.1 km (0.7 mi). turning almost 90° left, the most arduous climb follows, over some of the steepest terrain.

⚐ 9.7 km (6 mi) The trail reaches its highest point: 135 m (443 ft) above the lake. This is a good viewpoint and another place to rest and snack. Almost immediately, it begins to descend, losing more than 70 m (230 ft) in the next kilometre. Of course, it is not all at once; the terrain is rough, so there are constant small up-and-downs. There are also several lovely views available, even of the lake.

Another undulating climb follows, gaining back 50 m (164 ft) by 12.3 km (7.6 mi) before beginning the day's final descent. At about 12.9 km (8 mi), the trail skirts a small pond, staying above it on a ridge then dropping down to cross its outflow. The path follows this little trickle, descending toward Lake Superior, which you will soon begin to hear.

Emerging from the forest at 13.9 km (8.6 mi), turn left and walk along the beach. About 100 m/yd later, you will reach the mouth of the White Gravel River, which must be forded. We found the shallowest way was to keep close to Lake Superior's surf; we were able to cross at knee level on the gravel.

One campsite is found close to the river, but we used one of the remaining two, located near the far end of the beach. This final 500 m/yd section, traversing the small, round, loose stones of White Gravel Beach, was surprisingly disagreeable after the long day.

📍 **14.5 km (9 mi)** Arrive at the campsite near the end of White Gravel Beach. These sites are quite pleasant, each with its own outhouse and steel food shelter. Set just inside the treeline, they are sheltered from the worst winds but still close enough to enjoy an evening beach walk once the sun sets. If you have never seen the night sky from a remote location such as Pukaskwa, you will experience something memorable.

Our pace, rests included, was less than 2 km (1.2 mi) per hour. Navigating the rugged terrain, particularly while balancing a large backpack, is much slower than the usual day hike, and the fatigue level is much higher. Be prepared to hike slower than you expect.

28. Pukaskwa National Park – Day 4

MAGNETIC | TRUE

Contour Interval: 10M
1 KILOMETRE

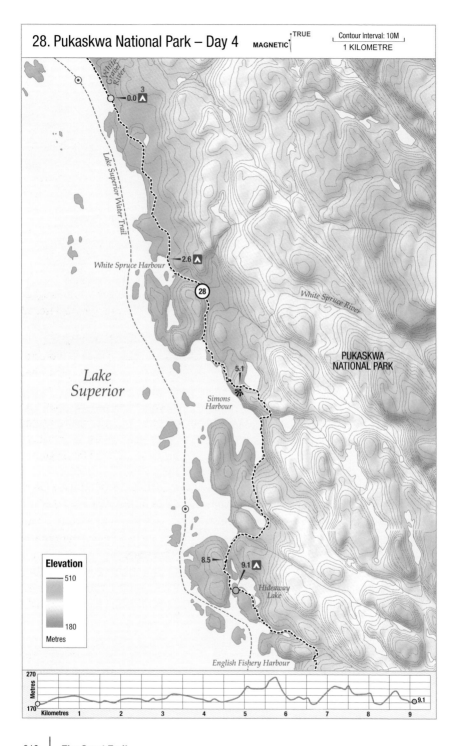

Day 4: White Gravel River to Hideaway Lake
Distance: 9.1 km (5.7 mi), one way
Ascent: 372 m (1,220 ft)
Descent: 372 m (1,220 ft)

Walk to the end of White Gravel Beach, about 200 m/yd; a sign marks where the footpath enters the vegetation. The trail immediately ascends a rock face, crossing a small brook at 600 m/yd. After this, the ground is distinctly spongy – fine when dry but certainly sodden after a shower.

This section is remarkably gentle compared to the previous day's trek. It passes through pleasant forest, a mixture of hardwoods and conifers and with little understorey to obstruct views. The footpath is distinct, often bordered by sphagnum moss, and there are fewer rocky areas. After the bog, the route remains separated from the lake by a buffer of vegetation. For much of this section, Superior's waves can be heard but not seen.

At about 1.4 km (0.9 mi), is an unexpectedly steep little gully, and a dry creek bed, to cross. At 1.9 km (1.2 mi), the trail curves left and climbs again, though relatively gently; 300 m/yd later it curves right and begins to descend,

2.6 km (1.6 mi) Reach the lakeshore at the White Spruce Harbour campsite. This is situated in a truly excellent location, bordering a small, well-protected cove. Alas, there is only one campsite, so it might already be occupied when you arrive.

Follow the beach to its end 200 m/yd later, where the path turns left into the trees and starts to climb. About 100 m/yd, later the path crosses a small creek. The trees here, young white spruce, are thick, forming a barrier on both sides of the path. Fortunately, the ascent is fairly easy, with the highest ground to the right.

The trail curves around this large hill and by 3.3 km (2.1 mi) has already begun to descend. To the left you might be able to see an open area or even a small lake. The relatively easy walking continues for another 400 m/yd, but as the angle of descent increases, more roots and rocks intrude into the treadway. To the left, and below, is a small stream, which your path parallels.

At 4.1 km (2.5 mi), you arrive at another small cobble beach, which you walk over. Somewhere along its length the White Spruce River – far smaller and less impressive than it sounds – flows into Lake Superior and must be crossed. (We hopped over it.) After about 100 m/yd in the open, it is back in the forest for 200 m/yd to work behind a headland.

From this point it is a more rugged track. Traversing more bare rock, the route tracks close to the lake, though not always alongside its shore. Superb views of the islands and inlets are available, especially as it climbs. At 4.8 km (3 mi), the trail turns 180° left and enters an extremely jagged area. Almost

Inland Beaches

One of the most curious features of the Coastal Trail is several large areas of rocky cobble set far from the Lake Superior coastline. They look like beaches but are clearly too far from the water to have been tossed by storm action — and Lake Superior has no tides, of course.

The reason, as with almost every other geological feature in the area, is glaciation. Only 10,000 years ago — the blink of an eye, geologically speaking — more than two kilometres of ice lay atop the rocks of Pukaskwa. They pushed all the topsoil into the United States, they scoured the innumerable bays and inlets, and they compressed the very rocks downwards with their weight.

In the millennia since the glaciers retreated, the land is still recovering. Each year, the ground in Pukaskwa rises more than 0.3 m (1 ft), almost like lungs re-inflating after an exhalation. So the vast cobble fields were beaches, but the rising landscape has pushed Lake Superior far away, and a little further each year.

immediately, it turns right again and confronts a near-vertical wall of rock. The route ascends this obstacle, and hands will be required to traverse the next 200 m/yd.

5.1 km (3.2 mi) Arrive at the end of the vertical ascent (but not quite the very top of the hill), where there is a wonderful lookout. If you are like me, a short rest might be in order as well. The trail climbs a bit more, but then drops slightly to a small lake only 100 m/yd further. The path works around its shore then climbs a little more.

The highest point along the Coastal Trail, about elevation 263 m (863 ft), is reached at 5.7 km (3.5 mi). The route then drops, curves right, and descends a narrow ravine alongside a small brook. About 300 m/yd later it reaches Simons Harbour, where it turns left. The trail remains under tree cover, though quite close to the lake. This section alongside Simons Harbour is a tough grind, very rocky and fractured. Care must be taken picking through the boulders.

The next interesting obstacle is at about 6.5 km (4 mi). A huge slab of granite, canted at 45°, slopes into the water of a creek. There is no route across the creek but this bare rock for 2 m/yd (7 ft). We managed to inch across without incident, hanging onto a few secure tree roots and with our boots gripping the dimpled granite. However, if it had been wet I do not think we would have been successful.

Another creek must be crossed less than 100 m/yd later, then, at 6.7 km (4.2 mi), the trail finally turns away from the water. However, it immediately begins to climb steeply. Nearby trees are mostly birch, some quite tall, but there are also other hardwoods. For the first time in the trip I heard thrushes.

By 7.3 km (4.5 mi), you are descending again, and a small lake should be visible ahead and below. The trail drops – almost – to its shore 100 m/yd later, then works around it for another 300 m/yd. The path edges past another tiny pool that is to the left, then drops down to Lake Superior at about 8.1 km (5 mi). For the next 200 m/yd, the route tracks alongside the water, including across a less steeply angled granite slope. Once at the end of this small bay, it turns back into the trees. The climb that follows next may be disconcerting, because the map doesn't reveal how difficult it actually is.

◊8.5 km (5.3 mi) The rise is only 40 m (131 ft) over the next 300 m/yd, but this includes a 2.5 m (8 ft) vertical rock wall that nearly defeated me. Again, footholds and handholds are necessary to scale that particular obstacle, made even more delightful with the added "backpack bonus."

It seems as if this entire climb is intended to bring you to one very fine view, which includes some (but, appropriately, not all) of Hideaway Lake. The remainder of the walk is relatively moderate by comparison. The descent is still fairly steep, and the terrain still rocky, but by comparison with what preceded it, easy.

At about 8.9 km (5.6 mi), the path reaches Hideaway Lake, and 100 m/yd later you cross its outflow, either by fording or on piled logs; it's a little awkward either way. Once across, only 100 m/yd remain.

◊9.1 km (5.7 mi) You arrive at the junction for the Hideaway Lake campsite, which is to the right about 50 m/yd. The site is actually in a tiny cove on Lake Superior and was perhaps my favourite. (They are all nice, but this one was cosy.) There are plenty of rocks to stretch out on and soak up some late-afternoon sunshine, and it is even easy to get into the lake if you want a swim. (I did, but the icy water soon drove me out.)

This was probably the most demanding day of the entire hike and included three of its most difficult obstacles. I did not have much energy remaining when I completed it.

Day 5: Hideaway Lake to North Swallow River
Distance: 4.8 km (3 mi), one way
Ascent: 173 m (568 ft)
Descent: 175 m (574 ft)

Return to the main trail and turn right. The trail approaches close to Hideaway Lake and meanders along the gentle slope beside it. The terrain is rocky, of course, though most in this thickly tree-shrouded section are covered in moss. It is hilly too, but these first climbs are so small as to go almost unnoticed, particularly after the previous day's exertions.

After an easy 500 m/yd close to this small lake, the footpath climbs out of the low ground surrounding it and heads to the Lake Superior shoreline, which it reaches in 200 m/yd. The terrain becomes much rougher, and once again your route is along the large rocks on the edge of this exposed coastline. On this day, offshore winds were lashing spray onto these rocks – and us – making them extra slippery and the footing treacherous.

At 850 m/yd, the trail turns left, just after crossing a small brook, which gurgles beneath the large boulders on which you are walking, and heads inland – climbing, naturally. Within 100 m/yd there is a large cobble field to the left, and soon your route heads directly across it. Be cautious negotiating across the small, loose, slippery stones. As the path works around a small pond, which is on the right, you cross more areas of cobble, including one that is sloped.

Leaving this pond, the trail climbs steeply between two hills, gaining more than 35 m (115 ft) over the following 300 m/yd of rough terrain. Any thoughts that this short section to North Swallow River would be easy are by now finally dispelled. An ugly little ravine crossing follows, down 15 m (49 ft) then up almost as much. In between you must work around a new beaver pond, which forces the path to stay high on the jagged hillside. At 1.7 km (1.1 mi), you cross the dam, descend a little further, then climb steeply up the rocky hillside.

This steep ascent ends after a breath-robbing 150 m/yd. A short gentle climb remains, but soon the path drops toward a long, narrow lake hugged by steep granite knolls on all sides. This section is surprisingly gentle, a pleasant gradual downhill through a healthy forest.

⚲**2.3 km (1.4 mi)** The trail reaches the north end of the fairly large lake, the most prominent feature on this section, though still 10-15 m (33-49 ft) above the water. Soon the path drops to water level and skirts along its rim on a narrow ledge of rocks, thick branches threatening to nudge you into the water. On your right, vertical slabs of granite, known as the Ramparts, tower high above, their tops obscured by a thick curtain of conifers.

After 300 m/yd tiptoeing carefully along the lake's perimeter, you turn right and climb about 5 m (16 ft). The trail curves left again and parallels the

28. Pukaskwa National Park – Day 5

MAGNETIC TRUE

Contour Interval: 10M

1 KILOMETRE

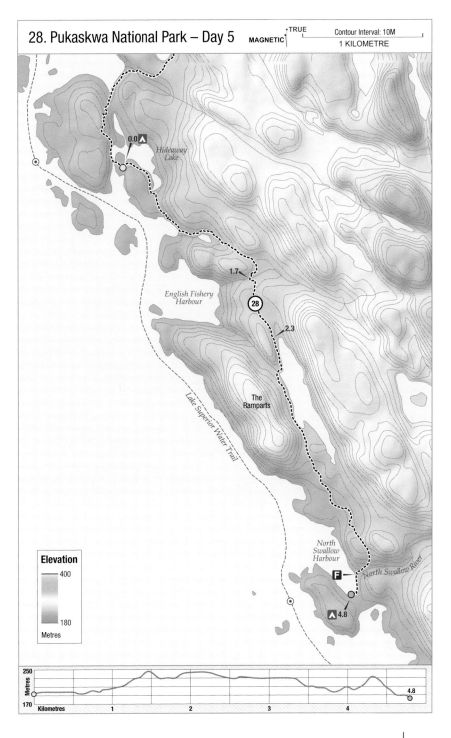

Hideaway Lake

0.0

1.7

28

2.3

English Fishery Harbour

The Ramparts

Lake Superior Water Trail

North Swallow Harbour

North Swallow River

F

4.8

Elevation

400

180

Metres

250

Metres

170

Kilometres 1 2 3 4

4.8

lake, though now high above the water. This is much easier walking, and there are nice views. And though it drops very gradually, the footpath never quite returns to lake level.

At about 3.1 km (1.9 mi), your route leaves this lake behind and begins to descend more noticeably. There are fewer rocks to scrabble over through here, and this forest stroll seems quite effortless. At 3.7 km (2.3 mi), the trail easily crosses a small creek; at this point you might hear the waves of Lake Superior, barely 150 m/yd on your right.

For another 100 m/yd, you follow the brook downstream, then curve left and begin the final climb of the Coastal Trail. Once again the trail works behind another rugged lakeshore hillock, and this climb would be considered

challenging on most day hikes. But this is Pukaskwa, and the end of the trek, so even though it is another 35 m (115 ft) trudge to the high point, at 4.3 km (2.7 mi), you probably will barely notice. It certainly will not seem especially difficult.

The descent is even more steep, and longer, because you are returning to the shoreline of Lake Superior. However, you have had considerable experience over the past five days. Probably you can think of little more than the return ride to the Visitor Centre. The path follows the North Swallow River for a short distance before reaching a crossing; there is no bridge. At 4.6 km (2.9 mi), you reach the lovely sand beach at the head of North Swallow Harbour.

4.8 km (3 mi) Arrive at the campsite, at the far end of the beach, where the hike ends – unless you are hiking back out again. A pair of Parks Canada's red chairs sits in the sand, facing the harbour, so you may relax and watch for the boat shuttle.

At this point, a certain measure of pride is permitted for completing Pukaskwa's Coastal Trail, one of Parks Canada's most challenging routes.

Further Information:
Ojibways of the Pic River First Nation: www.picriver.com
Pukaskwa Boat Shuttle: www.facebook.com/fishingcharterservice
Pukaskwa National Park: www.pc.gc.ca/en/pn-np/on/pukaskwa
Town of Marathon: www.marathon.ca

"Orphan" Sections

The Trans Canada Trail (TCT) was originally conceived as a land route only. Its five core uses, when introduced in 1992-93, were walking, cycling, horseback riding, cross-country skiing, and snowmobiling. If it ever achieved its ideal, the TCT wanted to be a nation-spanning off-road pathway, all of which incorporated the five core uses. In its first years, the TCT invited many already existing trails to become part of that vision, and many did.

When it became The Great Trail, the organization did more than merely change its name. It also adapted its vision to accept the reality it had observed over 25 years of effort. That included ideas such as incorporating water routes among its five core uses, designating extended stretches on roadways as temporary routes where no off-road pathways could currently be developed, and recognizing that there were some parts of Canada — such as Northern Ontario — where a connected land route represented a currently insuperable challenge.

As a result, previously designated land routes, such as Sleeping Giant, Pigeon River, the Voyageur Trail, and Pukaskwa's Coastal Trail, remained part of The Great Trail but unconnected by land routes to the remainder of the trail. That was a good decision, because many of these "orphan" sections provide some of the best hiking available in Canada.

Canada Jay

Sit for a few minutes anywhere in Canada's northern forests with open food, and you might be visited by this hungry and daring avian scrounger. Known alternatively as the grey jay or whisky jack, the Canada jay (*Perisoreus canadensis*) is a member of the corvid family, and like its cousins remains a year-round resident of the boreal forest. It survives by hiding small caches of food, as many as 1,000 a day, throughout its range. Apparently, it is able to remember them all, even months later during winter.

It also remembers food sources. Unwary hikers at popular picnic locations might see a moment's inattention result in portions of their meal disappearing into the beak of one of these fearless birds. One of its nicknames — camp robber — acknowledges the Canada jay's skill and audaciousness.

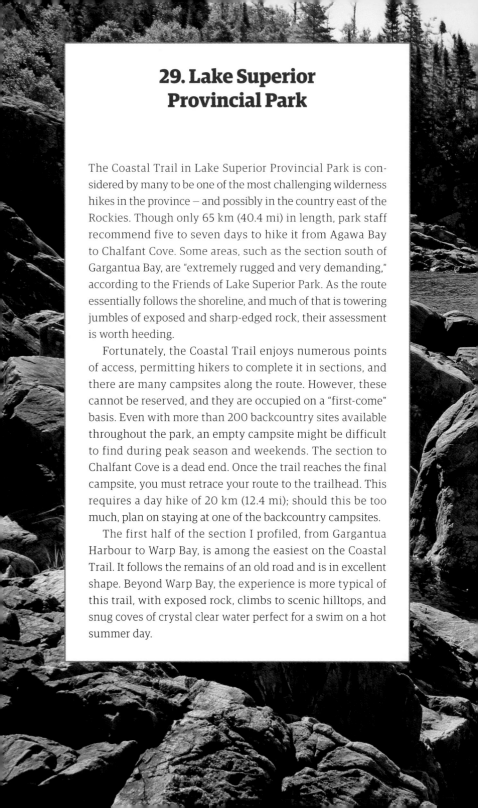

29. Lake Superior Provincial Park

The Coastal Trail in Lake Superior Provincial Park is considered by many to be one of the most challenging wilderness hikes in the province – and possibly in the country east of the Rockies. Though only 65 km (40.4 mi) in length, park staff recommend five to seven days to hike it from Agawa Bay to Chalfant Cove. Some areas, such as the section south of Gargantua Bay, are "extremely rugged and very demanding," according to the Friends of Lake Superior Park. As the route essentially follows the shoreline, and much of that is towering jumbles of exposed and sharp-edged rock, their assessment is worth heeding.

Fortunately, the Coastal Trail enjoys numerous points of access, permitting hikers to complete it in sections, and there are many campsites along the route. However, these cannot be reserved, and they are occupied on a "first-come" basis. Even with more than 200 backcountry sites available throughout the park, an empty campsite might be difficult to find during peak season and weekends. The section to Chalfant Cove is a dead end. Once the trail reaches the final campsite, you must retrace your route to the trailhead. This requires a day hike of 20 km (12.4 mi); should this be too much, plan on staying at one of the backcountry campsites.

The first half of the section I profiled, from Gargantua Harbour to Warp Bay, is among the easiest on the Coastal Trail. It follows the remains of an old road and is in excellent shape. Beyond Warp Bay, the experience is more typical of this trail, with exposed rock, climbs to scenic hilltops, and snug coves of crystal clear water perfect for a swim on a hot summer day.

29. Lake Superior Provincial Park

MAGNETIC ↑ TRUE

Contour Interval: 20M
2 KILOMETRES

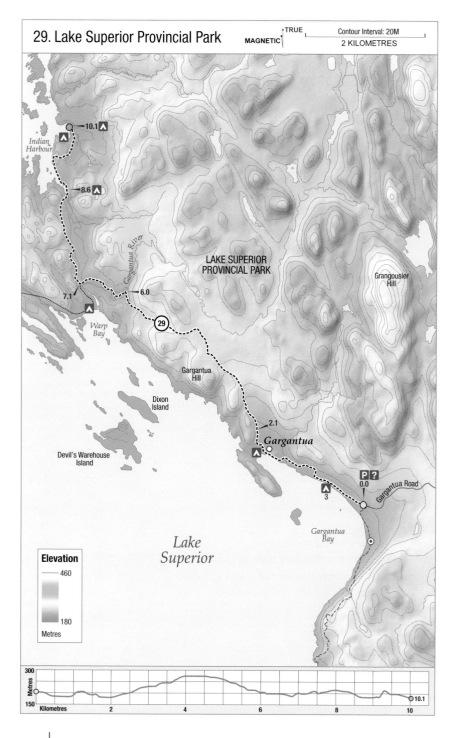

Indian
Harbour

10.1

8.6

Gargantua River

7.1

6.0

Warp
Bay

LAKE SUPERIOR
PROVINCIAL PARK

Grangousier
Hill

29

Gargantua
Hill

Dixon
Island

2.1

Gargantua

Devil's Warehouse
Island

3

P ?
0.0

Gargantua Road

*Gargantua
Bay*

*Lake
Superior*

Elevation

— 460

180

Metres

300

Metres

150

Kilometres   2   4   6   8   10

10.1

29. Lake Superior Provincial Park

Distance: 10.1 km (6.2 mi), one way
Ascent: 208 m (682 ft)
Descent: 230 m (755 ft)

Trail conditions: compacted earth, natural surface
Cellphone coverage: none
Hazards: isolated, wildlife

Permitted Uses							
Walking	Biking	Horseback Riding	Inline Skating	ATV	Snowshoeing	Cross-country Skiing	Snowmobiling
✔	—	—	—	—	✔	✔	—

Finding the trailhead: From the Agawa Bay Visitor Centre, drive 36.1 km (22.4 mi) north on Highway 17 to the Gargantua Road. Follow this to its end. (Please note that the road is gated in winter.) Although only 14 km (8.7 mi), the dirt Gargantua Road is rough and will require almost 45 minutes to drive.

Trailhead: 47°33'36.8" N, 84°56'54.6" W (Start: Gargantua Bay)
47°36'54.7" N, 85°00'39.5" W (Finish: Chalfant Cove)

Observations: This is a lovely and remote coastal hike on the rugged Canadian Shield shoreline of Lake Superior, on one of the country's most celebrated wilderness trails. I had originally intended to profile the section between Gargantua Bay and Orphan Lake, but I turned back after less than 5 km (3.1 mi), shortly before reaching the Buckshot River, defeated by the startlingly difficult terrain – something that had never before happened to me before or since. The coastal scenery was striking, but I slipped constantly on wet rocks and cut my hands on their many sharp edges. The climbs left me short of breath, and the descents in fear of falling onto jagged outcrops.

This was only the second hike I had attempted for the Western Canada book, and it was not a promising beginning to the project. I had to continue west, Lake Superior Park uncompleted and me unclear how I would include it. When I returned to the area two months later, after completing every other route except for Pukaskwa National Park, I explored the Coastal Trail from Gargantua Bay to the north toward Chalfant Cove. This proved to be much easier, though still with some challenging sections. The campsites at Chalfant Cove, the end of the Coastal Trail, were especially tranquil, and I could have

remained there contentedly for several days. If anyone truly wishes to challenge themselves, they should: try the route to the south!

Route description: The road ends facing a large trailhead pavilion, which features a map of the Gargantua area and some local history. Park there, but if no space is available there is a larger area to the left where you may find space. Return to the pavilion, where a sign indicates that the site of the former community (abandoned in 1930) is to the right – as is the route, along what appears to be a continuation of the old road.

The walking is very easy, with the wide track gently descending to lake level through an attractive mixed hardwood/softwood forest. Once close to the lake, the track curves left and parallels the shoreline, with backcountry campsites visible close to the water. In addition to a picnic table and a fire pit, campsites are serviced by an outhouse, should the need arise.

You will enjoy an easy stroll in view of Lake Superior and several small islands for the first 1 km (0.6 mi), until the old road makes a sharp turn right and climbs slightly. About 600 m/yd later, the trail crosses a small stream, and after this it curves left and returns to the lakeshore within 150 m/yd. A nearby spit of land across a narrow cove lets you know you have reached the sheltered Gargantua Harbour, and even though there are no permanent residents, there are a few cabins visible across the bay.

2.1 km (1.3 mi) A large beaver pond has blocked the road and submerged it. A new footpath, marked with a sign directing toward Warp Bay, enters the trees to the right just before you reach this new pond. This meandering path bridges a small creek 175 m/yd later, then rejoins the old road 50 m/yd beyond that. Another sign directs you right, to Warp Bay.

With vehicle access now cut off, vegetation has narrowed the former road to a broad footpath, though it remains relatively level and easy to hike. Where softwoods dominate, the track is somewhat wider. Lake Superior can no longer be seen or heard as the route heads away from the water and behind a row of low hills. On a calm day, such as it was when I hiked it, this section is abnormally quiet and the unstirred air hot and humid.

This section is quiet and uneventful, with no side paths and no views through the thick forest. The treadway is smooth and marked with a well-worn earthen strip in its grass-covered surface. Small bridges cross furrows created by tiny brooks, and it's a slow, steady climb all the way to the 4 km (2.5 mi) mark, on the slopes of Gargantua Hill, at 274 m (899 ft).

For 600 m/yd, the trail is absolutely level, after which a long descent begins. The trail appears to follow a narrow ravine downhill, which means that a small creek soon is heard trickling close by. The trail crosses it at 5.5 km (3.4 mi) and again 100 m/yd later. The vegetation shifts as you descend, with hardwoods

Problem Bears

For most, it seems without question that any bear encountered on the trail will be a problem, but in fact most bears are terrified of humans and will do almost anything to avoid them. However, a small percentage of these large omnivores come to identify people with food, usually through people's own carelessness, and become "problem bears."

What this means is that, instead of fleeing hikers and campers, they lurk on the edges of trails and campsites, hoping to pillage an easy meal. When camping, meals should be cooked away from where you camp, and all utensils should be cleaned immediately. Food should be suspended at least 4 m (13 ft) above ground and 100 m/yd away from your tent. Never offer food to an approaching bear; it will only want more.

Bears are intelligent and persistent. If they learn to connect people with food, they will certainly become a danger to both you and to themselves.

---

predominating. By 5.9 km (3.7 mi), the route no longer resembles an unused road but a single-track footpath.

6 km (3.7 mi) The trail reaches the Gargantua River, which a sturdy bridge traverses. On the opposite bank, a sign indicates that a waterfall is 75 m/yd to the right. Though small, it is quite attractive, and well worth the short diversion. It is also a lovely location for a short break and snack.

The main trail heads left, following the river downstream. It is much different now, unquestionably a hiking path: winding among trees, negotiating frequent rises and dips, and with the vegetation brushing against your clothing. Cedar is much more common among the trees, and route signage – a blue diamond displaying a white hiker – appears often.

After 300 m/yd alongside the river, the path turns sharply away to the right into a thickly wooded area. At first quite level, the path reaches a steep-sided ravine. It is not very deep, but it is still a sliding trek to the bottom, where a bridge spans another small creek.

7.1 km (4.4 mi) On the far side of this bridge is a signed junction: to the left is Warp Bay; to the right is Indian Harbour and Chalfant Cove. Your route heads right, but should you wish to explore a little further, the trail to the left continues to a dead end. It also features two scenic campsites overlooking Lake Superior.

The terrain is rougher now, with gullies and hills more frequent. There is much more up-and-down as the trail navigates the rockier slopes. It is still

not too difficult, but it is more difficult than any of the preceding sections. At 8.5 km (5.3 mi), after almost 500 m/yd of downhill, the trail crosses a larger creek; a larger body of water might be visible on the left

8.6 km (5.3 mi) You emerge from the tree cover next to Indian Harbour, a sheltered cove on the Lake Superior shoreline. This is a gorgeous little bay, lined with rocky knolls and islands and filled with calm, clear water. For the next 700 m/yd, the trail follows this coastline; the water looks so pristine that it will be tempting to swim, but remember that Lake Superior is always bitterly cold, even in the summer. Spruce dominate the coastal forest, with pine very common too.

About 9.2 km (5.7 mi), the trail makes its steepest ascent, climbing 30 m (98 ft) in the next 150 m/yd up a rocky prominence, with lots of tree roots and loose rocks to add to the challenge. You will enjoy magnificent views of Indian Harbour and Cape Gargantua, before the trail turns away from the water and quickly descends on the hill's opposite face.

The walking is much easier now, and the thick vegetation nearly obscures the path. Watch carefully for the blue diamond hiker markers. For what

Ontario's Provincial Parks

Although Algonquin Park was established in 1893, as late as 1954 there were only seven provincial parks in the entire province, and these were only found on lands considered unsuitable for settlement and farming. With the creation of a separate Parks Division within the Ministry of Lands and Forests and a new emphasis on creating tourism and recreation opportunities, this number had swelled to 72 provincial parks by 1960, 220 by 1985, and more than 300 today. From being remote, inaccessible, and visited only by a very few, Ontario's park system now hosts more than 9 million visitors annually.

To better manage the diverse needs of a massive and varied system, the Parks Division established six different classifications of their parks: Recreation, Cultural Heritage, Natural Environment, Nature Reserve, Waterway, and Wilderness. Lake Superior, Pigeon River, and Sleeping Giant Provincial Parks are in the Natural Environment category, which, in the words of the legislation, is dedicated to "protect the landscapes and special features of the natural region in which they are located, while providing ample opportunities for activities such as swimming and camping."

remains of the trail, it is all downhill, although only steeply so on the reverse of the viewing hill. At 9.6 km (6 mi), the vegetation to the right recedes, revealing a large wetland and pond. Less than 200 m/yd later, a side trail branches left; this is to one of the two campsites at Chalfant Cove.

10.1 km (6.3 mi) The trail ends abruptly at the final campsite, which is set in a charming spot overlooking Chalfant Cove and next to a sandy beach. Please remember that it might be occupied, so announce your arrival and say hello if it is.

This is the end of the Coastal Trail. Retrace your route to return to the Gargantua Bay trailhead.

Further Information:
Friends of Lake Superior Park: www.lakesuperiorpark.ca
Lake Superior Provincial Park: www.ontarioparks.com/park/lakesuperior

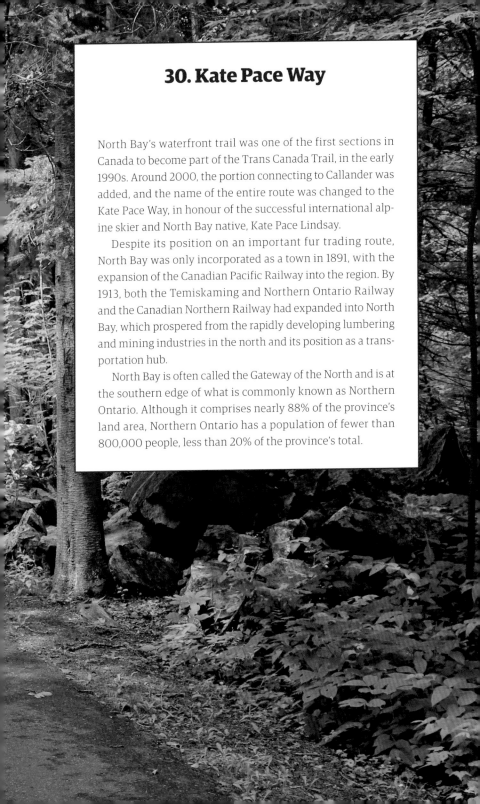

30. Kate Pace Way

North Bay's waterfront trail was one of the first sections in Canada to become part of the Trans Canada Trail, in the early 1990s. Around 2000, the portion connecting to Callander was added, and the name of the entire route was changed to the Kate Pace Way, in honour of the successful international alpine skier and North Bay native, Kate Pace Lindsay.

Despite its position on an important fur trading route, North Bay was only incorporated as a town in 1891, with the expansion of the Canadian Pacific Railway into the region. By 1913, both the Temiskaming and Northern Ontario Railway and the Canadian Northern Railway had expanded into North Bay, which prospered from the rapidly developing lumbering and mining industries in the north and its position as a transportation hub.

North Bay is often called the Gateway of the North and is at the southern edge of what is commonly known as Northern Ontario. Although it comprises nearly 88% of the province's land area, Northern Ontario has a population of fewer than 800,000 people, less than 20% of the province's total.

30. Kate Pace Way

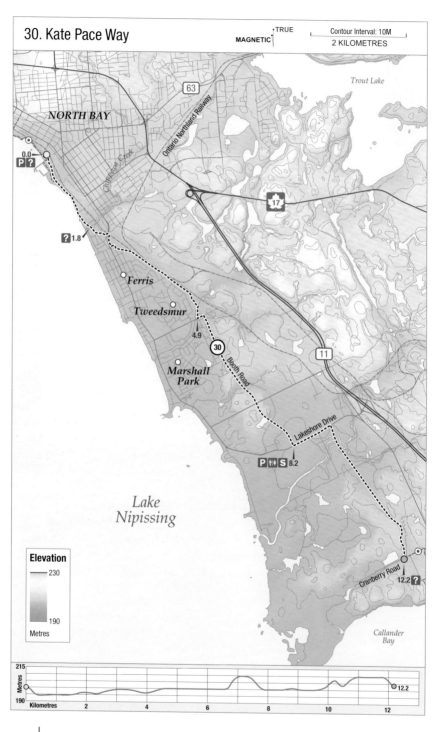

MAGNETIC · TRUE

Contour Interval: 10M
2 KILOMETRES

Trout Lake

63

Ontario Northland Railway

NORTH BAY

Chippewa Creek

0.0
P ?

? 1.8

Ferris

Tweedsmur

4.9

30

Marshall
Park

Booth Road

17

11

Lakeshore Drive

P ⫫ S 8.2

Lake
Nipissing

Cranberry Road

12.2 ?

Callander
Bay

Elevation

230

190

Metres

Metres						
215						12.2
190						
Kilometres	2	4	6	8	10	12

30. Kate Pace Way

Distance: 12.2 km (7.6 mi), one way
Ascent: 37 m (121 ft)
Descent: 33 m (108 ft)

Trail conditions: asphalt
Cellphone coverage: yes
Hazards: road crossings, on-road sections, ticks, wildlife

Permitted Uses							
Walking	Biking	Horseback Riding	Inline Skating	ATV	Snowshoeing	Cross-country Skiing	Snowmobiling
✔	✔	—	✔	—	✔	✔	—

Finding the trailhead: Begin this route at the Marathon Beach trailhead, on Memorial Drive, at the parking area on the east side of the road.

Trailhead: 46°18'50.9" N, 79°28'13.6" W (Start: Memorial Drive)
46°14'13.8" N, 79°23'05.6" W (Finish: Cranberry Road)

Observations: I found the ride along the Kate Pace Way quite pleasant and varied, although the on-road section in the middle of it was not particularly interesting. Its first few kilometres/miles are especially attractive, in sight of Lake Nipissing and adjacent to beaches and wonderful parks with excellent locations for a picnic. The wooded final part of the route, from the La Vase River to Cranberry Road, is sheltered from most human habitation and provides an enjoyable natural corridor.

I found the Kate Pace Way a rather short bike ride, but not having to spend the entire day cycling just to finish permitted plenty of time to stop and view any interesting sights. As a hike this route will require a full day, with most of the walking being inside an urban area, so it might be more pleasant to only travel the section from the Steve Omischl Sports Complex to Cranberry Road, about 8 km (5 mi) return.

Route description: The start of the trail is quite underwhelming, with a busy road flanked by parking lots. Concrete posts border and protect the small space, which is just large enough to contain a picnic table, a garbage can, and a map panel. The bidirectional paved pathway extends in one direction only, paralleling Memorial Drive and heading south. This is a busy area, with North Bay's downtown just across a railway track to the left, and Lake Nipissing to the right. It is also quite attractive, once you are away from the cramped starting point.

Sandy Marathon Beach lies just across the road, and in the first kilometre the trail passes a number of recreational facilities. On the right, King's Landing, with boat tours, is just 125 m/yd from the start. It is followed by the Waterfront Marina, then a large lakeside park with its own pathway, the Goulet Golden Mile. Numerous benches and picnic tables overlook the water on its wide lawns. On the left, 400 m/yd from the trailhead, is the Heritage Railway & Carousel Company, which runs a fleet of miniature trains. (I love trains, so I took a ride on one when I was there.) At 600 m/yd, an elaborate tunnel passes beneath the railway and connects to the Discovery North Bay Museum and the city's downtown.

Around 1 km (0.6 mi) from the start, Memorial Drive touches the lakeshore and the parkland ends. Only 300 m/yd later the trail, which runs alongside the road like a sidewalk, crosses Regina Street and passes in front of the Wastewater Treatment Plant. Those with olfactory sensitivity may find the next 200 m/yd a bit challenging. Once across Monk Street, you should enjoy less aromatic air again.

1.8 km (1.1 mi) Up ahead a large Trans Canada Trail Pavilion comes into view, which you reach after crossing Chippewa Creek and Stanley Street, at 1.8 km (1.1 mi). This is an important junction, with the Kinsman Way bike path heading into the city. Next to the pavilion, which sits in small Lee Park, is a trailhead map and a bike repair station. Inside the pavilion, a special plaque highlights Kate Pace Lindsay, the trail's namesake.

From this junction, the path curves left away from Memorial Drive, through the small park, to cross beneath a wide highway overpass (Main Street E) and runs adjacent to the railway tracks, 300 m/yd later. The trail immediately cuts sharply right, paralleling the road embankment and skirting the Veterans Soccer Fields until it reaches Judge Avenue at 2.4 km (1.5 mi). On the left is a washroom facility (only open when games are underway) and picnic tables.

At Judge Avenue, the path turns left again to parallel the road, and within 200 m/yd it makes another sharp left turn away from the street, where it heads toward a wooded area behind some houses. To the left lie more ball fields and soccer pitches, and about 50 m/yd from the road metal gates are positioned to bar vehicle entrance onto the wide, asphalt pathway.

Once past the gates, the pathway becomes a cosseted, though slender, forested laneway. Mostly young hardwoods, the leaves create a lush barrier that mostly hides the nearby houses and railway yards from view. Indeed, almost until it reaches a junction with Gertrude Avenue, at 3.7 km (2.3 mi), it seems as if the city has been left behind. Once the leaves have fallen from these hardwoods in the autumn, this is a very different experience.

From the Gertrude Street entrance, the path continues nearly straight for another 900 m/yd. Several bordering homes, on the right, have constructed their own sometimes elaborate bridges to create private connections to the trail. Just after crossing Parks Creek, the path makes a sharp right turn – somewhat dangerous if biking – and follows this minor waterway past Fire Station #3 to end at Marshall Avenue E.

9 4.9 km (3 mi) The off-road path ends, and for the next several kilometres/miles, the Kate Pace Way is a wide paved shoulder on both sides of the road. There is no crosswalk, but scoot to the opposite side of Marshall Avenue and turn left; there is a sign and directional arrow to guide you. About 150 m/yd later, at a T-junction with Booth Road, turn right.

For the next 3.2 km (2 mi), the route follows Booth Road. At first there is housing only on the right, and the left side of the road is forested. However, only 600 m/yd later, at a junction with Turner Drive, the new construction on the left suggests this may soon change. No crosswalks sign this road crossing, or any of the next several streets, so special caution must be taken by both cyclists and pedestrians.

There is an extensive wetland on both sides of an unnamed creek, at 6.6 km (4.1 mi), the most attractive portion of this roadway section. After that, there is a gentle climb to the busy intersection with Birchs Road 450 m/yd later. This is an extremely dangerous crossing to make during business hours, because the areas nearby host a wide range of commercial and industrial businesses. From here to Lakeshore Drive, about 1.2 km (0.7 mi), was my least favourite section of the route.

9 8.2 km (5.1 mi) Booth Road ends at Lakeshore Drive, which you cross. On the opposite side, the large Steve Omischl Sports Complex, with its several soccer and ball fields, lies directly ahead. In a building across the parking lot are public washrooms, and vending machines are visible from the trail.

Turn left and follow the broad paved pathway that runs alongside Lakeshore Drive. Continue past the playing fields, Sunset Park Public School, and a number of homes. Except for crossing Riverside Road, 600 m/yd from Booth Road, and several driveways, it should be a pleasant ride/walk to the junction with another off-road section of trail, at 9.1 km (5.7 mi). This is well signed, with a trailhead map, and there is even a transit stop. (Besides, the paved pathway ends here.)

The trail extends in both directions; turn right. This is a gorgeous, straight paved laneway – a rail trail – with fields and houses on both sides for the first 300 m/yd, until it reaches the La Vase River. After crossing on the most elaborate bridge of this route, the path enters a lovely forested area, in which

it remains for the balance of its route, except a brief interlude when it crosses Decaire Road, at 10.1 km (6.3 mi).

Numerous Trans Canada Trail Discovery Panels line this route, among them white-tailed deer, red-breasted nuthatch, and majestic pine. The vegetation crowds the edges of the path, but the effect is comforting rather than claustrophobic. Even piles of rocks at about 11 km (6.8 mi), left over from clearing the railway alignment, looked interesting.

At 11.6 km (7.2 mi), the trail emerges from its enshrouding vegetation. A significant wetland lies to the left, and the pathway varies from its straight path to curve along the edge of the dry land. For the first time, the pathway suffers from cracking, evidence of the soft ground beneath the trail.

12.2 km (7.6 mi) After another 650 m/yd, the Kate Pace Way ends at the gravel Cranberry Road, where the Osprey Links Golf Course bars further progress. There is no parking lot here, but in addition to the trailhead map, there is a large display for the municipality of Callander, with benches, and a map of the short Cranberry Trail walking path, which leads to a wetland on Lake Nipissing, a short distance to the right.

But this is the end of the Kate Pace Way; retrace your route to return.

Further Information:
City of North Bay Trails: www.cityofnorthbay.ca/living/recreation/trails
Discovery Routes: www.discoveryroutes.ca
Tourism North Bay: www.tourismnorthbay.com

Lake Nipissing

One of the largest lakes in Ontario, with the exception of the Great Lakes, shallow Lake Nipissing is also one of the most popular with anglers. Walleye, northern pike, and yellow perch are the principal species, and the lake's catch accounts for almost 5% of the entire province's recreational output.

Historically, Lake Nipissing was an important junction in the fur trade routes. It drains, to the west, into Georgian Bay and Lake Huron. To the east, routes following the La Vase and Mattawa Rivers reach the Ottawa River, and from there into the St. Lawrence. This water route was so important that an ambitious plan was developed to construct a canal from Georgian Bay to the Ottawa River, and it was only finally abandoned in the financial collapse of the 1930s.

North Bay & District Chamber of Commerce

Liam Quinn, Flickr, CC BY-SA 2.0

Acknowledgements

The number of people whom I have consulted for the routes in this book easily exceeds one hundred, so attempting to list them all would guarantee that I missed someone. A great many individuals provided valuable information that helped me write this book: provincial staff, trail managers, volunteers, tourism officials, government officials, and even fellow hikers and cyclists whom I spoke to along the paths. Each one made a contribution, and I apologize for not acknowledging you all individually.

In addition, when I travelled across the country researching this book, over fifty-nine consecutive days, a number of people provided their homes as a comforting overnight shelter, with the added bonus of delicious home-cooked meals. Ron and Ruth in Ottawa, Kirsten and Jack in Hurkett, Donna and Ray in Pinawa, Robert Champagne in Falcon Lake, my brother Dennis and Cindy in Chestermere – both heading west and returning east – Mandy and Colin in Canmore, Al and Marlene in Cranbrook, and Arne and Ann in Port Alberni: all welcomed me; none understood, I expect, how much their hospitality contributed to keeping me moving.

I also greatly appreciate several regional tourism agencies for providing me with a room when I worked in their area: the Beaver Motel in Nipigon, the Valhalla Inn in Thunder Bay (where I happened to see Bobby Orr in the lobby: major bonus!), and the Fairmont Winnipeg.

Even more than with Volume 1, I relied upon the provincial trail associations for their suggestions on what sections of their trail to profile. Most of the trails were located in areas where I had never before visited. These groups freely offered both advice and debate – at times quite lively, when we disagreed – and their contributions ensured that the field research became a genuine and exciting mission of discovery:

Trails BC: www.trailsbc.ca
Alberta TrailNet: www.albertatrailnet.com
Saskatchewan Trails Association: www.sasktrails.ca
Trails Manitoba: www.trailsmanitoba.ca
Trans Canada Trail – Ontario: www.tcto.ca

In Volume 1, I recognized the thousands of volunteers who have laboured for decades to build and maintain the trail. There is another group, much smaller, who also deserve to have their contribution acknowledged: the staff of the provincial trail associations. In most cases these organizations have only one or two full-time people. For example, from 1993 to 2003, I was executive director of the Nova Scotia Trails Federation – a part-time position, 30 per cent to 2000, 70 per cent thereafter.

No less than the volunteers, and usually hired from the volunteer ranks, these staff people work countless extra hours to achieve their goals, and always with extremely limited resources. Without their dedication, The Great Trail, especially during the early years of the Trans Canada Trail when the national organization was very weak, would not exist. The provincial staff carried the message of the Trans Canada Trail to communities throughout their territory, assisted the volunteer groups organize, and lobbied their respective governments for supporting legislation and improved funding – as they still do today.

One individual who deserves special acknowledgement is my friend Ron Hunt, who more than anyone else has been a supporter and confidant through the entire multi-year process of working on this project. When I visited Ottawa, I stayed at Ron's house. Whenever I was frustrated with the many obstacles I faced, he would listen and provide wise, measured counsel. He hiked the five-day Pukaskwa Coastal Trail with me, the final route I trekked for this volume, and with all the suppers and park entry fees he covered, he certainly became my greatest financial sponsor. No one else encouraged me to continue like he did. Thank you, Ron.

Finally, I want to recognize the contributions of the team at Goose Lane Editions. This is my twelfth work with them, an association spanning more than twenty years. Producing a book such as this is truly an arduous creative and collaborative process. If not for freelance cartographer Jim Todd, the maps would look far less professional; if not for creative director Julie Scriver, the design would not be so wonderfully attractive; if not for freelance editor Charles Stuart, my original manuscript might have been incomprehensible; if not for production editor Alan Sheppard, I might never have finished at all. And, of course, publisher Susanne Alexander who first gave me a chance to produce a work to help people venture into the outdoors and who has supported every project since then. If you enjoy this book, it is largely because of their contributions.

Index

Michael Haynes is one of the leading authorities on trail development in Canada. A travel writer whose articles have appeared in *Ottawa Magazine*, *Saltscapes*, and *Explore*, Haynes is a regular commentator for CBC Radio. He is the author of numerous trail guides, including *The Best of The Great Trail, Volume 1: Newfoundland to Southern Ontario on the Trans Canada Trail.*